"TO THE BEST OF MY ABILITY"

The Presidency and the Constitution

"TO THE BEST OF MY ABILITY"

The Presidency and the Constitution

DONALD L. ROBINSON

W · W · NORTON & COMPANY

NEW YORK   *LONDON*

Published simultaneously in Canada by
Penguin Books Canada Ltd.,
2801 John Street, Markham, Ontario L3R 1B4.
Printed in the United States of America.

The text of this book is composed in Janson, with
display type set in Bembo Bold.
Composition and manufacturing by the
Maple-Vail Book Manufacturing Group.
Book design by Margaret Wagner.

First Edition

Library of Congress Cataloguing-in-Publication Data
Robinson, Donald L., 1936–
"To the best of my ability."

Includes bibliographic notes and index.
1. Presidents—United States.   I. Title.
JK516.R49   1987   353.03'1   86-23867

ISBN 0-393-02426-1

W. W. Norton & Company, Inc.,
500 Fifth Avenue, New York, N. Y. 10110
W. W. Norton & Company, Ltd.,
37 Great Russell Street, London WC1B 3NU

1 2 3 4 5 6 7 8 9 0

FOR

Molly

AND FOR OUR CHILDREN

John   *David*

Kathy   *Paul*

Contents

ix

PART IV Crisis

PART V Renewal

Preface

This book, which examines the constitutional foundations of the American presidency and presents a set of proposals for revising them, takes its title from the oath the Constitution prescribes for a president as he takes office. It is an intensely personal oath and in some ways a poignant one. It reflects an understanding of human frailty ("to the best of my ability"), but it points to the president as the one who bears the ultimate responsibility to "preserve, protect, and defend the Constitution of the United States."

During the bicentennial era we pay tribute to the Constitution and the men who framed it. I hope this book reflects the respect I feel for them and for their achievement. We need also to recognize, however, that changing circumstances require a reassessment. In the pages that follow, we will examine these circumstances in some detail and analyze their impact on the constitutional framework—such developments as the democratization of the franchise, the emergence of an integrated national economy, the spectacular growth of federal bureaucracy, the assumption of a major role in world politics, the establishment of permanent armed forces, the invention of jet propulsion and nuclear weapons, and the spreading influence of electronic media of communication.

It is remarkable that the Constitution framed in 1787 has survived

these tremendous changes. It suggests that the fundamental principles of the system were sound. Yet a danger lurks in this achievement. The amazing durability of the system almost paralyzes us. It
seems a sacrilege to ask whether the framers' design still provides
effective, accountable government. We hardly dare inquire whether
our difficulty in coming to grips with the problems of our common
life—the length and high cost of political campaigns, the low turnout
of voters, budget deficits, the weakness of the bureaucracy, an inability
to make the exercise of war powers more accountable, disagreeable
cities, persistent poverty, obsolete factories, chronic distress on the
farms—may be rooted partly in the constitutional design.

This book focuses on the presidency because that office bears much
of the institutional strain that arises from modern conditions. It is
also the office that differs most from the framers' expectations. Article II, which establishes the executive branch, has been called the
"most loosely drawn chapter of the Constitution."[1] The framers
believed that it needed to be flexible because the executive branch
would have to grow as the government adjusted to developments.
What they did not foresee was the extent to which modern conditions would require the executive to take the initiative in the nation's
affairs. They certainly did not expect the president to become the
system's "chief legislator," and they hoped very much that he would
not become a party leader, to cite just two of the roles which Clinton
Rossiter identified as central to the modern presidency.[2]

The bicentennial is a good time to reexamine the system. It is a
time when we are particularly eager to understand the framers'
thinking and to ask why they constructed the presidency as they
did. It is also a time for looking forward, to ask what are the prospects that our constitutional system, given modern conditions and
demands, can provide effective, accountable government into the
third century.

This book is laid out in five parts. Part I (chapter 1) is introductory; it reviews some of the leading events of the past quarter century and finds that our last six presidents, selected and functioning
in an eighteenth-century constitutional framework, have repeatedly
stumbled in dealing with the challenges presented in the late twentieth century.

Part II examines the framers' design for the presidency. Many of the framers were thoughtful students of political philosophy and history, and all of them were experienced politicians. To understand why they shaped the presidency as they did, in chapter 2 we examine the books they read, and in chapter 3 we trace the evolution of the state governments in which many of them were active between the dawn of independence in 1776 and the gathering of the delegates at Philadelphia in the summer of 1787. Then, in chapter 4, we analyze the debates and decisions of 1787 which led to the establishment of a single separate and energetic chief executive. (Throughout the book, particularly in chapters 2 through 4, I have modernized spelling and punctuation in quoted material in the interest of ready comprehension.)

Part III identifies the principal stages in the evolution of the presidency through the past two centuries. Chapter 5 focuses on the domestic leadership of presidents. It begins with the organic laws which gave substance to the executive branch, then analyzes the improvisations (the party system, the regulatory commissions, the civil service, and the emergence of the president as "chief legislator") which enabled the system to cope with the evolving challenges of governance. Chapter 6 examines the way that various presidents, from Jefferson and Polk to Wilson and Truman, have met their responsibilities as commander in chief.

Part IV examines several specific aspects of modern American governance. The central argument of this book is that the demands of governance, at least since the middle of the twentieth century, have strained our constitutional system beyond its limits. The Constitution promises government that is both effective and accountable, but the institutions and procedures established by the framers have been unable in recent years to deliver on those promises. If we are to honor the ideals we still deeply share with the framers (a government of checked and balanced powers, based on laws enacted by a representative assembly and administered vigorously and fairly and rooted in the will of the people), we must be prepared to learn from our experiences and adjust the constitutional framework to the realities and demands of our own time.

The five chapters of Part IV analyze different aspects of recent presidential governance. Chapter 7 tells how recent innovations in the presidential selection process—the dominance of primaries, public financing, jet airplanes, and television—have brought to the presidency a succession of men who were estranged from the government they hoped to lead. Chapter 8 shows how presidents have had to share their appointment power with Congress, particularly senators, and how this has frustrated the framers' intention that presidents should control the administration of the national government and stand accountable for the results. Chapter 9 focuses on the president's responsibility to "take care that the laws are faithfully executed." It makes the somewhat complicated point that modern legislation delegates vast discretion to the executive branch, that much of this delegation is unavoidable, but that an institution headed by a single elected official, chosen once every four years, is unfit to exercise so much authority in a system committed to representative government. Chapter 10 examines the president's role as manager of the economy, in which his responsibilities, as defined in law and public expectation, far outstrip his powers. Chapter 11 notes how the invention of nuclear power and intercontinental missiles and the decision to enter "entangling alliances" have led us to abandon the framers' commitment that "no one man" should be able to take this nation to war.

We have noted that the adaptability and durability of the political system have inhibited American thinking about constitutional government. Yet if the performance of the system now fails in significant ways to satisfy either the framers' ideals or our own needs, we ought to consider whether modifications in the system might yield a net improvement. We can take courage for this enterprise from a dictum in George Washington's Farewell Address: "The basis of our political system is the right of the people to make and to alter their constitutions of government." Of course, changes ought not to be undertaken lightly. If they require formal amendment, the procedure established in the Constitution requires a broad consensus. Before such a consensus can begin to form, there must be creative thought about the alternatives. Part V (chapter 12) offers a contribution to that process. It presents several proposals for change in the constitutional framework and considers how they might fit with the existing system to provide more effective, more accountable national government.

I hope readers will accept these reflections in the spirit in which they are intended. My questioning of the Constitution may seem an impertinence. I do it because I believe that the best way to honor the framers is to follow their example. When they became convinced that the frame of government under which they were operating no longer met the needs of a free people, Washington and his associates reluctantly but with flinty resolution initiated the second revolutionary act of their generation. Today we stand in awe of their achievement, but our esteem for them is liable to become ironic if it paralyzes our critical and creative faculties and renders us immobile when we need to be acting to save democracy.

It is a great pleasure to acknowledge the assistance I have received while conceiving and writing this book. Among those who started me on the road that led to this book were Reinhold Niebuhr, John C. Bennett, and Robert MacAfee Brown at Union Theological Seminary; Clinton Rossiter and Theodore Lowi, my doctoral advisers at Cornell; and Dean Alfange and Everett Ladd, with whom I shared the rigors of graduate study some twenty years ago. Professors Lowi and Ladd were kind enough to read the book in manuscript, and while they are not responsible for faults that remain, they did save me from a number of egregious errors.

More recently I have had the benefits of friendship and association with James M. Burns, James L. Sundquist, Donald Lamm, Fred and Ruth Friendly, Shepard Forman, and James Munroe, whose wise criticism and encouragement have nourished me along the way. I would also like to thank Lloyd Cutler, C. Douglas Dillon, and Senator Nancy Landon Kassebaum, cochairs of the Committee on the Constitutional System, and Peter Schauffler, the committee's indefatigable coordinator, for inviting me to join in the deliberations of that group. Especially in light of their kindness, it is important to point out that chapter 12 contains my own ideas and bears little relationship to the consensus that has emerged from the committee's work.

For the past several years I have tried these ideas on my students and colleagues at Smith College and at several meetings of the college's alumnae. I would like to thank, especially, Leo Weinstein, Stanley Elkins, Nancy LeaMond, Susan Quantius, Ann Hoaglund, and Hope Babcock; Ginny Risk, who performed miracles of word processing; Kit Lee and Gretchen Locy, my extraordinarily capable research assistants; and Janice Daily, documents librarian at the William Neilson Library.

I want also to thank Smith College, which generously supported my work with leaves from teaching and other essential forms of assistance; Project '87, whose grant enabled me to do the research that led to chapter 2; the Center for the Study of Democratic Institutions in Santa Barbara, California, where as a fellow I drafted chapter 6; the American Enterprise Institute, whose kind invitation enabled me to deliver an earlier version of chapter 12; and the United States Information Agency, which gave me the opportunity to share some of the ideas in this book with scholars in Japan, the People's Republic of China, Hong Kong, and Israel.

Finally, I want to express gratitude to my wife, Molly Jahnige Robinson. Without her love, support, and assistance this book would not exist, and my own existence would be far less sweet.

Norton Hill
Ashfield, Massachusetts
September 1986

PART I

Challenge

CHAPTER 1

The Presidency
After Two
Hundred Years

This book is written in the light of two historic developments. The first is the bicentennial of the United States Constitution.* Americans are now celebrating the fact that through two centuries of turbulent change they have continued to be governed by the same set of institutions. France during the same two centuries has had five different republican constitutions, punctuated by military dictatorships, constitutional monarchies, and periods of rule by the puppets of foreign occupiers. Great Britain, though fairly constant in outer forms, has in substance proceeded from a constitutional monarchy in the eighteenth century, through the classic model of parliamentary government in the nineteenth, to a diminution of the House of Lords and an elevation of the prime minister in this century.[1] In Russia, Germany, and Japan, not to mention the nations we now call "developing," institutional revolutions have been even more frequent and profound. The United States, meanwhile, has stubbornly kept the same institutional structure and has to an amazing degree retained, at least in formal appearance, the original distribution of functions and pattern of interaction between parts of the structure.

*The bicentennial era commemorates the framing of the Constitution in 1787, its ratification in 1788, the inauguration of the new government in 1789, and the ratification of the Bill of Rights in 1791.

The second occasion for this book is even more compelling than the first. For the past two decades the American republic has undergone a continuing crisis. In the early 1960s there was a new sense of urgency about the need for governmental action on a number of fronts (overcoming racial discrimination, building a livable urban environment, coping with the demand for change in the "third world," coordinating a defense against Soviet aggression) but an apparent inability of our national institutions to generate an adequate response. On the very week that President John F. Kennedy was assassinated, the lead story in *Newsweek* magazine was an analysis of the deadlock between the president and Senate over his policy.[2] Many people worried about this paralysis, and many of the most thoughtful looked to the presidency to lead the way through the difficulties.[3]

Within two short years of Kennedy's death, however, the situation seemed to be reversed. In 1964 Congress passed an act which committed the nation to a historic assault on racial discrimination. In the heat of that year's national election campaigns Lyndon Johnson persuaded Congress to give him the Gulf of Tonkin Resolution, a virtual blank check to resist communism in Southeast Asia. He launched a "war on poverty," then won a tremendous electoral endorsement, enhanced by overwhelming majorities for his party in both houses of Congress. The next year he embarked on the Great Society and simultaneously committed the nation to war in Indochina.

Suddenly the system seemed not deadlocked but the opposite: utterly incapable of measuring its undertakings to fit its resources. The frenzy did not last long, however. By 1968 the Johnson administration was forced to choose between the Great Society and the war in Vietnam. It chose war, and the crusade in Southeast Asia turned into a ghastly parade of death and frustration, played out every evening on television. The presidential nominating conventions that year revealed a nation in the throes of a nervous breakdown. The Republican Convention in Miami was a brittle, surrealistic exercise in the avoidance of reality. A month later in Chicago the Democrats staged what Norman Mailer aptly called a "siege."[4] President Johnson's birthday occurred while the Democratic Convention was in session, but the man who had led his party to one of its greatest triumphs just four years earlier dared not appear in Chicago.[5]

Despite the disarray of the Democrats, the election of 1968 was no landslide. George Wallace, representing the frustrations of many deep southerners and blue-collar workers, got 13.5 percent of the vote. Hubert Humphrey and Richard Nixon split the rest almost evenly, but Nixon won a clear victory in the electoral college.

As he prepared to assume office, Nixon received a memorandum from his newly appointed adviser on urban affairs, former Johnson aide Daniel Patrick Moynihan. Moynihan noted that Nixon was assuming the governance of a deeply divided country and doing so at the helm of a divided government (that is, with Congress controlled by the opposition party). The situation was extremely dangerous, wrote Moynihan. "The sense of institutions being legitimate—especially the institutions of government—is the glue that holds societies together," he warned. The challenge of the Nixon presidency was clear: "to restore the authority of American institutions."[6]

At first President Nixon seemed to make some progress toward this goal, but gradually it became apparent that this president could not arrest, would in fact accelerate, the erosion of confidence to which Moynihan had called attention. He was too lacking in candor, too prone to the shrewd maneuver. Repeatedly he showed himself willing to "breach the faith" on which executive power in a republic rests—namely, a respect for civil liberties and for the traditions of fair play toward other political leaders.[7]

The 1970s were a time of deep despair about public affairs. People wondered whether our government was capable of meeting the challenge presented by modern conditions. In 1968 Richard Nixon had triumphed narrowly over an administration that had been shattered by its inability either to win or to abandon the war in Indochina. He had said during his campaign that he had a plan for ending the war, but as his first term drew to a close, there was little evidence of progress toward that goal. The president was apparently a shrewd man, but he seemed unwilling to take the people into his confidence.

The campaign of 1972 was a different story. The Democrats were still hopelessly divided. Their early front-runner, Senator Edmund

Muskie of Maine, bowed out early, following a nasty clash with a newspaper publisher in New Hampshire. For a time it seemed that Senator Hubert Humphrey might make a comeback, but after a disheartening primary campaign the party chose Senator George McGovern of South Dakota, a man with some innovative ideas but untested in presidential politics and virtually unknown to most voters.

On election day the alternatives seemed so unpalatable that almost half the eligible electorate failed to indicate a preference. In the wake of the election President Nixon held a remarkable press conference in which he characterized the American people as children. In order to give them the strong government they needed, he intended, he said, to make radical changes in the administration during his second term.

A freeze settled over the government.[8] Then evidence began to leak out that the investigation of a break-in at the Democratic National Committee headquarters had been obstructed, that "dirty tricks" had been played on the opposition candidates during the primaries, and that coveted appointments and other favors had been promised to those who contributed funds to the president's reelection campaign. Soon, almost incredibly, momentum began to gather to impeach the man who had won reelection by one of the largest pluralities in American history.

As these dismaying events came to a head, a device added to the Constitution in 1967 (the Twenty-fifth Amendment) came to the rescue.* Spiro Agnew, after pleading no contest to a charge of income tax evasion brought by the Justice Department, resigned from the vice presidency, leaving a vacancy to be filled by presidential nomination, subject to a confirming vote by both houses of Congress. By this time (October 1973) Richard Nixon's authority was so frail that he was forced to choose, as the new vice president, someone entirely acceptable to Congress. Gerald Ford, the minority leader in the House of Representatives, met that criterion, and so, by a process tantamount to the parliamentary method for selecting chief executives,

---

*Before the ratification of the Twenty-fifth Amendment there was no constitutional provision for filling a vice presidential vacancy. Without the new provisions, the man next in line for the presidency by statute would have been the speaker of the House of Representatives, Thomas P. ("Tip") O'Neill—a Democrat, just two years after voters had chosen the Republican ticket for the White House by a landslide margin.

Ford was nominated and confirmed as Agnew's replacement.

By the summer of 1974 the momentum of the Watergate scandal had become irresistible. A year earlier a White House aide, Alexander Butterfield, revealed to Senate investigators that President Nixon had made tapes of most of his conversations in the Oval Office. On July 24, 1974, the Supreme Court ruled unanimously that the president had no right to withhold evidence contained on the tapes of his conversations with aides. Three days later the House Judiciary Committee began voting, by margins of 27–11 and 28–10, in favor of articles of impeachment. On August 5, in compliance with the Supreme Court decision, Nixon released three transcripts of conversations of June 23, 1972, that clearly showed his participation in the cover-up, approving the use of the Central Intelligence Agency (CIA) to obstruct a Federal Bureau of Investigation (FBI) probe into the break-in. Overnight members of the Judiciary Committee who had voted against the articles of impeachment began calling the transcripts "a smoking gun" and indicated that they would reverse their position. Two days later Nixon announced that he would resign, and Ford was sworn in as his successor.

In his inaugural address President Ford offered reassurance to an anxious nation. "Our long national nightmare is over," he said. "Our Constitution works. Our great republic is a government of laws and not of men." But events quickly showed that faith could not be so easily restored. In September, just a month after taking office, Ford announced a "full, free and absolute pardon" for all offenses Nixon might have committed during his years as president. An outraged public wondered whether the laws would have treated a private citizen so leniently.

Many were concluding that the Watergate episode revealed the limits of the impeachment process for dealing with failed chief executives: that, in order to catch the president in a palpable crime, it was necessary to have evidence of criminal activity not likely ever again to be available; that it took a year and a half of public charges and dangerous confrontations to build the case for impeachment; and that, normally, the conviction or resignation of an impeachable president would install a man of his own choosing in his place.[9]

President Ford brought a stolid and impressive strength to his duties, but it was clear that a substantial part of the nation longed for a fresh start. Jimmy Carter, capitalizing on that feeling, won the Democratic nomination over several candidates who were far more experienced than he in national politics, and he rode it to a narrow victory over Ford in the 1976 election. When the new president and his wife walked down Pennsylvania Avenue to the White House following his inaugural, he symbolized the hope for a human-size chief executive, one eager to discharge his responsibilities in full view.

As president Carter scored some impressive victories. He developed and implemented plans for civil service reform and for the deregulation of the airlines, trucking, and railroad industries. He thwarted several weapons projects (the B-1 bomber, the neutron bomb) which he regarded as unnecessary or worse. He focused attention on the energy problem and helped the nation understand the need for conservation and a reduction of oil imports. He boosted the cause of fair play in the marketplace by appointing such strenuous advocates as Michael Pertschuk and Joan Claybrook to important regulatory positions. He changed the face of the American judiciary by appointing more women and members of racial minorities to the bench than all his predecessors combined. And in a remarkable post-election special session of Congress in 1980 he led the way to the enactment of legislation to protect vast tracts of land in Alaska and to establish a fund to clean up toxic wastes.

His greatest successes were in the field of foreign affairs. In his inaugural address he announced that arms control would be his top priority. On entering office, he ordered a fresh start on negotiations which, under Nixon, Ford, and Henry Kissinger, had been practically concluded, but by the time his version was ready for ratification the Soviet invasion of Afghanistan made it impossible to proceed. Despite that frustration, the treaty (called SALT II), though never ratified, put controls on the arms race well into the 1980s, through the tacit, voluntary compliance of Soviet and American leaders. Carter's treaty with Panama, ratified by two-thirds of the Senate despite vociferous popular opposition, removed a dangerous issue from the agenda of U.S. relations with Central America. With remarkable patience and persistence, he led Egypt and Israel to the so-called Camp David accords, an agreement which overcame deep, historic animosities. He cleared the way for a normalization of relations with the People's Republic of China by terminating a treaty with the government of Taiwan.

Notwithstanding these substantial achievements, President Carter gained a reputation for vacillation and for fruitless struggles with Congress which he was never able to shake.* His move to establish a federal Department of Education looked like a cynical payoff of a campaign debt, undermining his carefully cultivated reputation for moral rectitude. His persistent effort to terminate wasteful water projects antagonized many members of Congress. His plans for tax and welfare reform, for the reorganization of government, for the "containment" of hospital costs, for revisions in the FBI charter, and for a fee on imported oil and a $50 tax rebate found little support either in the nation or in Congress. Time and again he was forced either to accept defeat openly or to allow his initiatives to fall by the wayside. During the last two years of his presidency his administration seemed to stagger from one defeat to another. In the summer of 1979 he suddenly canceled plans for a televised speech to the nation on yet another set of energy initiatives, then summoned a group of leaders to Camp David to counsel with him about the state of the national character. When he came down from the mountain, he reorganized his cabinet and sought another new beginning, but to no durable avail. Almost immediately the government fell back to internal bickering. Sensing that the president was vulnerable, Senator Edward M. Kennedy of Massachusetts announced his intention to seek the Democratic nomination. The seizure of American diplomatic hostages in Iran created a new and crippling frustration, and when President Carter cited the need to concentrate on this situation as a reason for refusing to debate his differences with Senator Kennedy, he vastly increased his personal stake in a situation over which he had almost no control. In 1980 the economic picture worsened. There ensued a succession of substitutions and revisions of the fed-

---

*President Carter was sometimes hurt by a tendency to inflate his rhetoric. When he signed the act creating the Synthetic Fuels Corporation, for example, he said that the national effort to attain self-sufficiency in energy would be equal to the combined costs of the Apollo moon landing program, the interstate highway system, and the Marshall Plan.[10] That may have been true in unadjusted dollars, but the comparison was nevertheless ludicrous.

eral budget that contributed further to the impression that the government under Carter's leadership had lost its way.

It was never clear what even the greatest of presidents could have done to cope with the shocks that undermined the Carter presidency: the quadrupling of oil prices, which touched off far-reaching economic dislocations; terrorism in Iran; the Soviet invasion of Afghanistan. Perhaps any effort to deal more aggressively with them would have compounded the costs. Yet President Carter seemed almost to insist on being held personally responsible for the frustrations that engulfed him.

At several points in American history a presidential transition has signaled an abrupt change in the national spirit. The change from Herbert Hoover to Franklin Delano Roosevelt was one such occasion; so was the succession from William Howard Taft to Woodrow Wilson and from James Buchanan to Abraham Lincoln. In each case the retiring president seemed to have lost his grip on affairs, and people had lost confidence in him. The new president was an unknown quantity; but he was full of confidence and energy, and the nation expectantly braced for action.

Ironically in retrospect, the transition from Gerald Ford to Jimmy Carter at first seemed to be another such occasion. Yet by the end of Carter's term the national spirit was once again bogged down in confusion, and this time the difficulty could not be traced to an aberrant personality. Carter, on coming into office, had been inexperienced in national politics (like Lincoln? Wilson? both Roosevelts?), but he was manifestly an honest, highly intelligent, dedicated man. Evidently it took more than a personally laudable man to make the system work.

The widespread sense of disorientation at the conclusion of the Carter presidency was marked by the appearance of articles and books that traced the national "malaise" to faults in the system of government. The best remembered and most astute of these analyses, though by no means the only one,[11] was an article in *Foreign Affairs* magazine (Fall 1980) entitled "To Form a Government" by Lloyd Cutler. Cutler is a Washington attorney of vast experience, in and out of government, who had been called to join the White House staff in the wake of the Camp David conference. He had seen the ineffectiveness of the government up close during the Carter years. He traced it, though, not to the personal failings in his chief but to the inadequacies of the constitutional system for modern governance. It was impossible, he wrote, to "form a government" under this Constitution and thus impossible to enact an adequate energy policy or control the arms race.

The political opposition was quick to heap scorn on Cutler's article. Columnist George Will wrote in *Newsweek* magazine, in an article titled "The Administration's Alibi" (October 13, 1980), that the fault lay not in James Madison's checks and balances but in Carter's abysmal lack of political skill. The conservatives were not going to be cheated out of their chance to make the system work.

The succession from Carter to Ronald Reagan produced the usual sense of refreshment, very much as the transition from Ford to Carter had four years earlier. Yet this time, owing to Reagan's buoyant personality and his remarkable political skills, the popular sense of satisfaction with the president's performance proved far more durable.

During his campaign Reagan had capitalized brilliantly on the opportunity presented by Carter's frustrations. The decisiveness of the popular vote in his favor surprised many people who had based their expectation on polls taken before the final televised debate. Reagan accomplished two things in that debate: He fixed national attention on the disappointment and frustration that people felt with Carter, and he established his own standing as a man of presidential timber.[12] Popular ambivalence turned into a firm decision to try something new.

From the beginning of his first term Reagan seemed to belie the impression that the presidency could no longer provide leadership for the American constitutional system. Despite all the forces of inertia, the entrenched lobbies, and the control of the House of Representatives by the opposition Democrats, Reagan quickly proceeded to redeem his basic campaign promises: a tax cut, a military buildup, and a cut in domestic spending.

In foreign policy he was less successful. He was able to deflect Senate opposition to his proposed sale of arms to Saudi Arabia and to protect his policy of support for the government in El Salvador and for the guerrillas in Nicaragua from congressional interference.

In the Middle East, however, he ran into deep trouble. A prolonged struggle with Congress over the application of the War Powers Resolution to the dispatch of armed forces to Lebanon ended when a truck full of explosives crashed into a lightly guarded barracks in Beirut, killing 241 marines. The American retreat from this ill-advised mission was covered by a spectacular invasion of Grenada that same weekend. The Grenada action raised some troubling constitutional questions about the authority of a president to undertake aggressive military action in the absence of consultation with Congress and about the restraints placed by the military on press coverage of the invasion. The resistance in Grenada was somewhat stiffer than anticipated, but when the assault gained its principal objectives within a week, the political support for pursuing these constitutional objections melted away.

People who had concluded that the government was incapable of decisive, coherent action were astonished by Reagan's achievements, particularly during his first year in office. His performance was almost Rooseveltian. Hard times continued, but only partisan opponents blamed the president. In the face of a persistent recession which seemed to mock his faith in supply-side economics, Reagan himself remained optimistic, and throughout his first term talk of the need for a fundamental reform of political institutions was no longer heard in the councils of power.

The underlying realities, however, remained grim: high interest rates; a record trade deficit; an overvalued currency; the loss of manufacturing jobs; a surge in bank failures; a recession in agriculture; debt payment difficulties in Latin America and Africa that threatened to undermine the international financial structure. In the face of these problems it gradually dawned that the constitutional crisis that began in the early 1960s had not gone away. It was evident in the embarrassment President Reagan suffered when only 14 of the 178 Republican members of the House of Representatives voted in support of his strategy for enacting the top legislative priority of his second term, tax reform.* It was evident, most dramatically, in the

---

* Speaker O'Neill echoed many Republican legislators, and even a few White House officials, when he remarked, "I cannot believe that a president who won the votes of 54 million Americans cannot gain the support of his own Republican caucus for his No. 1 second-term initiative."[13]

inability of the president and Congress to agree on a plan to reduce the deficit. The president, who had made "fiscal responsibility" a centerpiece of his own drive for power, made gestures in the direction of concern about the deficit. He voiced support for a constitutional amendment to require a balanced budget and for legislative efforts to experiment with an item veto. Down deep, however, he seemed to believe that supply-side economics would solve the budgetary problems. He promised to veto any tax increase and continued to insist on higher spending for the military. He called for more reductions in domestic spending, but his own director of the Office of Management and Budget (OMB) and members of Congress, including hosts of fellow Republicans, warned that there was not enough money left in the budget for domestic programs to balance the budget, even if all discretionary programs were eliminated.

The deficit crisis revealed that the president and members of Congress were in basic disagreement. Everyone had a plan for reducing the deficit, but there was no way to fashion a consensus. The result was stalemate. In desperation Congress adopted a scheme for automatic, across-the-board cuts in spending, triggered in the event of a failure to meet legislated annual targets for reduced deficits. The mechanism was adopted in the rush for adjournment in late 1985, amid expressions of profound misgivings on all sides. The president himself signed the act without a public ceremony and admitted in a brief statement that he was not convinced that it was constitutional.* Others were even more blunt. The chairman of the House Budget Committee, William H. Gray III, Democrat of Pennsylvania, called it "horrendous public policy" and said that it violated "the most fundamental principles of congressional responsibility and accountability, the precepts of economic policy, and plain common sense."[14]

Thus, as the nation moved toward the bicentennial of the Constitution, many observers found a familiar pattern reasserting itself.

---

* In oral argument before the Supreme Court in April 1986 Reagan's solicitor general, Charles Fried, contended that the central feature of the act was unconstitutional. It interfered with the president's responsibility to enforce the law, he argued, for the comptroller general to resolve differences between the executive's Office of Management and Budget and the Congressional Budget Office over the size of the projected deficit, which was the basis for imposing cuts under the deficit reduction act. The Court accepted Fried's reasoning.

Once again it was proving virtually impossible to achieve coordinated action on the nation's most pressing problems. The government was unable to adopt coherent plans of action or to manage great enterprises effectively, and it was impossible to hold anyone, or any group, accountable for the frustrations.

As we think about the fitness of the constitutional arrangements for executive power, we cannot make better preparation than by going to school with the framers. We need to learn what they learned in preparation for their work. We need to know how their experiences shaped their thinking. Above all, we need to know why they chose as they did in designing the presidency. The deeper our understanding of this background, the better able we will be to judge whether the institutional structure and processes they left us are still serving the ideals we share.

PART II

Design

CHAPTER 2

The Idea of
the Executive

The framers of the Constitution were experienced political leaders, who trusted what they had learned in the course of public service. For most of them, however, there was another source of dependable knowledge: the writings of historians, philosophers, and jurists. Many of the framers were highly educated men; some could even be called learned—certainly James Madison and perhaps James Wilson, William Samuel Johnson, Alexander Hamilton, George Wythe, and George Mason as well. As practicing politicians they were duly skeptical of theories untested by experience, but they regarded the careful study of historical experience as a good way to examine the effects of ideas about politics. As John Dickinson remarked at the Federal Convention, "Experience must be our only guide. Reason may mislead us."[1]

Perhaps the best testimonial to this respect for sound learning came from the unschooled George Washington. In a letter to state governors at the close of the War for American Independence, the commander in chief wrote that the framers of American constitutions were fortunate to have at their disposal "the treasures of knowledge, acquired by the labours of philosophers, sages, and legislatures, through a long succession of years. . . ."[2]

Many leaders of that remarkable generation shared Washington's

appreciation of the contribution that "sages" could make to constitution making. Madison's preparations for the convention consisted
of an intensive, self-taught course in comparative politics. Hamilton
and Wilson also spent many hours getting ready to deploy an arsenal
of ideas gleaned from years of scholarly labors. Roger Sherman, a
cobbler by trade who had little formal education but an inquisitive
and powerful mind, spent the winter and spring months before the
convention reviewing his earlier studies in history and political science.

In this chapter we will be examining the ideas about executive
power found in some of the books which the framing generation
read. It will be obvious, as we pursue this inquiry, that the framers
ignored much of what they read—not always to their benefit—and
that they used what they read pretty selectively. We will nevertheless take a careful look at these sources because our purpose is not
just to see where the framers got their ideas but to sharpen our own
understanding of the role of the executive in a constitutional framework.

As the movement for American independence began to gather
momentum, colonial preachers and publicists drew heavily on the
literature of the "Atlantic republican tradition." Early Americans
read a wide variety of writers, from the deeply serious Algernon
Sidney to the satiric Jonathan Swift, from polished poets like John
Dryden and Alexander Pope and elegant essayists like Joseph Addi-
son and Lord Bolingbroke to literary journalists like Thomas Gordon and John Trenchard, as much for their brilliance as stylists as
for the profundity of their ideas. In their English setting these were
dissenting voices. In America they became the new orthodoxy. Their
central proposition was that liberty was perpetually threatened by
those who lusted after power. The only legitimate source of political
power was the consent of the people; the only authoritative statement of the people's will was the law, made by representatives chosen by the free suffrages of the people. All just use of governmental
power proceeded from such laws, never from a monarch. To Americans monarchy seemed an absurd institution. They simply did not
understand how a hereditary arrangement for choosing leaders could
reduce political conflict, how political elites (civil and military

bureaucracies) could use it to enhance the regime's stability. All Americans saw was wasteful pomp, the ignorant, mulish men wearing crowns, and the cringing sycophants surrounding them.

The English, through Tory reformism, saw the remedy for their ills in a purified monarchy, but such ideas fell on deaf ears in America. Other reformist implications of this critical tradition were, of course, greeted more sympathetically, and much of it had relevance for the framing of constitutions; but again, most of it was negative. It warned against standing armies and the "grasping" nature of power. Most of all, it warned against political parties. The British writers who had greatest influence in American political culture saw Robert Walpole's career as prime minister as proof that an astute man who controlled the crown's patronage could build a tremendous political machine and use it to win parliamentary elections. He could then use his leverage in Parliament to create more offices and appropriate revenues to pay stipends, thereby adding more loyal soldiers to his patronage army. The result was a tyranny as vicious as any ever practiced by despots of old.

Liberty and the preservation of civil virtue which was its essential foundation depended on breaking this corrupt connection between legislative factions and the government's powers of appointment. Bolingbroke's strategy—the elevation to the kingship of a man of incorruptible integrity and patriotism—offered one way to accomplish this goal. The framers thought they had such a man in George Washington. That solution, however, was obviously not permanent.

Again, the basic problem was that the dissenting tradition paid little attention to the constructive, institutional features of executive leadership. What exactly was the role of the executive in constitutional government? Here the American framers confronted a problem that was new in the Anglo-American tradition. Madison once remarked that in Europe charters of liberty had been granted by people in power, whereas in America a free people had granted charters of power.[3] In framing a constitution, Americans could not assume, as the British did, that the basic problem was simply to curb the power of the crown. Americans needed a positive definition of the role and functions of the executive and a means of curbing abuses that did not depend on a balance of social classes.

It was time for Americans to build political institutions of their own, and that required a new kind of study. As Benjamin Rush, a close friend of several framers, once remarked, "It is one thing to understand the *principles*, and another thing to understand the *forms* of government. . . ."[4] For the latter, many in the founding generation turned first to one of the most original thinkers of the Atlantic republican tradition, one who was fascinated by questions of institutional form, James Harrington (1611–1677).

According to John Adams, Harrington was the outstanding theorist of republican government. His ideas epitomized "classical republicanism" in seventeenth-century England. In his principal work, about a utopia, called *The Commonwealth of Oceana*, he presented a design for republican government in England which drew on his studies of the ancient Roman Republic, the political institutions of Renaissance Venice, and the teachings of Niccolò Machiavelli.

To Harrington and other men of the Puritan Revolution (1642–1660), a republic meant, first of all, a government without a king.[5] Harrington realized that the elimination of the king would not by itself produce civic happiness. It required two other fundamental conditions: the rule of law, made and executed by those who controlled the wealth of the community, and the broad distribution of wealth among the citizenry—if necessary, by land reform.

To prevent the abuse of power, the constitution of Harrington's utopia established elaborate procedures to ensure that power lodged only with the most able and public-spirited people, who would rotate in and out of office to forestall the consolidation of privilege. Another essential safeguard of liberty was the separation of powers. In Oceana the constitution provided that a council, rather than a single chief executive, carry out the law. A single initiator, a Moses or Lycurgus, would set the regime in motion. Once his work of founding was done, however, he would retire from the scene, lest by his awesome presence he undermine the institutions he had made. Harrington also provided a "dictator" to rule in emergencies, but in another significant departure from ancient designs, his dictator was a committee, which served for only a limited duration and then rendered an account of its actions to the community.

Like all republican theorists, Harrington was intensely concerned about the danger of factions, or parties, by which citizens, "laying their heads together or canvassing," might cause separated powers to be fused in the service of a single interest or passion. To meet this danger, he adopted a remarkably complex scheme of elections, combining deliberate choice and chance, so as to ensure winners who would not know "whom to thank, nor whom to challenge." The electoral processes set forth in *Oceana* are too complex even to summarize here. To understand the lengths to which Harrington was prepared to go, it is enough to look at the electoral process actually used for choosing the head of state in the city-state of Venice, one of Harrington's models.

> In the choice of the Doge, . . . all the members over thirty years old assembled and cast their names into a pot. In another pot was the same number of balls, of which thirty were gilt. A child then drew from the two pots until the thirty gilt balls had been drawn, with thirty corresponding names. The process was then repeated, the thirty names being put into one pot and thirty balls in the other, of which nine were gilt. The nine picked by this lot nominated forty, out of whom twelve were selected by lot, who nominated twenty-five. Nine of these were then picked by lot and proceeded to nominate forty-five, who were reduced by lot to eleven. The eleven chose forty-one leading members of the Senate, who then did the electing of the Doge, twenty-five votes being necessary for an election.[6]

Harrington once published, in a broadside, a marvelous drawing which illustrated how the balloting in Oceana would work.[7] To the modern eye it looks a little like a Rube Goldberg machine, with human parts. But Harrington insisted that his design would be simpler in practice than it appeared, and he warned that it must not be streamlined, for its safeguards against manipulation were crucial.

One of Harrington's strengths was his recognition that a commonwealth needed special procedures to cope with emergencies. Relying on the precedents of ancient Rome and Renaissance Venice, he provided for a dictator. He believed that the alternatives—holding rigidly to the republic's normal, slow pace or tolerating even a temporary deviation from constitutional procedure—were unacceptable. He agreed with Machiavelli: When a commonwealth once begins to take the easy path of resorting to nonconstitutional procedures to deal with emergencies, "she is dissolved, for the being of a commonwealth consists in her orders." Harrington's dictator, like the Venetian, consisted of a council, rather than a single individual. Once instituted by the Senate, it had full power to make war and peace, levy men and money, and enact laws, which were valid for one year unless repealed sooner by the Senate and Assembly.[8]

From the standpoint of the framers of the new American Constitution, Harrington's importance lay as one who identified problems and principles, rather than as an architect of solutions. They shared his concern for preventing the consolidation of power in a governing elite, though they rejected his insistence on rotation as a fundamental principle of free government. Like him, they were concerned that the election of the executive might be deeply divisive, and like him, they were prepared to go to great lengths in devising schemes to prevent this result.

We turn next to John Locke (1632–1704), whose political ideas were a fundamental source of the American ideology. His *Second Treatise of Government* contains analyses and prescriptions directly relevant to the problems the framers faced and to our assessment of their achievement.*

Locke contended that the legislative power was supreme in any well-ordered commonwealth.[9] Note, however, that the legislative assembly did not have a monopoly on legislative power. Locke expressed approval for a system (nameless, but obviously England's) in which "the legislative [was] placed in the concurrence of three distinct persons"—namely, "a single hereditary person," the supreme executive power; an assembly of hereditary nobility; and an assembly of representatives chosen by the people.[10] The prince as execu-

---

*Earlier we noted Rush's distinction between principles and forms of government. In that same passage, Rush goes on to say that, whereas "Mr. Locke is an oracle as to the *principles*, Harrington and Montesquieu are oracles as to the *forms* of government." This is a curious remark because the book of Locke's to which a modern political scientist would first turn, his *Second Treatise of Government*, is full of teaching about forms of government. The diminishing influence of Locke's ideas, to which Rush points, may have been owing less to his neglect of constitutional questions than to his insistence on facing awkward questions that the framers preferred to disregard.

tive thus "shared" in the legislative power, having in fact an absolute veto; but as commander of the force of the commonwealth and the one responsible for enforcing the laws, he was distinct from the rest of the legislative.

Locke offered two reasons for separating legislative and executive powers. First, laws can be made "in a little time," after which the legislative may disband until there is a need for new law; the executive, on the other hand, must operate constantly. Locke's second reason marked him as a true source of the American constitutional tradition. Because of the "temptation" of human frailty "to grasp at power," those who made the laws ought not be allowed to execute them.[11]

Locke here enunciated the principle that divides the British and American constitutional traditions. Americans remained closer to Locke. The British gradually moved away, toward a system that fused legislative and executive power in a cabinet of party leaders. For Locke, such a mixture of legislative and executive functions encouraged a soft but vicious form of tyranny.[12] He deplored the system of patronage and party loyalty which was already beginning to develop in England in the seventeenth century. He predicted dire consequences—popular resistance, the outbreak of civil war, eventually the dissolution of government—if political leaders pursued such corrupt practices. Nevertheless, he was content simply to issue warnings. He did not try to devise institutional means of prevention, apart from noting that in well-ordered commonwealths the executive and legislative are "often" kept separate.[13]

Locke's attitude toward the executive was ambivalent. At one point he called it "ministerial and subordinate,"[14] having neither will nor power of its own (that is, not until the legislature raised revenues and granted supplies). However, he also recognized that the legislative power, though supreme, was deficient in certain respects. There was, first of all, the problem of starting and ending legislative sessions. Theoretically a constitution could provide a regular time for convening and dispersing, but Locke said it was impossible to know in advance when new laws might be needed or how long an assembly ought to stay in session. Thus, in England it had become the "prerogative of the king" to summon and dismiss the legislature.[15]

In addition, Locke contended that "the good of the society requires that several things should be left to the discretion of him that has the executive power."[16] Legislators cannot foresee and provide by law for everything that may be "useful" to the community. Nor can legislatures remain always in being or act quickly enough to meet emergencies. Furthermore, it will not be in the public interest to have the laws executed with "inflexible rigour" on all occasions and on all persons. A power of pardon and other forms of administrative discretion must lodge somewhere. For all these reasons, there must be "a latitude left to the executive power, to do many things . . . which the laws do not prescribe."[17] Locke, the great Whig philosopher of the rule of law, here parted company with those who held that the executive must always "take care that the laws be faithfully executed" and helped prepare for what Clinton Rossiter called "constitutional dictatorship," in the United States as well as in England.[18]

Concerning the powers of government, Locke distinguished between the legislative, the executive, and the federative (the power to conduct foreign relations and to make war and peace). The executive and federative, though distinct powers, were "always almost united" in the same hands. Both required the use of force. To place them in separate hands would invite "disorder and ruin." Yet the federative could not be guided by antecedent, standing, positive laws. It must be entrusted to the "prudence and wisdom" of him who commands the force of the society.[19]

Locke's distinction here is vitally important. He realized that internal affairs, particularly taxation, present quite different problems from external affairs. In matters of war and of treaties with foreign powers, it is not possible to subject the government to the sort of prior control that is possible in domestic affairs.[20] Thus, Locke's prince operated alone in making alliances and in deciding whether, when, and where to go to war. If his policies required material support, he was, of course, dependent on the legislative power to raise taxes. Nor, practically speaking, could he compel the nation to do what it was determined not to do. Nevertheless, only he could take the lead in foreign affairs, and he had discretion in this arena that he did not have in his domestic capacity.

The prince, in Locke's theory, combining executive, federative, and a share of legislative authority, had enormous power. What if he abused it? Locke wrestled with this problem at some length—he was writing, after all, in a century of revolution—but his conclusions were not clear. He noted that the person who holds the supreme executive power cannot be punished by the legislature since he is himself part of the legislative power, equipped with an absolute veto to defeat hostile resolutions or enactments, and thus, "he is no more subordinate than he himself shall think fit, which one may certainly conclude will be but very little."[21] On the other hand, executive power placed anywhere but in the person of the prince was "visibly subordinate and accountable," both to the prince and ultimately (through its power of granting "supplies") to the legislature. Furthermore, if the legislature put the means of execution into hands other than those of the prince himself, they had power when they found cause to resume it out of those hands and to punish those guilty of any maladministration against the laws. The same held also in regard to the federative power, "that and the executive being both *ministerial and subordinate to the legislative.*"[22] These considerations implied a power of impeachment lying against the king's ministers and suggested that the legislative could withhold the means needed to execute any designs that the prince might have when they were contrary to the will of the people's representatives.

Beyond these powers of discipline in particular cases lay the ultimate sanction: dissolution of government. Whenever the executive set his personal will against the laws, whenever he hindered the legislature from assembling or interfered with its freedom of debate, whenever he altered the mode of election to legislative assemblies contrary to the interest and consent of the people, whenever he delivered the people into subjection to a foreign power, whenever he neglected or abandoned his responsibility to enforce the law, leaving the people in a state of anarchy—whenever the executive abused his power in these ways, the people, seeing the ends of government violated and the constituted frame of government broken, might consider their allegiance dissolved.[23]

But these potential incitements to dissolution and resistance were all acts of the executive. Even if legislative assemblies were inclined to act contrary to the people's will and interest, they could not do so, by Locke's theory, without the concurrence of the executive (the executive having an absolute veto). Thus, the executive, for Locke, was potentially both the savior of the commonwealth, by prerogative, and its betrayer.

Locke recognized that his theory, taken literally, invited anarchy.[24] If government dissolved every time the prince set his personal will above the law or interfered with the free operation of legislative assemblies, there would be perpetual chaos. But the people, said Locke, were patient. It was difficult to persuade them to amend even acknowledged faults once they had grown accustomed to them. Only when there had been "a long train of abuses, . . . all tending the same way,"[25] would people rouse themselves and resist the outlaw. A wise prince would avoid this degree of popular alienation above all other perils.[26]

There was a considerable measure of political prudence in these observations. Locke was concerned about political obligation and abstract right, but he also had a finely tuned sensitivity to political reality. He recognized that there would be emergencies, even in a perfectly well-ordered commonwealth, and he knew also that foreign relations presented special problems, to which the strict rule of law was ill suited. No matter how emphatically the constitution forbade prerogative, no matter how carefully it sought to distribute the powers relating to foreign relations and war making, he saw that its viability would depend on the chief executive's ability to take effective action and on his ability to win and keep popular support for what he did in these emergencies. The refusal of most of the framers to face this problem did not lessen its challenge to the system they were creating.*

We turn next to Montesquieu (1689–1755), whom Madison, in *The Federalist*, Number 47, identified as "the oracle who is always consulted and cited" on the separation of powers. Yet when one passes beyond his elegant argument in *The Spirit of Laws* for the separation of powers, it is difficult to discern any influence on specific features of the Constitution's design. Indeed, his teachings on the executive seem a trifle eccentric from an American perspective.

The basic point of his treatise taken as a whole is not that govern-

---

*Hamilton is the obvious exception. See especially *The Federalist*, Number 23.

mental powers should be separated—he used the term *separation* only once[27]—but that liberty and "tranquillity" depended on a balance of political and social forces.[28] What made Britain work so well, Montesquieu thought, was that the powers of government were dispersed through an ancient social structure. Thus, the rich and wellborn constituted a separate class, with distinct interests requiring protection. "[W]ere they to be confounded with the common people, and to have only the weight of a single vote like the rest, the common liberty would be their slavery, and they would have no interest in supporting it, as most of the popular resolutions would be against them."[29] Therefore, the legislative power was committed to two separate bodies, one comprised of the nobility and another "chosen to represent the people."[30] This is doubtless an elegant formulation and might have appealed to some of the planters of South Carolina and Virginia—but not to the likes of Roger Sherman and Elbridge Gerry.

Another teaching that must have seemed peculiar to most framers came in the discussion of impeachment. Montesquieu insisted that the legislature ought not to have the power to impeach "the person, nor the conduct, of him who is entrusted with the executive power." If the monarch himself were vulnerable to accusation and trial, the legislature might act against him arbitrarily, putting an "end to liberty." But was it necessary to move directly against the chief executive himself? No abuse could be committed "without bad counsellors."[31] Who then would try the charges? Not the courts, for the legislature ought not to have to "demean itself before the ordinary tribunals, which are its inferiors," and were in any case common people like themselves, who might be "swayed by the authority of so powerful an accuser. No," concluded Montesquieu, "in order to preserve the dignity of the people and the security of the subject, the legislative part which represents the people must bring in its charge before the legislative part which represents the nobility, who have neither the same interests nor the same passions."[32]

The framers in 1787 were to have great difficulty with the question of impeachment. In formal terms their solution resembled the one Montesquieu "found" in England. But in political and social substance Montesquieu's scheme was totally different. What made the House of Lords a fit tribunal for impeachments in Montesquieu's eye was that it represented something entirely distinct from the accused and the accusers. Partaking of neither the lonely eminence of the monarch nor the vulnerability of the common people, the nobility could, he thought, judge objectively. The British social system provided the key ingredient to this solution. The six-year term for senators in the American plan gave them a measure of security, but senators were in no sense drawn from separate and distinct parts of the social system.

The "mixed" constitution, rooted in multiple, balanced social forces, was an essential part of Montesquieu's ideal, but the materials for it were not available in America.* From Montesquieu's model, Americans abstracted the mechanism of separated powers and fashioned a balance of institutions. It is highly doubtful, however, that Montesquieu would have had much confidence in their scheme. The truth is that except by lending his authority to refinements of the separation of powers, Montesquieu had very little influence on the framing of the presidency.

William Blackstone (1723–1780) opposed repeal of the Stamp Act in 1766, a notoriously unpopular stand in America, but his *Commentaries on the Laws of England*, initially published between 1765 and 1769, was the "first complete description of English law ever written,"[33] and it brought its author immediate renown in both England and America. There was much about this Tory's outlook that rubbed Americans the wrong way; but among lawyers and law students his work carried enormous authority, and there is no doubt that many of the convention's trained lawyers read the *Commentaries* carefully.

The layout of Blackstone's book fitted neatly into the evolving American sense of what a constitution should look like. It began with a chapter on the "absolute rights of individuals" (a discussion of the Bill of Rights), followed by a chapter on Parliament (matters found in Article I of the U.S. Constitution), then eight chapters dealing with the king, his councils, duties, and powers (equivalent to Article II).[34] Apart from the heavy weighting toward the executive, this format would have seemed familiar to the American framers.

---

*Charles Pinckney attempted to come to terms with this fact, in his speech to the convention on June 25, 1787.

Blackstone is best known for his commitment to parliamentary supremacy. He believed, as Thomas Hobbes did, that "absolute despotic power" had to lodge somewhere in every government. The English constitution gave it to Parliament, which had "sovereign and uncontrollable authority" to do anything that was "not naturally impossible."[35]

This did not mean, however, that the king was subservient to the House of Commons. He was, in fact, a constituent part of the British Parliament. Besides his veto, which was (at least theoretically)* absolute, he had exclusive power to convoke and dissolve Parliament. Thus, the crown and the legislative assemblies, though distinct parts of the constitution, shared its powers, which were divided into two branches: the legislative, consisting of the king, lords, and commons, and the executive, consisting of the king alone. There was no separation, though. The king bound the government together.[37]

Through the mist of his fictions about royal prerogative, Blackstone's book presented a thoroughly realistic picture of the role of the executive in constitutional governance. In his discussion of patronage, for example, he showed how honors and government jobs could be used to advance the crown's policy. In the context of his analysis of Parliament, his description of this process was duly censorious. Attempts to influence elections by patronage were "illegal and strongly prohibited," he wrote. When alluding to the same subject in the context of the crown's powers, however, his tone changed. Government required "a due subordination of rank," to encourage the people to respect authority. The law, knowing that "no one can be so good a judge" of merit in public officials as the king, gave him "the sole power of conferring dignities and honors, in confidence that he will bestow them upon no one but such as deserve them."[38] He did not connect the distribution of offices by the king's men with the corruption of legislative elections until the last paragraphs of his chapter on the crown's place in the constitution. Organic laws passed since the execution of Charles I, he wrote, had greatly diminished the powers and prerogatives of the crown, and the elimination of

---

*As Hume had pointed out a quarter century earlier (in 1741), "the royal assent is little better than a form," inasmuch as "whatever is voted by the two houses is always sure to pass into a law."[36]

many ancient sources of royal revenue further "impoverished" the crown. These developments had weakened the constitutional position of the crown and seemed likely to throw its mechanism out of balance.

There were, however, countervailing developments. A vast national debt had accumulated, resulting not only in a sharp increase in taxes but in the proliferation of officers, appointed by the crown, to collect them. In addition, military forces had grown, giving the administration a disciplined army "raised by the crown, officered by the crown, commanded by the crown." It was true that the army was "kept on foot" by annual appropriations, but once raised, it had, by the nature of the constitution, to be "at the absolute disposal of the crown."[39] This added greatly both to the king's patronage and to his influence over the course of national policy.

Blackstone concluded that though the crown's nominal power had been reduced by organic statutes passed since the Glorious Revolution of 1688, its actual domination of the country had been increased by developments over the past century. The resulting constitutional imbalance did not need to be permanent, however. "When . . . our national debts shall be lessened; when the posture of foreign affairs and the universal introduction of a well-planned and national militia will suffer our formidable army to be thinned and regulated; and when, in consequence of all, our taxes shall be gradually reduced; this adventitious power of the crown will slowly and imperceptibly diminish, as it slowly and imperceptibly rose."[40]

Americans by 1787 had already experienced the accumulation of a national debt, however modest in comparison to England's, and though they had no standing army and no foreseeable need for one, their immersion in the literature of the dissenting Whigs filled them with fear of a permanent military establishment. Lacking Blackstone's reverence for the crown and being less inclined than he was to rest on "hope," most of them (possibly excepting Hamilton) would have viewed this situation with less equanimity than he did. Might future developments create an opportunity and demand for executive dominance along the lines indicated by Blackstone? Lacking monarchy, where would it come from, and how would it be kept accountable? Would the Constitution provide sufficient leverage for countervailing institutions? A thoughtful reader of the *Commentaries* had to recognize that Blackstone's analysis posed a serious challenge to the American framers, without providing clear answers.

David Hume (1711–1776) was one of a remarkable group of Scottish social scientists whose books on ethics, political economy, history, and psychology became standard texts in American colleges during the late colonial period.[41] The framers who were graduated from Princeton (Madison, Oliver Ellsworth, William Paterson, Luther Martin) were steeped in these works by John Witherspoon, the great Scot who was president of the college during these years; so were James Wilson, a graduate of St. Andrews, in Scotland, and Alexander Hamilton, who quoted them at the convention and in *The Federalist*.

Hume combined the spirit of an iconoclast with a lucidity, moderation, and brilliance of expression that made his ideas resonate in the mind. He did not write deliberately for an American audience, and he candidly asserted his preference for monarchy and his skepticism about republicanism, which he associated with the excesses of the Puritan Revolution and the utopianism of the dissenting Whigs. Yet these opinions did not seem to diminish his authority with the "young men of the Revolution,"[42] who first encountered his bracing ideas during their late adolescence.

He made his greatest contribution to American thought with his reflections on representative government. Before Hume, it was commonly believed (by Montesquieu, for example) that popular government could exist only in a small territory, where citizens could discuss their differences until a consensus emerged. Over a large territory, according to this theory, factions would develop and tear the fabric of government to pieces. Hume argued that this "common opinion" was false. He thought the contrary more likely: that representative government, once established over an extended territory, would be more stable and durable than in a single city. Interests, to achieve the support of majorities, would have to reach out and form alliances, which would induce them to moderate their demands.[43]

Concerning executive power, Hume was less creative. He was, in fact, fairly comfortable with the existing hereditary monarchy in Britain. He saw constitutional balance as essential to the preservation of liberty and good order. Like Blackstone, he recognized that modern conditions posed new threats to this balance. The king had enormous political resources at his disposal, including the power to fill civil offices, collect taxes, and make military and ecclesiastical appointments. This power, which had grown enormously since the Glorious Revolution of 1688 and was still increasing, made it not improbable, in Hume's judgment, that Britain would "incline" toward executive dominance in the years ahead.[44]

Although he was concerned about these trends, Hume was no republican. He affirmed the rule of law, but he warned that purely popular government, without the balancing factor of magisterial authority, was inherently unstable and prone to suppress liberty. The tumultuous history of Rome showed what happened when a popular assembly became dominant. So did the Puritan Revolution: the triumph of the Roundheads was fatal first to Charles I, finally to Parliament itself.[45]

Hume's approach to the reform of political institutions was cautious. He warned that it was never wise to tinker and try experiments in government "merely upon the credit of supposed argument." A wise ruler must adjust his innovations to the "ancient fabric" and try to preserve its "chief pillars and supports." Yet he encouraged utopian speculation. Mariners, he pointed out, kept trying to perfect the design of ships, even though existing models achieved marvels. The form of government was a chief ingredient in the happiness of men. "Why may we not inquire what is the most perfect of all, though the common botched and inaccurate governments seem to serve the purposes of society?" Who knows? If the "wise and learned" could agree on the best form of government, there might be an opportunity in some future age to reduce theory to practice, either through the collapse of some old government or by men coming together to form a new one "in some distant part of the world."[46]

In this spirit Hume addressed several problems that confronted the framers of the presidency. Ought the chief executive to be elective or hereditary? "To a superficial view," he admitted, election seemed a better method of "filling the throne." But contested elections inevitably divided the people into factions, inviting civil war. The stakes were too great to be decided on merit alone. With candidates and their friends using force, money, and intrigue to win votes, superior merit was no more likely to gain office than where the selection of the sovereign was left to birth alone.[47] England had been correct at the end of the seventeenth century in returning to the hereditary monarchy, he thought.

Though he deplored the spirit of partisanship, which caused people to ignore all virtue in their opponents and excuse all folly in their mates, he appreciated the uses of a party system. Rejecting the conventional view, he contended that a division into "court" and "country" parties (what we might call "government" and "opposition") was not only inevitable, in view of the British constitution of crown and elected legislative assembly, but useful. It provided a check on power and encouraged cohesion between the executive and legislative branches.[48]

Nor did he flinch from admitting that the crown would probably use its patronage in service of the court party. We may disparage this influence, he wrote. We may call it corruption or dependence. But it is inseparable from the very nature of the constitution and necessary to its preservation.

In his constitution for a "perfect" commonwealth he sought to reduce corruption by providing a plural executive, chosen by the Senate from its own membership. He suggested that at the end of their terms in office departing senators be "shut up in a conclave like the cardinals, and by an intricate ballot, such as that of Venice or Malta," choose a "protector" (or chief executive), a treasury commission, and six councils, consisting of five members each, dealing with foreign affairs, education, trade, legal appeals, war, and admiralty. These officials would be salaried, though no legislator would receive any remuneration. Hume defended the indirect mode of election by arguing that the "lower sort of people" are capable enough of judging someone not very distant from them in rank or dwelling place but are unfit for electing the higher officers of the republic. Their ignorance enabled the "grandees" to deceive them.[49]

Several inventors of the presidency read Hume's *Essays* carefully. No doubt they saw themselves as a fulfillment of his hope that someday, somewhere people would have an opportunity to build a "perfect" commonwealth. Perhaps he reinforced their own growing sense that republics especially needed the stabilizing influence of a strong executive. Only a few,* however, could have seen any positive value in the executive's ability to encourage the growth of an administrative party through the adroit use of patronage and electoral influence, and fewer still (only Madison, so far as we know) shared Hume's willingness to approach political parties in an analytical frame of mind.

The significance of these writers was not that they provided practical answers to specific questions of structure and process. Hume probably came closest, in his essay on a utopian constitution, and it is no coincidence that Hume's speculations held great fascination for the most fertile minds among the younger framers (Madison, Hamilton, Wilson).

What they did do—and it mattered greatly that they did—was to teach that strong executive leadership arose not solely from the ambition of princes but from the nature of government. This argument was not incontrovertible and not unanimous. Harrington disputed it. But it came to the framers of the presidency backed by the leading authorities of the Anglo-American tradition.

As Americans turned from the dissenting Whigs to look for more positive guidance, they found in this body of literature, centering on Locke, Blackstone, and Hume, a conviction that the executive, however chosen and mounted, was the core of government.† The popular impulse—to insist on the rule of law and to entrust lawmaking to an assembly of representatives—was still dominant in the American culture, but philosophers lent powerful encouragement to those

---

*See the speeches by Nathaniel Gorham and Alexander Hamilton on June 22, 1787, at the Federal Convention. Hamilton cited Hume as his authority for the view that "influence on the side of the crown, which went under the name of corruption, [was] an essential part of the weight which maintained the equilibrium of the [British] Constitution."[50]

†As Clinton Rossiter has written, "In the last resort, it is always the executive branch in the government which possesses and wields the extraordinary powers of self-preservation of any democratic, constitutional state. . . . Locke could champion the supremacy of the legislature and bespeak the Whig fear of overweening executive power, but even he had to admit that it was the undefined power of this organ . . . that was the ultimate repository of the nation's will and power to survive. It is never so apparent as in time of crisis that the executive is the aboriginal power of government."[51]

who were beginning to sense that it was the executive that gave coherence and energy to government. The challenge for framers of constitutional government was to figure out how to hold executive power accountable without vitiating its capacity for leadership.

CHAPTER 3

First
Experiments in
Government

The founders of the American constitutional tradition were not doctrinaire. In approaching their work of nation building, they would far rather have relied on their vast experience in colonial and early state politics than on book learning or theorizing. As John Adams wrote in 1776, framers of the new state constitutions would be well advised to "proceed in all established modes to which the people have been familiarized by habit."[1] The difficulty was that "established modes" offered no clear pattern for the executive in a republic, certainly not in 1776 and not even by 1785. Beyond that, the isolated situation of the states, coupled with the fact that foreign relations were conducted for the most part by agents of the federal Congress, enabled them to ignore crucial aspects of the executive's business.

Nevertheless, if we are to understand what the framers did in Philadelphia, and why, we must know how ideas about the executive evolved during the decade before they met. To that we now turn. It is a story of evasion, yielding only gradually to a greater willingness to face the harsh demands of reality.

Throughout the colonial period the thirteen governments that declared independence as the United States of America had been led by strong chief executives. Two of them, Connecticut and Rhode Island, operated under charters that provided for popularly elected governors. In three others—Pennsylvania, Delaware, and Maryland—governors were appointed by proprietary families. In the other eight the crown appointed the governors.[2]

When independence came, government continued virtually as before in Connecticut and Rhode Island. But in the other eleven it had to be reconceived. Should they simply lop off the colonial governorship and allow government to proceed entirely from the assembly? Or ought they give the crown's functions to someone else? If so, should it be a single person or a council? How should it be chosen? What exactly were the functions and powers of the "executive"? How did they relate to the "rule of law"? The preamble to the Constitution of New Hampshire (1776) neatly stated the predicament: "The sudden and abrupt departure of his Excellency John Wentworth, Esq., our late Governor, . . . leaving us destitute of legislation, and no executive courts being open to punish criminal offenders; . . . *Therefore*, for the preservation of peace and good order, and for the security of the lives and properties of the inhabitants of this colony, we conceive ourselves reduced to the necessity of establishing a FORM OF GOVERNMENT. . . ."[3] Note the indistinct separation of powers: The departure of the governor left them "destitute of legislation" and with no "executive courts" to punish criminals. Behind these expressions was the concept, still prevailing in the eighteenth century, that the monarch was the source of *all* government, however much he might be obliged by custom and the realities of public finance to win the cooperation of others.[4]

The crown governors had been figures of considerable magnificence, and they wielded enormous powers. Many of them viewed their service in America as a chance for quick enrichment or a step in a career of civil service. Careerism sometimes made them energetic, but in order to advance, they had to satisfy the bureaucracy in London, not the Americans.

The charters under which they operated were strongly centralized. Governors had total command of military forces. They appointed most public officials, including customs collectors, justices of the peace, and sheriffs, giving them considerable patronage. They exercised judicial power, not only through the appointment and removal of judges but by having the power of pardon and by serving, with their councils, as the final courts of appeal in the judicial process. They had substantial legislative power, too. They convoked, disbanded, and dissolved legislative assemblies. They had an absolute veto over legislation, but whereas the crown's veto was almost never used (not since the reign of Queen Anne in 1708), governors frequently used their vetoes to impose the policy of the Colonial Office in London.

Nor did most governors depend upon the assemblies for their personal income. They relied on fees, such as rents on crown lands. This arrangement often put governors at odds with American settlers. In Pennsylvania during the late colonial period Governor Thomas Penn sequestered lands in the western part of the colony, then held them vacant, waiting for prices to rise. When Indians made raids on the thinly settled frontier, colonists blamed the governor's policy.[5]

Not all colonial governors were rogues. Even those who were conscientious, however, became object lessons on the dangers of power that served a distant ruler. Colonial administrators in London appointed American-born Thomas Hutchinson royal governor of Massachusetts because he had shown respect for imperial authority as lieutenant governor during the Stamp Act crisis and as chief justice in the controversy over the writs of assistance. As governor he sought to be an honest broker between London and his fellow Americans. But in this polarized situation his pragmatic approach utterly failed. The Colonial Office in London repeatedly withheld timely support, while the Americans despised him for his maneuvers. In an attempt to shore up his position he distributed patronage to supporters of the government, but the device backfired. Americans knew this game; they identified it with politicians like Robert Walpole, whose party-building tactics their favorite journalists had deplored for many years. Even loyalists had to refuse his patronage for fear of incurring the wrath of the revolutionaries. In the end, his efforts only confirmed the growing impression that American interests would not be safe until all vestiges of imperial authority were banished from the land.[6]

The men who framed the first state constitutions vividly remembered the unpopular, unlawful acts of colonial governors. Most of them had been legislators themselves in the late colonial period. To them, liberty meant that the legislature had to keep officials on a short tether. It meant no more vetoes and no more corruption by those who appointed public officials. It meant government by law, not by the will of any one man.[7]

In the intensity of these convictions the early framers showed little regard for the claims of executive power. Thus, in January 1776* the Assembly of New Hampshire, noting the departure of the royal governor, proclaimed the colony independent and sovereign and announced its intention to select "twelve persons" to serve as a "separate branch of the legislature," called the council.[8] That was all. There would be no other attempt to replace the governor. The council would have a "president," but the president would have no power other than presiding over the meetings of the council. (Note that "president" in this usage was a far less imposing title than "governor.") All public officers would be appointed, not by the president but by the council and Assembly. This New Hampshire Constitution of 1776, which lasted eight years, showed the instinctive reaction of one colony when forced to establish a form of government quickly. It centered on the legislature (note the immediate fabrication of a second chamber), but it made virtually no provision at all for an executive.[9]

If one work captures the popular feeling that underlay this constitutional instinct at the dawn of independence, it is *Common Sense*, by Thomas Paine, published in January 1776. *Common Sense* was a brilliant rhetorical performance, converting hosts of Americans to the cause of rebellion by gathering up their most profound prejudices and hurling them in the face of George III, the reigning monarch.

The crown had become the final refuge for Americans who hoped to avoid dismembering the British Empire. The colonial leadership had repaired to this position in 1774, when James Wilson, Thomas Jefferson, and John Adams each developed a version of the "dominion" theory, arguing that the colonies owed their allegiance not to

---

*New Hampshire was the second state to proclaim an independent government; Massachusetts had been the first, in July 1775.

Parliament (they had their own legislatures) but to the crown alone.[10] So long as colonial theorists could blame the troubles in America on Parliament or on the king's ministers, the drive for independence stalled. When George III in 1774 ordered troops in Boston to enforce the Coercive Acts, most Americans hesitated. Renouncing the crown was an awful act, almost a kind of patricide.

Tom Paine, however, was ready. He aimed his pamphlet directly at the institution of the monarchy. After a brief introductory section on the origin of government ("Government, like dress, is the badge of lost innocence; the palaces of kings are built on the ruins of the bowers of paradise"), he got down to business. Monarchy, he said, is idolatry. Paine recalled how the Israelites (in 1 Samuel 8) had asked Samuel to "make us a king to judge over us like all the other nations." God directed Samuel to warn the Israelites what to expect from a king: He would draft their sons to drive his chariots of war, reap his harvest, and make instruments of war; he would take their daughters to be confectioners and cooks and bakers; he would seize their best fields and give them to his servants; he would take a tenth of their servants and livestock for himself. And when all these things were done, said God, "Ye shall cry out in that day because of your king which ye shall have chosen, and the Lord will not hear you in that day."[11] In a popular culture thoroughly familiar with biblical history, these vivid images were a powerful warning against monarchy.

Paine saved his most caustic language for hereditary succession. It is unnatural to choose rulers by heredity, he said; "otherwise [nature] would not so frequently turn it into ridicule by giving mankind *an ass* for a lion." The founders of most dynasties were "nothing better than the principal ruffian of some restless gang," the "chief among plunderers." Nowhere was this more true than in England, where "a French bastard landing with an armed banditti" established himself "against the consent of the natives. . . ." Royalists contended that hereditary succession "preserves a nation from civil wars," said Paine, but this was "the most barefaced falsity ever imposed upon mankind." Since the Norman Conquest, Paine counted "no less than eight civil wars and nineteen rebellions."[12]

Toward the end of his pamphlet Paine acknowledged that if there were "any true cause of fear respecting independence," it was that the colonies had no plan for government of their own. To relieve this anxiety, he would offer some "hints," to stimulate abler and wiser men to develop better ideas.

What followed was a design for government by legislature, "with a president only." He specified no duties for his president. However, lest he grow into something more formidable, Paine limited his term of office to a single year and provided that the office be rotated through each of the thirteen colonies in turn. Having set forth this simple design (earlier he had written that "the more simple anything is, the less liable it is to be disordered"), Paine capped the most effective polemic in the history of American popular culture with these words: "But where, says some, is the king of America? I'll tell you, friend, he reigns above, and does not make havoc of mankind like the royal brute of Britain. Yet that we may not appear to be defective even in earthly honors, let a day be solemnly set apart for proclaiming the charter; . . . by which the world may know that . . . in America the law is king."[13]

Despite its shrill tone, Paine's pamphlet vividly articulated the impulses that dominated the popular mind at the time of the Revolution. Two themes were fundamental: revulsion against monarchy and attachment to a government of laws, made by elected representatives. Related to these was a populist suspicion that complexity and subtlety were the tools of unscrupulous men.

John Adams praised Paine's stirring call for independence but added, in a letter to his wife, that if he (Adams) had written the pamphlet, the recommendations for a new plan of government would have been stronger.[14] A few weeks later, in response to a request from the Assembly of North Carolina, Adams wrote a twelve-page pamphlet, entitled *Thoughts on Government*, in which he outlined his own recommendations.[15]

At the beginning of his pamphlet Adams identified himself as a republican. Good government, he said, is an empire of laws, not of men, and the best of republics is "that form of government which is best contrived to secure an impartial and exact execution of the laws." Who makes the laws? Adams answered: An assembly of representatives, "in miniature an exact portrait of the people at large."[16]

So far Adams was safely within the consensus of revolutionary ideas. Next, however, came a critical question. Should all powers of government be committed to the assembly of representatives? Adams's answer was unequivocal. "[A] people cannot be long free, nor even happy," he warned, "whose government is in one assembly." Legislative assemblies were unfit to oversee the enforcement of laws and to decide particular controversies over statutory interpretation. Even in the exercise of their lawmaking responsibilities, they needed to be checked. Being human, legislators always favored their own interests. The structure of government needed to prevent them from taking unfair advantage of their position, so that nobler, more generous passions would have a chance for expression.

It went almost without saying—though Adams never tired of saying it—that the power which controlled the assembly would itself have to be controlled, that the system needed checks and balances. He suggested that the assembly choose a second chamber, with full powers of legislation, from among its own members or from the state at large. Then these two houses by joint annual ballot should choose executive officers (a governor and lieutenant governor, secretary, treasurer, commissary, and attorney general; at this stage Adams was recommending a long ballot). Concerning the powers of the executive, he said only that the governor should have command of the militia and an absolute veto over legislation, powers he could be trusted not to abuse because of his annual election by the legislature.

These ideas of Adams, composed in the spring of 1776, were obviously primitive. He had given very little consideration to the means for ensuring that the separated powers would remain truly independent and vigorous in their own proper sector. Thus, prior to the Declaration of Independence, at least one important leader of the Revolution was already convinced that elected assemblies needed to be checked.

The early returns (Massachusetts, New Hampshire, and Pennsylvania) had leaned toward Paine's simplistic ideas. The Constitution of Virginia was the first to embody significant aspects of Adams's design for the "mixed" constitution.

Like the other constitutions framed in 1776, Virginia's reflected the deep suspicion of executive power produced by decades of struggle between ambitious colonial administrators and an assertive local elite. Thus, although its Declaration of Rights boldly pronounced a commitment to the separation of powers, it closely fettered executive power by holding the governor's term to one year, limiting him to three successive terms, denying him a veto, and requiring him to obtain the consent of a privy council before making administrative appointments, exercising military command, or taking any other kind of executive action. It left the bicameral legislature in control of the government, not only in the making of laws but in the choice of governor, privy councillors, and judges.[17]

Jefferson's career under this constitution dramatically revealed its strengths and weaknesses. He had served in the House of Delegates (the lower house of the legislature) from October 1776 until his election as governor in 1779. As a legislator he had developed a broad program for the "reformation" of Virginia, including the abolition of primogeniture and landholding by entail and the establishment of religious freedom.[18] In all, his program included 126 bills, at least 100 of which were eventually enacted into law (some not until the mid-1780s). In later years Jefferson cited this program as his greatest contribution to humanity.

His service as governor was another story. He was elected for a one-year term in June 1779 and reelected the following year, but the constitutional limitations on Virginia's governor, coupled with his own reticence, made him a poor leader, particularly during the British invasion in the spring of 1781. By the end of his second term he had virtually abdicated.[19] Later the Assembly conducted an investigation of charges that as governor he had been sluggish in military preparations and lax in command. In the end the inquiry vindicated him, and the Assembly adopted a resolution of thanks for his services; but his years as governor left painful memories.[20]

In his famous *Notes on the State of Virginia*, written shortly after his retirement as governor, Jefferson described the defects of the revolutionary constitution, tracing them to a failure to provide adequately for the separation of powers. "All the powers of government, legislative, executive, and judiciary, result to the legislative body," he wrote.[21] At the same time he strenuously deplored the desire of some Virginians in 1776 and again in June 1781 to create a "dictator" to cope with the British invasion. The second time, he noted, the resolution "wanted a few votes only of being passed."

Jefferson argued that dictatorship could never be justified by a plea of necessity. "Necessities which dissolve a government do not convey its authority to an oligarchy or a monarchy. They throw back, into the hands of the people, the powers they had delegated, and leave them as individuals to shift for themselves." Other states—he mentioned Massachusetts, New York, and Pennsylvania among others—survived invasion without abandoning the republican form of their governments. (Jefferson neglected to mention, though he probably knew it, that South Carolina had conferred dictatorial powers on John Rutledge during the invasion of 1780.) If Virginia had adopted a dictatorship, warned Jefferson, it would have given all oppressors "a proof, which they would have trumpeted through the universe, of the imbecility of republican government, in times of pressing danger. . . ."[22]

In an appendix to the 1787 edition of his *Notes*, Jefferson published his 1783 draft of a revised constitution for Virginia. It was remarkably stingy toward executive power. It provided a governor, elected by the legislature for a five-year term, but retained for the legislature the power to appoint the state treasurer and attorney general, all general military officers, and all judges of state courts. It gave the veto to a "council of revision," on which the governor served, along with five other officials, including three judges; two-thirds majorities in both houses of the legislature could override the council's veto.

Jefferson's draft was most noteworthy for its attempt to define the scope of the executive in a republic. He explicitly denied to the governor the "prerogative powers" of erecting courts, offices, corporations, markets, ports, or lighthouses; of laying embargoes; and of naturalizing aliens. Certain other powers, he noted, were left "under the authority of the confederation" (that is, the federal government); among these were the power to declare war and conclude peace, contract alliances, raise armies and navies, coin money, and regulate weights and measures. He added, however, that if any of these powers should ever fall to the state, they should be exercised by the governor, under the regulation of the laws.[23]

His trials as wartime governor had evidently not persuaded Jefferson that republics needed vigorous executive leadership.

At the helm of affairs in South Carolina was a man of different kidney, a future framer of the United States Constitution and justice of the Supreme Court, John Rutledge. Rutledge was one of the new nation's wealthiest planters and merchants and, like most of them, a reluctant revolutionary. He was doubtless horrified by almost every word in Paine's pamphlet, including its constitutional prescriptions.

The constitution under which South Carolina began its existence as an independent state was brief and tentative, having been promulgated in March 1776, when Rutledge and his neighbors still hoped to reach an accommodation with Great Britain. In form it replaced the royal governor with a president, to whom it gave an absolute veto. Two years later, having been elected president by the legislature, Rutledge used the veto, while simultaneously resigning, in a vain attempt to block a new constitution that was even weaker, from the standpoint of executive power, than the one issued in 1776.[24]

The period of "phony war" in the South ended in 1779. From their base at Savannah, Georgia, British troops marauded inland and northward. In May 1780 the Americans suffered the heaviest defeat of the war, surrendering the 5,500-man garrison, including four ships, at Charleston. A month later the British general Sir Henry Clinton left for New York, leaving behind about 8,000 men to maintain and, if possible, extend British control by campaigns inland.

In these parlous circumstances the state government of South Carolina became, in effect, the junta for a band of guerrillas. Harking back to Roman precedents, the Assembly voted in March 1780 to make John Rutledge dictator of South Carolina, to rally the effort against the British occupation.[25] There was no constitutional warrant for the Assembly's action, but since the constitution was itself only an act of the legislature, never popularly ratified, the legislature apparently had power to amend it, as the Supreme Court of South Carolina later ruled.[26]

Rutledge's tenure as dictator belied his grandiose title. There was not much he could do, except lend encouragement to the guerrillas. After the war South Carolina reverted to its weak constitution, to Rutledge's dismay.

The response of leaders in New York to military occupation was both stronger and more principled. During the autumn of 1776 British troops, advancing northward, chased George Washington, commander in chief of the American forces, out of New York State. In these dire circumstances revolutionary leaders in New York turned to the question of permanent government for the state. The committee of the Assembly empowered to frame a constitution for New York was a band of men on the run. They met in seven different locations during that dreadful first winter of American independence.*

There were other circumstances, too, which impelled New Yorkers toward a relatively powerful executive. Its colonial government had been centralized, and its social structure, aristocratic (though it should be noted that a similar inheritance seemed to push Virginia in the opposite direction). Of greater weight in New York was the presence, prominent among New York's framers, of an extraordinary group of lawyers, bold, energetic young men, such as John Jay (age thirty-two), Gouverneur Morris (twenty-five), and Alexander Hamilton (only twenty-two in 1777). These young eagles, particularly Morris and Hamilton, were visionaries. Their "state" might now be a frail pretense of a polity, but they were already dreaming of empire. They knew their constituents' commitment to republicanism, and they themselves were firm believers in the rule of law and "popular government"—that is, government arising from the will of the people. But unlike many, perhaps most, of their countrymen, they valued political leadership, and they believed that vigor in statecraft required a unified executive. Under the circumstances, this commitment to the executive was not conservative but the opposite. Indeed, a relatively strong executive turned out to be the most notable feature of the New York Constitution. It was manifest, first of all, in the fact that the governor's term extended for three years.[28] Only Delaware's was that long. South Carolina's was two years; all the rest were one year. In addition, New York's governor was to be

---

*Chief Justice Charles Evans Hughes, writing for the Supreme Court in 1934, argued that we did not need to suspend the Constitution during emergencies because its grants of power were framed "in a period of grave emergency."[27] That may be an exaggeration of conditions in 1787, but it does fairly describe those in which the harried New Yorkers framed their new constitution in 1777.

popularly elected, the first of the new governors so chosen. This was a significant feature. In other states the executive owed his office to the legislature, but in New York he had an independent political foundation. Separation of powers was no longer just a formal aspiration, invoked mainly to justify a strengthening of the legislative assembly. It was beginning to take on political substance and to be linked to the notion of balance.

New York's provision for its chief executive represented a milestone in American constitutional development in another respect, too: the list of his powers. During the late colonial period there had been much talk of the separation of powers, but very little about the proper role of an executive in a balanced constitutional system.

The framers of New York's Constitution began to address this oversight. They included a list of powers for their governor. Besides his responsibility to "take care that the laws be faithfully executed," he became commander in chief of the armed forces and was authorized to convene the legislature, recommend measures, grant pardons and reprieves, and conduct relations with other states.[29] Furthermore, in the exercise of these powers New York's governor, uniquely among governors before 1787, was not attended by an executive council.*

In two respects, however, the governor of New York did have to share his power. The constitution provided for a veto over legislation but gave it to a council of revision, composed of the governor, the chancellor (the state's presiding judge), and at least two other judges of the supreme court. The council of revision could send any bill "about to be passed" back to the legislature, along with suggested revisions challenging either its constitutionality or expediency. The legislature could override by passing the original version by two-thirds majorities in both houses.[31] No other state up to that time permitted its governor even this much involvement in the legislative process.

The other shared power was over appointments, and here the framers made a mistake. Virtually every American politician at that

---

*William Morey says that New Jersey shared this distinction,[30] but in New Jersey, in military matters and on pardons, the governor had to consult with a privy council, composed of members of the upper legislative chamber.

time accepted the testimony of British journalists that the crown's patronage had been used to corrupt Parliament.[32] Several of the early state constitutions (North Carolina, New Jersey, Rhode Island) tried to solve the problem by giving the power of appointing administrators to the legislature; several others (Connecticut, South Carolina, Virginia) made the legislature responsible for judicial appointments. Even in states where the chief executive was the creature of the legislature (Pennsylvania, Delaware, New Hampshire), he was attended by a legislative council, the consent of which he had to obtain before making any appointments.

After considering various schemes, the framers in New York chose a variation on the latter alternative. They created a council of appointments, composed of the governor and four senators, the latter chosen annually by the legislature.[33] As a device for curbing corruption, this council was a dismal failure, as Hamilton reported in *The Federalist*, Number 77. With the emergence of parties in New York, senators on the council of appointments usually formed a caucus which dispensed the state's patronage in accordance with partisan goals. The governor, who had only a casting vote in the event of ties between the other four members, thus lost control over the administrative branch, unless he was able to dominate the factional conflict in the legislature, a difficult undertaking in light of the separate electoral processes for the two branches.

Despite its flaws, the Constitution of New York represented a bold step in the direction of a distinct and vigorous chief executive. It clarified the executive function, gave military command to the governor, extended his term, and rooted his authority in a popular election. It created a powerful figure capable of taking leadership in the state's political life.

The following year (1778) produced another vital clarification of the emerging American concept of the executive. It came not in the form of specific constitutional provisions but in an influential essay written during the drive to revise the Constitution of Massachusetts.

In the early stages of the Revolution (1775) the Massachusetts Assembly sought to establish independent government simply by declaring that its own acts were "lawful and valid to all intents, constructions and purposes whatsoever."[34] It proceeded to administer the state's affairs by improvisation, with the predictable result of inefficiency, duplication, and, at times, virtual anarchy, particularly in the western part of the state. By 1778 demands for constitutional revision grew insistent. The legislature responded by producing a draft constitution, which it sent out for ratification in March 1778.

The voters of Massachusetts decisively rejected this 1778 version, partly because of defects in its form but mostly because people resented the legislature for seizing the power to establish a frame of government. In fact, no other state constitution had been drafted by a specially elected convention; none yet had been popularly ratified. Public opinion in the Commonwealth now insisted on both of these marks of the special character of a fundamental law.

The most significant result of this failed attempt of 1778 was a critique written by Theophilus Parsons, a twenty-eight-year-old lawyer and future chief justice of the commonwealth. Parsons's analysis was adopted by a convention of delegates from towns in Essex County and came to be known as *The Essex Result.* It contained an analysis of the executive function which was unique, among writings of that period, for its realism and candor.

Parsons first divided the executive into external and internal components. The former, which consisted of war, peace, and foreign relations, including the sending and receiving of ambassadors, had been "lopped off" from the American states and given to the federal Congress. "We [at the state level] have therefore only to consider the internal executive power, which is employed in the peace, security and protection of the subject and his property, and in the defense of the state. The executive power is to marshal and command her militia and armies for her defense, to enforce the law, and to carry into execution all the orders of the legislative powers."[35] This was far from a complete definition of the executive, even as it was then operating in such states as New York, Virginia, and South Carolina. It omitted the executive's typical interactions with the legislature: convening and adjourning it, recommending measures, and casting vetoes. Nevertheless, it was one of the first attempts in America, and the fullest up to that time, to define analytically the constitutional role of the executive.

Parsons put the case for a vigorous executive very strongly. The executive ought to be free to execute the laws "without opposition."

He needed on occasion to operate secretly, to be able to surprise suspected lawbreakers and conspirators. For these reasons, and in the interests of military efficiency and civilian control, Parsons argued, the executive ought to be a single person, just as, for the sake of adequate representation, the Assembly needed to consist of a large number of people.[36]

Parsons was especially keen that the power of appointment lodge with a single chief executive. Any public official is likely to bring his own friends into office, regardless of the public interest. The smaller the number appointing, the fewer would be their "connections," and the greater the probability of competent administrators. Also, if one man makes the appointments, the people can watch him closely. (The latter argument was better than the former. A leader's "connections" did not need to be personal friends. They could be part of a patronage machine.)

The Essex Result did not simply parrot the argument for separation of powers and balanced government. It sought to relate a theory about political man and the nature and direction of American society to an analysis of constitutional form. The analysis was plainly inadequate. Most important, in setting aside what he called the "external" aspects of the executive, Parsons made it easier to ignore the fact that law could not in all circumstances direct the actions of public authority. What Parsons did achieve was the clarification of the independent executive function and the articulation of an argument for executive power—unified, vigorous, capable of secrecy and dispatch. With George III's armies still in the field, this represented a striking psychological breakthrough, providing other young patriots, notably Hamilton, Morris, and Wilson, with a lead they were eager to follow. Hamilton, in particular, must have been a close student of *The Essex Result*. Not only did he follow much of Parsons's analysis of the executive in *The Federalist*, Number 71, including much of the same terminology, but he ended *The Federalist*, Number 85, with the same passage from David Hume's *Essays* that Parsons used to conclude *The Essex Result*—the one about the need to revise constitutions after experience had revealed their defects.*

---

*Parsons, though he quoted Hume virtually verbatim, apparently did not cite him.[37] Hamilton, however, did.

In certain respects the new Massachusetts Constitution of 1780 followed the ideas of *The Essex Result*. John Adams, home for a brief visit from his post as commissioner to France, drafted it. There were marked differences between Adams's *Thoughts* of 1776 and Parsons's *The Essex Result*, and the striking thing, if we are to judge by Adams's draft constitution, was that he seemed to accept Parsons's ideas in preference to his own earlier design. For example, whereas in 1776 Adams would have allowed the legislature to choose the governor, Parsons in 1778 presented a strong argument for popular election, and the Adams draft in 1780 provided for the direct popular election of the governor.

Overall, though, the concept of the executive in the Massachusetts Constitution of 1780 marked a move in the direction of New York's. In the hands of men like John Hancock and James Bowdoin, it would prove nearly as strong as New York's under the determined and resourceful George Clinton. It provided for a "supreme executive magistrate," elected annually by popular vote. It saddled him with an executive council (nine persons chosen from the Senate) to confirm his appointments and advise him about administration. It made him commander in chief of the armed forces and empowered him to direct them "agreeably to the rules and regulations of the constitution and the laws of the land, and not otherwise." It gave him the power of pardon and guaranteed him an "honorable" salary. And uniquely among these early constitutions,* it gave him a veto, subject to a two-thirds override.[38] Although no Massachusetts governor until 1825 vetoed a bill,[39] the power to do so made him potentially a formidable figure in the legislative process.

Concern with constitutions did not lapse between 1780 and 1787. Agitation for revision continued in New Hampshire. New Hampshire, it will be recalled, had decided in 1776 simply to vest government in the colonial Assembly, much as Massachusetts had. But as the War of Independence reached a successful conclusion, nearly everyone agreed that the state needed a new constitution. Despite the examples of executive vigor set by New York and Massachu-

---

* As we have noted, the short-lived South Carolina Constitution of 1776 was a partial exception. It gave its "president" an absolute veto.

setts, however, New Hampshire resumed the pattern of a weak executive. The "president" of New Hampshire, in the new constitution inaugurated in 1784, had no veto power and shared virtually all administrative powers, including powers of appointment, with a council of legislators chosen by the legislature.[40] The New Hampshire Constitution of 1784 was the last new state constitution ratified before 1787.

Meanwhile, in Pennsylvania partisan furies raged over constitutional questions. On one side were the Constitutionalists, ably led by the Irish-born Philadelphia lawyer George Bryan, claiming such distinguished and active adherents as Charles Willson Peale, David Rittenhouse, and Tom Paine[41] and consisting mainly of Scots-Irish and German farmers from the frontier counties to the west of the capital. These fierce populists took their stand on the Constitution framed in 1776—a time, they said, "when the flame of patriotism shone its brightest."[42] On the opposite side were the Republicans, the mercantile elite and their shrewd and articulate attorneys, led by Robert Morris and James Wilson, whose political support centered in Philadelphia and in the older communities to the west.

The primary constitutional issues were questions of focus and pace. The Constitutionalists thought government should center on the legislature and be kept simple and made to move slowly, so that the general public could understand and monitor the actions of its stewards. In this view, owners of great wealth deserved no special consideration. The crucial thing was to keep government harnessed to the will of the common people. A unicameral legislature, with a plural executive, seemed well designed to do this.

The Constitutionalists were ascendant in 1776, and the frame of government instituted that year in Pennsylvania reflected their ideas. Its plural executive consisted of a council with twelve members, chosen by direct popular ballot. The "president," chosen by joint ballot of the council and Assembly from among the elected councillors, had no special power, other than to preside over meetings of the council. All executive acts required the concurrence of a majority of the councillors. The council had no veto and no power to dissolve the Assembly, but with respect to powers not legislative, it was, in fact, a rather strong executive. Besides power to "take care that the laws are faithfully executed," it had exclusive powers of appointment (that is, without legislative confirmation) to both administrative and judicial positions; it commanded the armed forces; it had powers of pardon and reprieve; and it conducted the state's external relations.[43]

The Republicans of Pennsylvania were at first called "Anti-Constitutionalists" for their opposition to the Constitution of 1776. Gradually, however, their ideas clarified and became more positive. So simple a constitution as that of 1776, they thought, encouraged faction, the bane of republics. It tended to divide the people in two: the group that controlled the unicameral legislature and the opposition. The dominant group then absorbed the other two branches of government (executive and judicial) and used the whole government for its own ends. The remedy, they thought, was to introduce "balance," a genuine separation of powers, and enable each branch, particularly the executive, to defend itself.

The simmering quarrel came to a boil in 1784. The Constitution of 1776 provided for the election of a "council of censors" every seven years, to inquire whether the Constitution was being "preserved inviolate in every part" and whether the executive and legislative branches had usurped "other or greater powers than they are entitled to by the constitution."[44] The censors got down to business in early 1784, and it was soon apparent that a majority of those in attendance were Republicans—that is, critics of the Constitution to whose preservation "inviolate" they were supposedly committed. Instead, they resolved to consider whether the Constitution was "perfect in all its parts" or ought to be revised. The Constitutionalists cried foul, insisting that this broadening of the inquiry was unconstitutional. The Republicans plowed ahead and appointed a committee composed entirely of their own number to report those articles of the Constitution which were "materially defective" and needed amendment.[45]

The censors' preliminary report, presented a little more than two weeks later, contained a scathing indictment of virtually every aspect of the Constitution. Offering few particulars of the government's performance since 1776, the report instead attacked its fundamental design. The vesting of executive power in a "president and council" came in for especially severe criticism. Its constant sitting was "expensive"; it lacked "decision," especially in sudden emergencies;

its mistakes could never be pinned on any individual; and the president, being chosen by joint ballot of the council and Assembly, had "nothing to fear from the legislature," being a leader of its prevailing faction. The only remedy, said the Republicans, was a new constitution, rebuilt from the ground up. It should have a bicameral legislature and a single governor, chosen annually by the freemen of the commonwealth. Besides normal executive powers (including those of appointment without legislative confirmation and military command), the governor should be authorized to recommend legislation, convene the legislature, and veto bills, subject to a two-thirds override.[46]

This was the most extreme statement of executive power in the entire preconvention period. It set forth a solitary chief executive, popularly elected, sharing legislative powers, having exclusive control over the administrative branch, with his status as "chief of state" reflected in military command and the expectation that he would "inform the general assembly, at every session, of the condition of the Commonwealth." All that was missing were "external" powers, and even those were adumbrated in the provision that he "correspond" with the governors of other states. The report said that the proposed revisions were "not experiments, but were founded on reason and the experience of our sister states."[47] In fact, no other state, not even New York or Massachusetts, had an executive this strong. The Republicans of Philadelphia wanted the strongest chief executive in the land, stronger even than the future president of the United States. What makes this especially significant is that James Wilson, a major framer of the United States presidency, was the intellectual leader of the Pennsylvania Republicans.

The preliminary Censors' Report of January 1784 was adopted by a vote of 12 to 9. The Constitutionalists immediately issued a powerful dissent, scolding the majority for perverting their mandate as censors. The 1776 constitution, they said, framed when the land was mercifully free of ambitious or mercenary factions, had stood well the test of time, despite the Republicans' persistent attempts to subvert it. Now its foes wanted to substitute an aristocracy for the existing popular government and place a chief magistrate at their head, vesting him with greater powers than kings normally exercised.

It was soon apparent that the Republicans in their excitement had misjudged popular sentiments.[48] Several months after the bitter exchange of January the Constitutionalists, now a majority of the Council of Censors and joined belatedly by their leader, George Bryan (elected to fill a seat vacated by resignation), set about the work for which the censors had been elected: to assess the operation of the 1776 frame of government. They admitted that it had not worked perfectly. There had been occasions when the branches of government—particularly the legislature, but also the executive council—had acted unconstitutionally. Listing specific acts and dates, they pointed to instances in which the Assembly had regulated prices, settled disputed land titles and granted divorce settlements, remitted fines, adjusted pensions, appointed revenue officers, and served as a court of appeals, granting summary relief and staying prosecutors' hands. They noted several instances in which the Assembly had introduced "resolves" and passed them in the same session, ignoring the constitutional requirement that bills not be enacted until the session following their introduction, "except on occasions of sudden necessity." Among the resolves cited for skirting this requirement were one authorizing a military draft in 1778 and another granting extraordinary powers to Washington and the Executive Council in the dire winter of 1777. Not all were of an exigent character, however. One resolution, passed in 1778, authorized the Council to "place chains across Chestnut Street (a public highway) in Philadelphia city, whilst Congress, etc., be sitting, to prevent the passing of carriages." Another, in 1783, provided money for a triumphal arch and illuminated paintings to mark the occasion of the treaty of peace with Great Britain. Nor was the abuse limited to resolutions. An act for erecting Dickinson College at Carlisle had been "introduced September 2, 1783, and passed into law seven days later."[49]

The censors did not confine their criticism to the Assembly. During the revolutionary war, they said, the Executive Council had violated the Bill of Rights by seizing blankets, lead drain spouts, and wagons and by denying fair trials to loyalists. It had established boards of war without legislative authorization, declared martial law without clear authorization from the Assembly, allowed persons who were not elected members of the council to sit with them as a council of safety, and committed numerous other minor infractions (not keeping minutes properly, meeting without a quorum, allowing councillors to sit before taking the oath of office, and so on).

Despite these lapses, the censors strongly defended the Constitution of 1776—"clear in its principles, accurate in its form, consistent in its several parts, and worthy of the veneration of the good people of Pennsylvania." To the Constitutionalists, the proper remedy was greater care and commitment, not the fundamental revision sought by the Republicans.[50] They ascribed the lapses to inexperience, carelessness, or misunderstanding and traced them to bad habits carried over from the colonial era. With patient clarification, men of goodwill could correct these errors and make the Constitution function as its framers intended. The Republicans, on the other hand, traced the malpractices of the Assembly to the absence of checks and balances. In their view, only a completely revised constitution could correct a defect so profound.

The struggle for the soul of Pennsylvania was desperate during the 1780s. Allies of the Republicans had won in New York and Massachusetts and to a lesser extent in Maryland. The Constitutionalists had powerful allies in Virginia and New York, however, and even where their ideas were regarded as inapplicable to state government, they were sometimes seen as relevant to government at the national level. That, of course, raised other issues, including whether a slow, strictly accountable political process was appropriate for "external" functions. At the end of the first round of American constitution making, wherever men were determined to keep government small and weak, whenever they tended to withhold trust from public institutions, the ideas of the Pennsylvania Constitutionalists had a following.

Thus, from Paine to Parsons and from George Bryan to John Rutledge, there was a broad spectrum of opinion and practice about the executive during the first decade of independence.

At first, in 1776, there had seemed to be a consensus. Most agents and friends of royal power had fled or gone into eclipse. Those who seized power in the former colonies took their stand on the "natural" right of freemen to be governed strictly in accordance with laws made by elected representatives. In the constitutions framed during this period one can see a fairly coherent image of the executive. In every state there was a chief executive, a "governor" or "president," but in every state the chief executive shared power with an executive council. Except in New Jersey, the executive council was distinct from the upper house of the legislature. Usually it was composed in whole or in part of members of the legislatures, although in some cases (Pennsylvania, Delaware, North Carolina) persons were specially elected as members of the council.

Another feature common to these constitutions framed in 1776 was that the executive was chosen by the legislature. Except in Delaware and South Carolina, he was chosen annually because of a conviction that "where annual elections end, tyranny begins." This profound suspicion of all power was further reflected in the principle of rotation, which limited most chief executives to three or four successive terms, in order, as the Pennsylvania Constitution put it, to forestall "the danger of establishing an inconvenient aristocracy."[51]

Concerning the functions of the executive, the consensus was mainly negative. He was to "take care that the laws be faithfully executed." The dreaded "prerogative" had no place here. In some states (Pennsylvania, Delaware, Maryland, Virginia, and Georgia), the executive (that is, the governor and the council) made most administrative appointments by itself, without legislative confirmation, but in others (New Hampshire, Massachusetts, New Jersey, and North Carolina) the constitution withheld even this basic requisite for responsible administrative action. In several states (New Jersey, North Carolina, and Virginia) the legislature kept for itself the power to appoint judges.

In other respects, too, the constitutions of 1776 fettered the executive. Commander in chief powers were typically assigned to the chief executive and council. Only in South Carolina did the executive have a legislative veto (there, curiously, the president's veto was absolute). In a few states the executive could call the legislature into session, but there was no power to disband it and certainly none to dissolve it and call new elections.

In short, the spirit of 1776 kept the executive on a short tether. The legislatures which framed these constitutions embodied the forces which brought the Revolution into being, and they intended to keep power in their own hands.

Soon the pendulum began to move in the direction of stronger executives—not everywhere, but in key areas. New York, as we have seen, chose in 1777 to have a popularly elected governor, make him commander in chief, and give him a share in the veto power. New York's Constitution was the first sign that the spirit of 1776, so hostile to the executive, would not last.

By the mid-1780s the revolutionary consensus on constitutional form had collapsed. Not only New York but Massachusetts (in 1780) had set up a chief executive whose authority rested on an independent constituency. They had given him a share in the legislative process and had begun to define a distinct, positive executive function. There was a powerful movement to make similar revisions in Pennsylvania. In several other states, too, and at the national level there was a growing conviction that legislatures were incapable of using their enormous powers effectively and that republican government needed a strong executive to resist legislative "encroachment" and to ensure that the laws were enforced evenhandedly, without interference by legislators.[52]

The problem, for the framers of 1787, was that Americans had had so little experience with a constitutional executive. As Parsons noted, the states, having consigned "external" government to the federal government, had no experience with foreign relations. Furthermore, as both Massachusetts and New York were beginning to realize, the problem of appointing government officals (administrators, judges, diplomats) had not been satisfactorily solved. Nor was anyone thinking very clearly about the problem of political leadership. The ablest minds were by now convinced that legislative dominance led to government by factions, which they considered the bane of republics. The political leadership of the executive was not yet understood, except perhaps dimly in New York, where Governor George Clinton was moving strongly to take charge. No one anywhere was giving consideration to the mechanisms by which such leadership might fuse the authority of the executive and legislative branches into a coherent, accountable government.

Thus, as the movement for a revised federal constitution neared its crisis, the question of the executive's role in the system was perhaps the least well understood. Yet, for the fate of republican government, it was the most crucial question of all.

CHAPTER 4

The Convention
of 1787

SHOULD THERE BE ANOTHER REVOLUTION?

During the first decade of independence the United States had no
viable national government. The Congress of the Confederation
struggled to support and coordinate the armed forces and conduct
foreign policy, but it was not much more a national government than
the General Assembly of United Nations has been a world government since World War II.

By the mid-1780s Congress was, in the words of Louis Otto, the
French chargé d'affaires in America, "only a phantom of sovereignty, destitute of powers, energy and respect," and the government was "falling in ruins."[1] A few delegates to Congress tried to
persuade the states to grant to the national government some of the
basic attributes of sovereignty, such as the power to regulate commerce or levy taxes to pay off the war debt. Under the Articles of
Confederation, however, amendments required the unanimous ratification of the states, and it was impossible to fashion a proposal so
innocuous as to receive universal assent.

Affairs were at an impasse. Government under the Articles was
impotent, but amendment was virtually impossible. The problem
was compounded by the fact that leading Americans, many of them

lawyers, were deeply committed to lawful processes, and they longed for legitimacy. They had supported the Revolution against Great Britain, but their instincts made them doubt that the American union could survive a second overt act of revolution against lawfully constituted authority within a single generation.

In this context what happened between the early months of 1786 and the summer of 1788, when the president of Congress declared that the nation had a new constitution, was quite simply a miracle, a "glorious revolution" in which a few intrepid men carved a stone of order from a mountain of confusion.

Yearnings for a stronger national government had been felt by the younger revolutionaries as early as 1780,[2] but the movement for constitutional revision did not begin until January 21, 1786, when James Madison persuaded the legislature of Virginia to send five commissioners to a convention to consider what might be done to remove the impediments to commerce among the states. The resolution paid obeisance to the rule that any recommendation issuing from such a convention would take effect only when ratified by each of the thirteen states, although every sensible person in America knew that strict compliance with this condition would make reform impossible to achieve. Nine other states followed Virginia's lead in appointing delegations. Yet when the convention opened at Annapolis, Maryland, on September 11, 1786, the twelve delegates in attendance represented only five states. It was a pitiful showing. Even the official report of the convention stated that the commissioners deemed it inadvisable to proceed on the basis of "so partial and defective a representation."[3]

The Annapolis Convention may have been pathetic, but its leaders were unwilling to accept defeat. In a statement drafted by Alexander Hamilton, the commissioners boldly traced the difficulties in interstate trade to "defects in the system of the federal government" and declared that they could not be corrected without a "corresponding adjustment of other parts of the federal system." The situation of the nation, they insisted, was "delicate and critical," and they called upon the states to send delegates to a convention "at Philadelphia on the second Monday in May next." In bold terms they defined the purpose of the proposed meeting: "to take into consideration the situation of the United States, [and] to devise such

. . . provisions as shall appear to them necessary to render the constitution of the federal government adequate to the exigencies of the nation. . . ." Having declared their radical purpose, they added the reassuring note that the results of such a convention would take effect only when ratified by Congress and then by the legislature of every state[4]—once again, the impossible condition. There was something almost manic about this report. Only a soul as sanguine as Hamilton could sit in such an assembly and issue a call for a constitutional revolution.

Madison knew the odds against Hamilton's plan, but he, too, was a desperate man. The only hope lay in a virtual coup d'état, a strategy that skirted Congress and the procedures established in the Articles while seeming to respect them. He set to work first in Virginia. One month after the fiasco at Annapolis he steered through the Virginia legislature a resolution endorsing the idea of a special constitutional convention, announcing that the Old Dominion would send a delegation, and bidding the other states to come along. The resolution noted that a special convention was preferable to a "discussion" in Congress, which might be interrupted by ordinary business and where the valuable contribution of men who were not members of Congress could not be had. (Madison's resolution did not mention the other reason for skirting prescribed channels: that opponents of reform in Congress could easily block it there.) The Virginia resolves concluded by promising that the convention would send its recommendations to Congress and to the states and that the provisions for amending the Articles, including unanimous ratification, would eventually be followed. This promise, in one form or another, was contained in every states' enabling resolution except New Jersey's.[5]

It was more than a month before a second state followed Virginia's lead. New Jersey's brief authorization, passed on November 13, was even broader than Virginia's, reflecting the confident grasp of New Jersey's governing elite, who had decided that it was time for a change. The way to get it, they knew, was to give the convention leeway, then trust their delegates to obtain revisions that did not sacrifice the state's vital interests.

By mid-February seven states (a bare majority of the confederacy) had acted to send delegations to Philadelphia. But there were some crucial holdouts. From New England only New Hampshire had responded. The nabobs from South Carolina had not yet chosen their men, and Maryland hung back. The most troublesome delinquent, however, from the standpoint of the reforming nationalists, was New York. Governor George Clinton regarded the national visions of Hamilton and his associates with profound suspicion, and before he would consent to send a delegation, he wanted assurances that the convention would stay within narrow bounds.

Part of Clinton's strategy was to put Congress itself on record with a confining resolution. The nationalists had submitted a resolution by which Congress, noting the "inefficiency" of the federal government, would have "strongly recommended" that the state legislatures send delegates to the proposed convention. The New York delegation, inspired by Clinton, countered with a resolution which, without criticizing the existing government, would have recommended that the states send delegates to a convention strictly "for the purpose of revising the Articles of Confederation." New York's motion was defeated, but Massachusetts, another cautious state, offered a compromise which alluded to "defects" in the existing government, acknowledged the need for "a firm national government," and authorized a convention "for the sole and express purpose of revising the Articles of Confederation." Congress passed the Massachusetts version.

There was a little something for everyone in this diffident resolution. For the nationalists it acknowledged that the existing government was defective and specifically endorsed the special convention at Philadelphia. For the opponents of revision it made Congress insist on the established mode for amending the Articles, thus placing an insurmountable hurdle in the path to fundamental reform. The nationalists wisely accepted this language. It gave legitimacy to a special convention, while lulling diehards into thinking that the barriers to revision were secure.

The congressional resolution apparently satisfied Governor Clinton, for a week later New York agreed to send a delegation to Philadelphia. The credentials of the New York delegates incorporated the restrictive congressional language: that the "sole and express purpose" of the convention would be to draft revisions of the Articles of Confederation and submit them to Congress and the states for ratification.

In the spring four more states joined the federal procession, leaving tumultuous Rhode Island the lone holdout. Never mind. Madison and Hamilton had laid a workable foundation for a miracle. If the great men of the Revolution could be persuaded to overlook the crippling terms imposed by the enabling resolutions and lend the authority of their presence to the enterprise, it was possible to hope that a single sovereign nation might yet emerge from the movement for independence.

As the delegates gathered, most of them knew that the task before them involved two features heretofore unknown at the national level: a scheme of representation that reflected the varying sizes of the states and an executive constitutionally separated from the legislature. The two issues presented quite different challenges. Although the delegates wrangled bitterly over representation, the structure of the so-called great compromise, resulting in a popular House of Representatives and a Senate representing the states, was clear almost from the start of the convention. The trick was political: to get politicians from large and small states to accept the deal.

The shaping of the executive, on the other hand, required genuine creativity. No nation in the world offered a model of a republican executive. The Articles of Confederation, which described the existing national government, had no provision at all for an executive. Delegates came from states that had governors (or, in three cases, presidents), but the states' constitutional arrangements showed several different patterns, none of them fit for direct application to the federal government.

In short, there was no consensus on the proper form for a republican executive. The convention had to hammer one out.

THE INVENTORS OF THE PRESIDENCY

The term *framer of the Constitution* refers to the fifty-five delegates who attended the federal constitutional convention of 1787. Of the fifty-five, twenty-one played important roles in the creation of the presidency. Perhaps a dozen had clear concepts of the executive to set forth and defend. The rest distinguished themselves by offering key motions or by their service on the committee that gave final shape to the presidency. These twenty-one were the inventors of the presidency.[6] As a group, what sort of men were they?

They were, first of all, highly educated sons of the Enlightenment. This fact is so large and so familiar that its significance is easily overlooked. Compare the framers of the first Canadian constitution, known as the British North America Act of 1867. Of the thirty-seven framers of that confederation, only four had a college education, and only one of those (a medical doctor) had any formal training beyond college.* By contrast, of the fifty-five delegates to the convention in 1787, twenty-five had college degrees, six had read law at the Inns of Court in London, at least three had studied medicine abroad, and one was a graduate of St. Andrews in Scotland. Of this convention as a whole, John Conway has written, "Probably never before or since has there been assembled in North America for political discussion a group of men so intellectually distinguished."[8]

In age, these twenty-one men were perhaps a young group by twentieth-century standards, though ripe enough by standards of their own time. Charles Pinckney, at twenty-nine, was the youngest of this group. Six of them were in their thirties, and eight in their forties. Hugh Williamson, John Dickinson, and George Washington were in their fifties; George Mason was sixty-two, Roger Sherman sixty-six, and Benjamin Franklin the eldest at eighty-one. It was a group of men young enough to be vigorous yet old enough, most of them, to have experienced both the need for leadership and the value of consultation and compromise.

They were not a cross section of American life; they were an elite. Several of them had rude beginnings. James Wilson was a son of rural poverty in the lowlands of Scotland. Alexander Hamilton came from acutely humble origins in the Caribbean. Sherman had supported himself as a tradesman most of his life. Rufus King and Luther Martin had gotten their starts as scholarship students, so to

*Speaking of the era when the Canadian constitution was written, John Conway writes, "In Great Britain and western Europe, the decorum of the middle decades of the nineteenth century was singularly inhospitable to originality or innovation in art or political speculation," and the situation in the provinces, he adds, was even worse.[7] The contrast with the end of the eighteenth century could hardly be more marked.

speak, at Harvard and Princeton. By 1787, however, every one of them had made a pile of money, married a wealthy woman, or committed his professional life to the service of wealthy clients.

By profession they were mostly lawyers.[9] Fourteen of them had practiced law extensively, two who lacked formal training (Washington and Sherman) had served as county judges, and two others (Madison and Mason), who had no formal training and did not practice regularly as attorneys, were nevertheless close students of the law. Perhaps it was partly due to the preponderance of lawyers that the convention was so firmly committed to government by law. Many delegates worried about the capacity of elected legislatures to enact proper laws, but they did not doubt that the proper way to order human affairs was through laws, enacted by representatives, duly promulgated and vigorously enforced. Any assertion that the executive might sometimes have to act in the absence of lawful authority, or even against it (as Locke argued in his *Second Treatise*), could expect a chilly reception in this assemblage.

Another striking quality about this group was its self-confidence as an elite and its high expectations for the future of the nation. Again, there are exceptions. Elbridge Gerry was a chronic worrier, afraid that the masses might suddenly erupt or be misled by designing men. Mason feared the loss of republican virtue as the nation grew more urban and more sophisticated. Indeed, most of them thought the nation was approaching a crisis, and no one clearly foresaw a way through it. But if the constitutional crisis could somehow be resolved, if a firm republican national government could be established, most of them expected a glorious and happy future for the United States of America.

It was a relatively cosmopolitan group. Only two (Wilson and Pierce Butler) were born, reared, and educated abroad. William Paterson had migrated from Ireland as a baby, and Hamilton came from the Caribbean when he was a teenager. The others had been born and reared in America. But Dickinson and John Rutledge had read law at the Inns of Court in London. Williamson had studied medicine in Scotland and Holland. Franklin had traveled to England as early as 1724 and spent much of his adult life on diplomatic missions in England, France, and Holland. Oliver Ellsworth and Butler made business trips to Europe in the 1780s. These experiences abroad exposed the framers to other modes of governance and patterns of political development than those found in the young American states and gave them a sense of the world with which the United States might one day have to contend.

For most of them, however, Europe's constitutional systems served as warnings, not models. Holland, for example, was degenerating (as the framers saw it) from a republic into a corrupt monarchy. France was a terminal Bourbon autocracy. England was a paradox: a cruel and ignorant tyranny toward its colonies but a great, if corruptible, constitutional monarchy at home. Several of the inventors of the presidency (Gouverneur Morris, Hamilton, Dickinson, Nathaniel Gorham) admired Britain's government a great deal. But even for them, the British model was problematic. The monarchy and peerage were essential components of the British system in the eighteenth century, and no one knew how to supply, or get along without, those features in America. (The parliamentary system as it developed in the nineteenth century was an embryo in Britain at the time, and no one could have predicted its evolution, much less adopted it as a model, in 1787.*)

Although several of the leading framers were well acquainted with the broader Atlantic civilization, all of them had deep roots in their home states and local communities. Only of Washington and Franklin could it be said that they were framers primarily by virtue of their national reputation, and even these two had long since won the confidence of the state legislatures that chose them as delegates. Morris was a recently adopted son of the state he represented, and King was in the process of moving away from the one he represented. But every one of the men who helped frame the presidency, except Gouverneur Morris and David Brearly, had held elective office in the state he now represented. Morris, having represented New York in Congress in 1778 and 1779, had moved to Philadephia in 1779; Brearly was a presiding judge of New Jersey's supreme court.

There was a very powerful sense in 1787 that the United States was a confederacy of states and that its constitutional system must leave real authority at the state level. Some of the delegates—Morris,

---

*I owe this astute observation to the late Donald Morgan, professor of political science at Mount Holyoke College.

Hamilton, and perhaps Paterson and Brearly—seemed to have little attachment to the states as such, but most of the others, including such strong revisionists as Madison, Edmund Randolph, Pinckney, and Rutledge, had no intention of allowing the states to be undermined or dismantled.

Several of them were military men, veterans of the long and dangerous struggle for independence.[10] Washington, of course, was America's greatest and most honored soldier; but Hamilton, Pinckney, Paterson, and Butler had also served in battle with distinction, and Williamson had performed under fire as a military surgeon. Several belonged to the Society of the Cincinnati, an organization of revolutionary war veterans.

On the other hand, Old Republicans Mason and Gerry were almost paranoid about the Cincinnati. The society was holding a major convocation in Philadelphia as the convention gathered, a coincidence which some found ominous. Fears of the military fed on the myth of Oliver Cromwell, who in England a century earlier had used the military to bring the Puritan Revolution to a dictatorial climax. Opposition journalists in England, much admired in America during the half century before the Declaration of Independence, had used the myth of Cromwell to reinforce the argument against standing armies, and the Old Republicans took this warning to heart. In their minds, the Society of the Cincinnati was not only a potential lobby for a standing army but a cadre already in place for a militarist regime.

In fact, Washington was probably the only man in America who could have led a military coup; certainly none that he opposed could have succeeded in the last quarter of the eighteenth century. His stony opposition to an attempted coup in 1783 put an end to that danger for the foreseeable future—at least until a new war could cast up another hero. Nevertheless, men like Gerry and Mason, whose anxieties projected far into the future, sought desperately to erect permanent constitutional safeguards against militarism.

Many of these framers were themselves experienced political executives, yet none, except perhaps Washington and for a brief period Rutledge, had held an office the powers and responsibilities of which remotely resembled those of the presidency they would create. Four (Franklin, Dickinson, Rutledge, and Randolph) had been or were currently chief executives of their states, and at least three others (Sherman, Madison, and Ellsworth) had been members of their states' executive councils. But these truncated offices were a far cry from the Constitution's presidency. Others had held administrative positions at the federal level: preeminently Washington, but also Gerry as a member of the Treasury Board, Franklin as postmaster, Williamson as surgeon general, Gorham as president of Congress, and Sherman, Dickinson, and Wilson, as well as several of the younger men (Madison, Hamilton, King, and Morris), as members of various administrative committees. Still, only Washington and Rutledge could be said to have exercised true executive power.

Finally, these men belonged to a constitution-writing generation. At least eight of them (Franklin, Dickinson, Gorham, Hamilton, Madison, Morris, Randolph, and Rutledge) had played leading roles in framing their states' constitutions. One other (Wilson) had fought hard for fundamental constitutional revisions at the state level. Two (Dickinson and Sherman) had been prominent drafters of the Articles of Confederation, and several of the younger ones (Madison, Hamilton, Pinckney, Morris, and King) had promoted amendments to the Articles. Thus, at a time when leading political men were thinking hard about constitutional questions, several of these framers had devoted their best energies to the drive for constitutional change.

As the debates began, three basic issues emerged as central to the framing of the executive:

1. *The Question of Unity*   Should the Constitution vest executive power in a single individual or in a council, or should there be some combination of the two: a council sharing certain powers with a single chief executive?
2. *The Process of Selection*   How should the executive be chosen?
3. *Distributing Functions*   What powers should the Constitution vest in the executive, and should the executive share any of them with the legislature or with a part of it?

THE QUESTION OF UNITY

It is hard for us to take seriously the question of whether executive powers should inhere in one person or a council. If all the states by 1787 had a single chief executive (they did), how could the framers have decided otherwise?

The convention of 1787 was not so solidly committed to the solitary chief executive as we sometimes think. Roger Sherman of Connecticut, for example, believed that the executive was "an institution for carrying the will of the legislature into effect" (the legislature being "the depository of the supreme will of the society") and that the legislature should be free to vary the number of executives from time to time, as circumstances might require.[11] This is exactly how it works today in parliamentary regimes, where the size of the cabinet varies from time to time, as party leaders adjust to changing circumstances.

Others feared that a single chief executive would be the "foetus of monarchy." Everyone knew about the drift of the Puritan Revolution in seventeenth-century England toward military dictatorship under Oliver Cromwell. Several delegates (Williamson, Butler, Franklin), having sojourned in Holland, knew at first hand how the Dutch had gone from an elected chief executive at the end of the seventeenth century, through a succession of foreign intrigues and internal disorders, to the establishment of the House of Orange as an hereditary monarchy during the eighteenth century.[12] Would America be immune from such dynamics? "Why might not a Cataline or a Cromwell arise in this country as well as in others?" asked Pierce Butler.[13] In fact, several of the delegates were almost fatalistic about it.*

The profound opposition to a single executive on the part of some delegates stemmed from orthodox republican doctrine. George Mason, the old colonel from Virginia, was the leading spokesman for this faith at the convention. He acknowledged the "advantages" of a unified executive, especially in time of war (secrecy, dispatch, vigor),

---

*Williamson put it this way: "It was pretty certain . . . that we should at some time or other have a king; but he wished no precaution omitted that might postpone the event as long as possible."[14]

and he admitted that monarchies possessed these qualities more than republics. Republics, though, had virtues of their own. They could count on far more intense patriotism. Citing several ancient republics that had resisted large imperial armies, Mason argued that America's victory in the late war—which it began "without arms, without soldiers, without trade, money, or credit, in a manner destitute of all resources"—was owing to the superior patriotism of republican citizens.[15]

There was more than antique faith behind the idea of a plural executive. Franklin, Sherman, and Mason, noting the extent and variety of the country, stressed the dangers that would come from placing the nation's forces in the hands of a man whose personal experience and loyalties tied him to one state and one region more than others. Even if the chief executive were trying to be fair, the situation would be dangerous. What if a foreign army invaded New Hampshire when the "single supreme magistrate" happened to be a citizen of Georgia? Would not the people of New Hampshire ascribe any delay in defending them to this circumstance? asked Mason.[16] The fear was not entirely hypothetical. Older delegates vividly remembered the fury of South Carolinians and Virginians when Washington kept his main forces up north while the British, virtually unopposed, mauled their plantations and ransacked their villages. Imagine if Washington had been from Massachusetts! Mason's remarks also foreshadowed New England's feelings during the embargo of 1808–1809. President Jefferson said that he felt the Union tremble under his feet during that crisis. Wouldn't it be safer and more stable to commit executive powers to a council drawn from the various regions?

The advocates of a single executive contradicted this argument directly. If sectional interests were deliberately represented in the executive branch, there would be continual conflict within the administration. One person, more decisive and vigorous than a council, would be better able to carry the effects of government to the nation's remotest regions. Nathaniel Gorham thought the issue went to the root of the nation's viability: If it couldn't trust executive powers to a single person, perhaps the United States was not a political society.[17]

Those who opposed the idea of a single chief executive had another fear, too: that a single executive might seek to promote his own designs rather than those fashioned into law by Congress. A plural executive seemed less likely to evolve in that direction. It would have a broader sense of accountability, and its members would check one anothers' personal ambitions.

The concept of a single executive took its inspiration from George Washington, though James Wilson gave it articulation. Again and again the eloquent Scot insisted that America needed a separate, independent executive, a single man, elected for short terms directly by the people. America's late troubles with England, he insisted, came from a corrupt multitude in Parliament, not primarily from a malignant tyrant.

Wilson peppered his argument with examples from ancient Greece and Rome and with citations from Montesquieu. Plurality in the executive (as in the case of the Roman triumvirate of Antony, Lepidus and Octavian) encouraged factions, bitter rivalries, and civil war, and it was these disorders, not vigorous administration, that paved the way to tyranny. No one wanted an American chief executive to have the powers of the British monarch, he said. The king's prerogative included powers that were clearly legislative, such as war and peace. The executive's proper task was to enforce the law.[18]

Early in the convention Williamson asked Wilson if he meant to "annex a council" to the executive. Wilson answered no. All authority in a republic arises from the people, he said. To prevent the legislature from becoming the instrument of a faction, you must divide it into two chambers; to control the executive, you must fix responsibility on a single individual.[19]

Madison took the lead in relating this concept to prevailing republican doctrine. For Americans of the revolutionary generation, one principle of constitutional engineering was fundamental: power, having a natural tendency to be grasping, had to be checked.[20] "Ambition must be made to counteract ambition." But the application of this principle to the executive, Madison argued, involved a paradox. The great danger to republics came not from executives who practiced tyranny but from legislatures that wrote unjust laws and intrigued to put their cronies into public jobs. In a constitutional monarchy the king appointed public officials, dispensed public honors, commanded the armed forces, conducted foreign policy, and wielded an absolute veto, which was a potent weapon, even if he rarely used it. The concentration of these powers in one individual, who served for life and passed power to his son when he died, posed a danger to public liberty. Only by guarding the purse could the legislature keep a monarchy accountable for the discharge of so much power. In a republic, on the other hand, the legislature controlled the actions of government. Unless the internal mechanics of the system counteracted the tendency, the legislature would hold full sway.

Events in Pennsylvania had already shown the consequences, argued Madison. According to the Censors' Report of 1784, the Assembly had passed legislation which, instead of laying down principles applicable to all cases equally, attempted to deal justice in individual property suits, divorces, claims against the government, and the like. Experience in Pennsylvania and elsewhere had taught how to control legislature: divide it into two chambers.

The executive in a republic lacked the prestige and prerogatives of monarchy. The danger here was that the legislature would swallow it up, take over its functions, and use them to perpetuate a majority faction in power. The remedy: Fortify the executive. Give him at least a qualified veto, fix his term and salary, make him eligible for reelection, and, above all, keep power focused in the hands of a single individual. Do not permit internal squabbling to weaken the executive.

Madison's argument represented an amazing shift in republican doctrine over the preceding decade.[21] During the Revolution, particularly its early days, all forms of governmental power were feared. In the meantime, said Madison, we had learned to fear governmental impotence as much as the abuse of power. Unchecked executive power might become tyrannical, but an executive unable to carry out the laws and incapable of defending itself might plunge a community into chaos and cause the people to clamor for competent authority, without much concern for whether it was "republican" or not.

It was a great achievement for Wilson and Madison to transform the republican suspicion of power into an argument for a fortified and unified executive. They were less successful, however, in bending the separation of powers to the service of their conception. In conformity with that doctrine, early drafts of the Constitution had made members of Congress ineligible to hold executive offices during their term as legislators and for one year thereafter. Gorham moved to strike that clause and was supported by Wilson, who said that the provision would deprive the nation of the services of many capable people. Charles Pinckney added that if Gorham's motion succeeded, the Senate might become a "nursery of statesmen." Others (Madison, Rufus King, Hamilton) pointed out that ineligibility would not prevent corruption; it would only lead members of Congress to seek offices for their kin and cronies. Hamilton cited Hume's argument that the influence which the executive might garner from astute appointments, sometimes called corruption, was essential to maintain the equilibrium of the Constitution.

But the adherents of separation stood firm, insisting that the intrigues of legislators for public offices and honors had been an endless source of corruption in England. In the end Madison was able to reduce the prohibition to cover only sitting legislators, thus opening the way for senators and representatives to resign during their terms in order to accept administrative appointments.[22] Nevertheless, the bar to a parliamentary system was set in place. A member of the cabinet could not continue to serve in Congress.* In that crucial respect the separation of powers stood, and stands still, in the path of evolution toward a parliamentary regime.

What is missing in Wilson's and Madison's discussion of constitutional balance is any recognition that an astute politician in the presidency might use the powers of his office to shape policy. One searches their speeches in vain for signs of concern, or hope, that the president, by the exercise of his discretion over law enforcement, might change the practical effect of the laws or, by his foreign policy or his decisions as commander in chief, drastically alter the nation's course.

No aspect of the proposed Constitution seemed more dangerous to the Old Republicans, especially Mason, than the lack of an executive council. In rejecting it, the old colonel exclaimed, "we were about to try an experiment on which the most despotic governments had never ventured."[23] It is indeed curious that the convention adamantly refused to compromise the unity of the executive. Besides

---

*Woodrow Wilson believed that this clause was the gravest defect in the Constitution.

Mason's desperate pleas for a council to review and confirm appointments (for Mason, and for several others, including Wilson, the involvement of the Senate in the appointment process was a mistake, mixing power that ought to be separated and laying seeds for the development of an aristocracy),[24] several supporters of a strong presidency proposed that the Constitution provide a "privy council" to assist the chief executive with his responsibilities. By mid-August, however, the principle of a unitary chief executive was settled, and the convention was turning to other questions related to the executive establishment, such as the mode of election. Toward the end of the convention Gouverneur Morris and Charles Pinckney, both proponents of a strong presidency, proposed to establish, in the Constitution, a council of state, composed of the chief justice of the Supreme Court, plus six department heads, serving at the pleasure of the president. The function of the council would be to provide formal advice for the president, though he would remain free and responsible for his own actions.[25] The proposal was referred to committee. When it emerged two days later, it included the president of the Senate and speaker of the House. Its status, however, was the same: advisory, not controlling.

No more was heard of this idea until the waning hours of the convention, when Morris obliquely referred to it, stating that the committee which had just resolved the outstanding issues relating to the president's election and his relationship to the Senate had decided to omit any reference to an executive council in the Constitution, in the conviction that such a body would qualify the president's responsibility for his acts without affording any real protection against the abuse of presidential powers.[26]

With the evaporation of Morris's idea and the defeat of Mason's, the president was left alone. It was a remarkable outcome, the most shocking decision of the convention. These framers were careful men. Few politicians in American history have been less prone to flights of enthusiasm than James Madison, Roger Sherman, and John Dickinson, each of whom eventually gave full support to the solitary presidency. How could these political Calvinists, so well acquainted with the history of abused power and failed republics, have lent themselves to the creation of such an office?

Partly it was because they knew that weakness had its perils, as well as excessive strength. They were determined to seize the opportunity to build a strong national government, which required, they believed, strong administration. Partly it was because they saw corruption in legislatures as a greater threat to liberty than ambition in executives.

Most fundamentally, however, it was their conception of the executive role that led them to accept the risks involved in a unitary presidency. As commander in chief and enforcer of the laws, the president would have command over all the military force he would need to stage a coup, if he were so disposed. They discounted this fear because they thought the electoral process would keep the presidency out of the hands of men disposed to stage coups and because they thought that the cultural ingredients for a politics of coup were not present in America. In these respects their gamble has paid off.

What they failed to foresee was a fundamental shift in the role of the executive. They did not expect the nation to wait for the president to initiate the federal government's "program" each year. They did not anticipate that he would be held responsible for economic prosperity and full employment. They did not foresee the extent of the federal government's lawful involvement in people's lives or the opportunity a president would have, as chief executive, to shift the direction of government by imposing his own interpretation on the laws.

Had they anticipated the role that modern presidents would play, would they have insisted so strenuously on separating the executive from the give-and-take that characterizes the deliberations of Congress and ensures that a broad range of public interests are taken into account before laws are made and implemented? Would it have seemed such a virtue that the executive was capable of secrecy, or able to act quickly, without second thoughts?

No doubt, then as now, there needed to be some authority in the system capable of decisive action and rapid reaction to emergency and danger. However, when foreign relations loom so large on the nation's agenda, ought that person to be brought to account just once in four years, short of impeachment? Ought he to share his responsibility for executing the law and conducting foreign relations only with persons of his own choosing, without political weight of their own?

I do not mean to imply that the framers would have moved away from the separation of powers if they had foreseen the scope and procedures of modern government. I do not know that. I do know that their conception of the constitutional role of the executive was far from modern practices and that their reasons for preferring a single executive do not cover the modern case. Rather, by the framers' own logic, an executive that exerts vigorous leadership over the whole operation of government, as modern presidents do, needs both greater authority and broader accountability than the framers provided.

THE PROCESS OF SELECTION

The decision for a single chief executive brought the convention to its most vexing issue: how to choose him. The models offered by the state constitutions were unacceptable for various reasons. A genuine act of creation was required. What kind of electoral process would give executive power to a person who would discharge it vigorously and effectively yet be trustworthy not to abuse it?

From their historical studies the framers gathered that "popular" governments, those based on the will of the people, tended to degenerate into despotism. Conventional wisdom held that popular governments over a large territory were particularly prone to abuse power because it required strong discipline to maintain order over far-flung regions. Also, people exposed to danger because of a weak regime soon demanded more vigorous and capable authority, even, if need be, at the cost of democracy.

Madison, following Hume's lead, replied to this famous theory by insisting that popular government had a better chance of durability in large territories than in small ones. In a large population there would be greater variety, giving rise to many factions. None would constitute a majority by itself, and none alone could dominate. In a legislature that represented such a plural society, tyranny by a single interest would be virtually impossible.*

---

*Madison's argument was presented in the convention[27] and elegantly summarized in *The Federalist*, Number 10.

The trouble with this brilliant defense of popular government was that it afforded no comfort in the case of a single chief executive. Here vast power would fall certainly into one person's hands. Madison's reassurance about popular government, based on the notion that a single chamber would contain many conflicting interests, was simply not applicable.

Was it possible, then, to have an elected chief executive? Could a single individual be relied upon to respect the law? What process of recruitment and selection would cause the executive powers to fall into the hands of a vigorous and independent, yet moderate, character?

From the outset the convention recognized two basic options: The chief executive could be chosen by the legislature, or he could be elected by the people. Popular elections, in turn, could be either direct or indirect, via electors. The crucial decision was the choice for or against congressional election.

Of some of the implications of this choice, the framers were well aware. They knew that the electoral process would have a bearing on the relative independence of the executive. They knew that it would determine whether the governing process was more likely to be coordinated or confrontational. What they could not know was that they were deciding whether to institutionalize the opposition of law makers and the executive, in the fashion of Europe's constitutional monarchies, or to set the world's first modern democracy on the road toward parliamentary government.

From the beginning of the convention virtually to its end, selection of the chief executive by the legislature was the preferred mode. In the Virginia Plan and in the leading alternative, the New Jersey Plan, as well, the legislature chose the executive. Several of the leading delegates (Sherman, Williamson, Charles Pinckney, Rutledge) favored this method, and by the end of the convention some of its strongest foes seemed reconciled to it. Mason, for example, who had said early in the convention (June 2) that the selection of the executive by the legislature violated the "fundamental principle of good government" (that is, checked power), declared on July 26 that this mode was "liable to the fewest objections." Even Wilson, who was the convention's strongest advocate of direct popular election, by the end of July was trying to iron out certain problems that stood in the way of legislative choice.

If it violated the separation of powers, why did so many delegates prefer this method? The answer is that it seemed only natural for lawmakers to choose the person who would carry out the laws. This mode was familiar to most of them from the state constitutions, in eight of which (all states south of New York), the legislature chose the chief executive. It was also the practice that had evolved nationally under the Articles of Confederation. Opinion varied about the quality of administration under the Articles,[28] but if there were problems, why not try to correct them with the minimum adjustment: by establishing a constitutionally separate executive, with a set term of office? Why was it necessary to alter the method of selecting the chief executive? Men active in national political life would be most likely to know the people under consideration. Having written the laws, they would know best how to give them effect. Delegates might even have thought about the problem in personal terms. Everyone assumed that George Washington would be the first president under the Constitution. He had been chosen by Congress to serve as commander in chief during the revolutionary war. Why not let Congress choose him again and choose his successor when the time came?

What, then, was wrong with this method? Two things, one theoretical, the other practical. First, it violated the separation of powers. The framers believed that legislative and executive powers needed to be kept separate because if they were not, the legislative branch would dominate the government, weakening law enforcement and corrupting administration. People seeking the position of chief executive would connive with legislators, making promises about the way they would conduct the executive office, particularly in filling administrative positions. Part of the remedy might be to forbid members of Congress from serving in the administration, but that would not prevent legislators from seeking places for their friends and supporters. A few of the framers (notably Gorham and Hamilton) recognized that such patronage was the glue that held the republican elements of the British constitution together. Gorham regarded it as a dangerous experiment to expect a constitution to function without this force for cohesion, but he was virtually alone on this point. Most delegates considered the separation of executive and legislative powers "absolutely necessary" to prevent corruption and came to believe that it could not be achieved if Congress chose the president.[29]

Not all the framers were ready to yield to the principle of separation on the corruption issue. Some thought that if the executive's term were made long enough, and if he were ineligible to succeed himself, the incentives for corruption would be decisively weakened. James McClurg, Madison's lucid but naïve friend, even proposed that a president selected by Congress might serve during "good behavior"—that is, indefinitely, as judges do. Hearing this proposal, Gouverneur Morris enthusiastically exclaimed, "This is the way to get a good government!"[30] But most of the delegates preferred a more moderate solution, one with a better chance for ratification.

Besides, giving the president a long, nonrenewable term did not answer all the questions. What if a chief executive grossly abused his powers? Could he be impeached? If so, by whom? No matter how long his term, if he were vulnerable to removal by Congress, he would still be dependent. Other delegates worried about making him ineligible for reelection. Vividly Hamilton described this suggestion as an invitation to a coup d'état. Would a strong leader, coming to the end of his term in a time of national crisis, go quietly home while the public clamored for him to defy the Constitution?[31]

In addition to these theoretical and hypothetical problems, there were the practical problems. How would Congress ballot for a president? If the answer were by a joint ballot of all members in both chambers, then the states having the largest delegations in the lower house would probably control the outcome, and that seemed to violate the spirit of the compromise on representation. If the houses voted separately and both had to concur, a bare majority from thinly populated states, banding together in the Senate, could paralyze the government, holding it hostage to their preference for a particular candidate.

In all this consideration of selection by Congress, there was very little talk about the role that parties might play. Parties are, of course, fundamental to the classical parliamentary model, in which the majority party chooses the prime minister and the cabinet. Yet at the Federal Convention, the idea was anathema that the government might be controlled by officials and voters bound together by an organization espousing a political program—especially so, ironically enough, among those most favorable to selection of the president by Congress. Their notion was to allow Congress to choose the executive, then encourage his independence in law enforcement and appointments by every possible constitutional device.

Against this instinctive preference for familiar forms, no matter how badly flawed, Wilson, Gouverneur Morris, and eventually Madison threw the weight of a new idea: a leader whose authority rested on the fact that he was chosen by the same people who chose the lawmakers. To these men, an independent chief executive was "indispensably necessary."[32] A republican government drew its strength from a firm grounding in the sentiments of the people. Just as the legislature drew authority from frequent elections, so the executive needed the strength and independence that would come from direct popular election.

The idea of popular election for national legislators was itself a radical notion in 1787.* Delegates to Congress under the Articles of Confederation were chosen by state legislatures, and it was not at all clear, early in the convention, that this feature would be changed in the new Constitution. In the end members of the House of Representatives were to be chosen directly by the people, but senators by the state legislatures. (The latter provision was changed by the Seventeenth Amendment, ratified in 1913.)

Everyone agreed that the question of electoral process was fundamental. When Wilson introduced his proposal for "election by the people," Sherman replied that he favored "appointment by the legislature" in order to make the executive "absolutely dependent" on the body whose will he was to carry into execution. In his opinion, independence in the executive was "the very essence of tyranny if there was such a thing."[34]

Gouverneur Morris had a different conception of the executive function, requiring a different approach to the question of electoral choice. The executive, he said, was to be "the great protector of the

---

*Even Thomas Jefferson had his doubts. In 1776, opposing the direct election of senators in the Virginia Constitution, he wrote, "I have ever observed that a choice by the people themselves is not generally distinguished for its wisdom."[33]

mass of the people." He must be able "to control the legislature." Lawmakers would continually seek to enrich themselves and enlarge their power and constitutional prerogatives. The executive must be "the guardian of the people, even of the lower classes, against legislative tyranny, against the great and the wealthy who, in the course of things, will necessarily compose the legislative body." The way to ensure such loyalties and to equip him for such a task was to provide for election by the people.[35]

At first the idea of popular election for presidents was greeted with skepticism by almost all the delegates. Asking the people at large to choose a chief executive was like referring the choice of colors to a blind man, said Mason.[36] Mason's vivid remark is often cited as evidence that the framers were antidemocratic. It seems fairer to recognize that his simile, taken literally, is not unsympathetic to the people. A blind man cannot choose colors, not because he is stupid or evil but because he cannot see. The people at large cannot make a wise choice for president because they cannot know the character and qualifications of the candidates. Mason spoke in an era without daily newspapers, magazines, radio, and television and without rapid means of transporting candidates to communities around the country. It was not unreasonable of him to wonder how citizens would develop an impression of the candidates.

Gouverneur Morris, however, replied that the people at large would be more likely than Congress to choose a man of truly "continental" reputation. People around the country knew the nation's heroes (Washington, Franklin, Adams, Jefferson). As men by their deeds and words stamped their characters on the public mind, the people would develop an impression and be able to make an informed choice. Besides, he added, the selection process in Congress would be marked by intrigue, "like the election of a pope by a conclave of cardinals." Intrigue was less likely where greater numbers of people were involved.[37]

There was another serious objection. Sherman and Williamson argued that popular election would result in the dominance of large, heavily populated states. A man who achieved fame in a large state, where lines of commerce and communications intersected, would be far more likely to win a national election than one who had displayed his talents on a smaller, more remote stage. To this, Madison and

Gouverneur Morris replied that the interests of the large states were not unified and that even if they were, legislators from those states could cooperate far more easily than popular majorities.[38]

Thus, the objections of the Old Republicans, while substantial, were not unanswerable, and alone they would not have sufficed to repel the drive for direct popular election of the president.

There was, however, one other crucial consideration. It is only rather fleetingly evident in Madison's record of the debates,* but it was absolutely decisive. It stemmed from the institution of slavery. Because slaves did not vote, southern electorates were a smaller percentage of total population than northern. In distributing representation between the states in Congress, weight at the rate of three for five could be given for the southern population in slaves. But in a direct popular election for president, how could these persons be counted if they did not vote?

Williamson, from North Carolina, appears to have been the first to realize the weight of this consideration. On July 17 he noted that direct popular election would be tantamount to choice by the largest states. But not Virginia, he added; "her slaves will have no suffrage."[40] Two days later Madison picked up this point. Southern states would have "no influence in the election on the score of the Negroes."[41] For himself, he said, this objection was not decisive. He cited two countervailing considerations: a prediction that "republican laws" in the southern states would gradually reduce the differences between the sections (did he mean to suggest the eventual emancipation and enfranchisement of blacks?) and his conviction that "local considerations" should yield to the general interest. As an advocate of direct popular election he was personally willing "to make the sacrifice," he said.[42]

As a southern politician Madison was unique in this respect. The disfranchisement of slaves was, in fact, the decisive consideration against the direct popular election of the president in 1787. No North or South Carolinian or Georgian, and not more than a handful of Virginians, would have accepted any constitution that included it.

---

*Throughout the convention and in his notes on its deliberations, Madison treated slavery with extreme care, by circumlocution whenever he could.[39] Like Jefferson and Washington, he knew that slavery posed the greatest threat to American union, and he was determined not to exacerbate it unnecessarily.

They did not simply oppose it. It was unacceptable. When south-erners cast an issue in these terms, it was time to yield and move on or to give up the common enterprise. As the weight of Williamson's point sank in, the notion of the direct popular election of the presi-dent was effectively dead.

The rejection of the choice of a president either by Congress or by direct popular vote left the convention in a quandary. The idea of assigning the choice to electors had been mentioned several times, but it, too, had difficulties. The usual model provided for electors, specially chosen for this responsibility, convening at the national capital to perform a single act of public service. To strengthen the separation between the legislative and executive branches and to dis-courage the rise of patronage-based parties, it was stipulated that legislators and other federal officials would be ineligible to serve as electors.

What made many delegates skeptical about electors was the expense and the doubt that good people would serve so limited a function. Delegates from remoter areas, especially the Carolinas and Georgia, noted that it would be costly and inconvenient for people from their states to serve solely as electors, so far from home.[43] And while some of the old patriots (Franklin, Gerry, Sherman) thought that public-spirited citizens would consent to serve, the younger realists were skeptical.

So there was little enthusiasm for the electoral scheme on its own merits. Yet delegates were repeatedly led back to it because it seemed the only way to satisfy the demands of popular accountability and the separation of powers. In addition, it might provide a way to deal with the problem of slaves not voting.

From July 17 throughout the month of August the convention picked away at this knot, trying to devise some way to ensure the independence of the president from Congress or some way to choose electors, staggering back and forth between problem-ridden propos-als, at one point in desperation considering a scheme of selection by lot. It was Wilson who moved that the executive be chosen "by elec-tors to be taken by lot from the national legislature." On a scrap of paper he worked out his scheme. Let ninety balls be prepared, with as many of them gilded as the proposed number of electors. Each representative and senator would then draw a ball; those drawing gilded balls would be electors. The scheme was a delightful echo of the electoral process of the Venetian Republic, which, as we have seen, had a lot of appeal for framers who knew the Atlantic republican tradition. But Gerry and King opposed it on the ground that, as King put it, "We ought to be governed by reason, not by chance."[44]

Finally, on August 31, the convention selected a committee on unfinished business and assigned it to wrestle with the problem of presidential selection. It was a group of the convention's leaders, weighted on the side of those who favored a strong and independent president: Gouverneur Morris (rather than Franklin) of Pennsylvania; Madison (not Randolph) of Virginia; King of Massachusetts; Dickinson of Delaware; Butler (not Pinckney or Rutledge) of South Carolina. But it contained two of the most astute older republicans as well: Sherman of Connecticut and Williamson of North Carolina. The other four (David Brearly of New Jersey, Abraham Baldwin of Georgia, Daniel Carroll of Maryland, and Nicholas Gilman of New Hampshire) had not taken strong positions on the executive. It was this committee, meeting for the first time three weeks before adjournment, that made the crucial decisions on the president: how he would be elected; the extent of his appointment powers; his role in foreign relations.

The committee made its initial report, which dealt with the electoral process, on September 4.[45] The scheme it presented is the one that appears in the Constitution, except that electoral deadlocks were to be referred to the Senate rather than to the House of Representatives.

The Senate differed from the House both in makeup and powers. The committee was apparently thinking mostly of the difference in makeup—that is, the fact that the states were represented equally in the Senate. The electoral college, like the House of Representatives, gave an advantage to the more populous states. To refer electoral deadlocks to the House would have extended that advantage. The small states insisted on referral to the Senate, where states were represented equally.

On the floor of the convention, however, attention focused on the Senate's unique powers: to confirm appointments; to decide in cases of impeachment; to advise and consent on treaties and ambassadorial appointments. If the electoral process gave the Senate a crucial role in choosing the chief executive, the president would become, in Wilson's words, "not . . . a man of the people as he ought to be, but the minion of the Senate."[46]

It was not clear how often this fallback feature would need to be invoked. Gouverneur Morris and Baldwin thought that the vote of the electors would almost always produce a majority for a single candidate, particularly as the nation knitted together.[47] But most of the delegates thought otherwise. Mason predicted that in nineteen cases out of twenty the choice of president would fall to the Senate. Among those who agreed were Madison, Sherman, King, Randolph, Hamilton, Charles Pinckney, and Rutledge.[48]

Williamson suggested that the electors meet at the capital and work together until they produced a majority among themselves, rather than refer the choice to the Senate. Such a provision might have led to electors assuming a substantial political role, somewhat akin to delegates at a party's nominating convention. But his motion was rejected on a vote of one state to nine, a measure of the intensity with which most delegates were determined to avoid "cabal."[49]

For a moment it seemed that the electoral scheme might fail for lack of an expedient on this point. Then Williamson and Sherman had another idea. Why not refer deadlocks to the House, with each state delegation casting a single vote? This proposal broke the threatened link between president and Senate but preserved the equality of states in choosing between candidates nominated by the electors. In the event of an election that produced no majority of electors, the larger states might dominate the first stage, but the smaller states would have more influence at the end. This proposal was immediately accepted.[50]

The newest feature of the plan prepared by the committee on unfinished business was that the electors were to meet in their own states, on the same day, thus saving the expense of traveling to a single place and, not incidentally, preventing any collusion between them. This small adjustment seems to have been crucial in making the electoral scheme acceptable. As Gouverneur Morris pointed out, the primary attraction of the committee's proposal was that it would prevent "cabal" and "intrigue" in the selection of a president.[51] Meeting in dispersed state capitals, in this era of primitive communications, seemed to guarantee it.

One other feature of the plan is worth special notice. Delegates who were particularly attached to the states (men like Sherman, Williamson, Dickinson, and Butler) saw to it that states retained control over their own participation in the electoral process (electors were to be chosen in each state "in such manner as the legislature thereof may direct"). This provision turned out to be crucial to the shape of the national party system, as states discovered the advantage of casting their electoral votes en bloc. The effect was to make presidential politics a mosaic of state pieces rather than a single national unit.

In these final deliberations about the election of a president, we catch a glimpse of the framers' expectation about the political process that would emerge under the Constitution. That the choice of president might help shape the nation's sense of purpose seems hardly to have been considered. The president was to be a "patriot king," strong, but aloof, almost judicial in bearing, sternly transcendent over the concerns that animated political factions. He was to have extensive political powers, including the power to appoint administrative and judicial officials and to take the lead in foreign relations, but he was to do all this without having played any active role in shaping a national political coalition. In fact, what Alexis de Tocqueville called "the art of associating together," the cultivation of which he deemed vital in a democratic (that is, egalitarian) society, was never considered by the convention of 1787, except negatively, as something to be discouraged.

It is hardly necessary to dwell on the inadequacies of the electoral college or the faultiness of the analysis on which its acceptance rested. In the first contested election under the Constitution (1796), several framers were themselves prominently involved in a partisan process which subverted the convention's design. And not nineteen out of twenty but only two elections (1800 and 1824) in two centuries have been referred to the House of Representatives, the former owing to another flaw in the system (the failure to distinguish presidential and vice presidential ballots).

Perhaps no major proposal at the convention was less adequately analyzed and studied than this one. When it was proposed on September 4, after three exhausting months of maneuvering and compromising, the delegates seemed to heave a collective sigh of relief and give themselves to the hope that their troubles were over. With a bit of fine tuning, but with no serious reflection, the scheme was accepted.

On the central issue dividing them, the proponents of a strong and independent presidency won a complete victory, as they had on the question of unity versus plurality. There would be a single chief executive, and he would be chosen by the people, as directly as the existence of slavery would allow. The role of those who would serve as electors, and whether they would exercise independent judgment, were not discussed. Hamilton's glib theorizing in *The Federalist*, Number 68—to the effect that the electors would be "men most capable of analyzing the qualities adapted to the station [of chief executive] and acting under circumstances favorable to deliberation"—was his personal gloss. There is no indication in the records of the convention that any delegate gave thought to this question.

DISTRIBUTING FUNCTIONS

The one great virtue of the electoral scheme was that by satisfying the demand that the chief executive have an electoral base independent from Congress, it cleared the way for a strong presidency.

As early as June 1 the convention assigned the executive a general authority to execute the law. In the draft of the whole Constitution prepared by the committee on detail in early August, a list of presidential powers drawn from the Constitution of New York State was set forth virtually as it appears in the U.S. Constitution today.[52] The president—as he is called here for the first time in the convention[53]—was given authority to report on the state of the Union, to recommend measures for congressional consideration, to convene Congress on extraordinary occasions and adjourn it in case the houses disagree, to execute the laws, to commission all officers of the United States, to receive ambassadors, to grant reprieves and pardons, and to be "commander in chief of the army and navy of the United States, and of the militia of the several states."

These familiar statements of executive power masked several important issues that were still unresolved. Not until the beginning of September, when the convention found an acceptable electoral scheme, was it possible to resolve these outstanding issues.

As it turned out, the most controversial powers were those relating to the appointment of federal officials, including judges, and the conduct of foreign relations, including the power to "make" treaties and appoint ambassadors. Each of these powers affected the relationship between the president and the Senate. That relationship, with its potential for corruption and for nurturing aristocracy, proved to be the main source of contention about presidential powers.

Reviewing the debates, one is struck by differences between the framers' initial notions about the proper distribution of powers and our own easy assumptions. In their early drafts the framers sidestepped the difficulty of drawing the line between legislative and executive powers by assigning to the executive, "besides a general authority to execute the national laws, . . . the executive rights invested in Congress by the confederation"—without specifying what those "executive rights" were.[54] When the convention returned to this resolution on June 1, Madison sought to refine it by assigning to the executive "power to carry into effect the national laws, to appoint to offices in cases not otherwise provided for, and to execute such other powers not legislative nor judiciary in their nature as may from time to time be delegated by the national legislature." Other delegates suggested that the clause about delegation was unnecessary, being included in the "power to carry into effect the national laws." Madison agreed that the power to "appoint to offices, etc." was "perhaps included in the first member of the proposition." With that, the convention decided to eliminate the refinements and stick for the time being to the fundamental proposition. There the matter rested, while the convention wrestled with other controversial questions, until the committee on detail went to work at the end of July.

In fleshing out the convention's resolutions, the committee on detail inserted the list of powers drawn from the New York Constitution and greatly enhanced the powers of the Senate. The powers of appointment were given to the president, with unspecified exceptions to be "otherwise provided for." As it turned out, the principal exception was the appointment of judges, which the convention assigned solely to the Senate.[55] The committee on detail, of course, incorporated this provision into its draft but, in addition, gave the Senate an exclusive power to appoint ambassadors and "make treaties."

These assignments of responsibility, however strange they may seem to us, reflect a reasonably coherent conception of the separation of functions. The appointment power generally, with the exception of judges, ambassadors, and the treasurer,* was given exclusively to the president. On the other hand, the power to make treaties was conceived as a legislative power. It was assigned not to Congress as a whole but to the Senate, because that chamber, being less numerous, was considered better able to conduct confidential negotiations and because it represented the constituent states more directly than the House. Following the habit of the Articles of Confederation, the states were still seen as having a vestigial sovereignty, particularly in the field of foreign relations. In addition, treaties were regarded as a species of legislation and thus appropriately the business of a legislative body.

During the month of August, when so much time was spent devising the electoral scheme, there was little attention given to the question of presidential powers. Finally, at the end of August, the deadlock on the presidency was handed over to the committee on unfinished business. It proposed several significant additions to the role of the Senate. Besides referring electoral college deadlocks there, it made the Senate, rather than the Supreme Court, the locus of trials of impeachment. And it made the president and Senate cooperate in all major appointments, including ambassadors and judges, and in making treaties.

How these sharings of power were to be accomplished was left vague. There are, of course, a great number of ambiguities in the Constitution, many of them deliberate. In this case, however, the

---

*In this draft, the power to appoint the treasurer was given to Congress as a whole, creating the potential for congressional responsibility in budgeting and programming as well as monitoring governmental expenditures. This provision was finally eliminated on September 14, two days before adjournment.[56] Had it survived, we might have had an official comparable to the chancellor of the exchequer in a parliamentary regime. At any rate, Hamilton's position in Washington's administration would have been different.

new arrangements were left uncertain at least partly because the convention was weary from three months' labor.

Two questions in particular were left hanging. First, what does the word *advice* mean with respect to the Senate's responsibility in appointments and treaty making? Was it intended to be collective or individual? Secondly, who was to have authority to *remove* officials from office? Sympathetically one might observe that the untidiness in the Constitution on these points has been creative. It has left, for subsequent political resolution and re-resolution, the question of who shall determine the direction of American policy. At least in regard to the appointment of federal district judges and regional administrators, however, the practices which unfolded represent a clear defeat for the intentions of the framers.

It is commonplace to note that legislative and executive powers are shared between Congress and the president in the Constitution. What is less often realized is that this mingling, particularly between the Senate and the president, was the source of very profound misgivings by several leading delegates. For Mason, it was the "fatal defect" in the new system.[57] It meant, he said, that the government would begin as a "moderate aristocracy" and develop finally into either tyranny or a corrupt aristocracy. The other nonsigners, Randolph and Gerry, agreed. Authority in government, they held, ought to lie with a popularly chosen legislature. In the Constitution too much of it was mounted very high, in a mutually dependent chief executive and small upper house, composed of representatives of the political elites in each of the states.

These were dissents, however. It was the spirit of James Wilson and Gouverneur Morris which finally prevailed. Morris wanted the government to be energetic and glorious. He thought of the House of Representatives as a sufficient and proper forum for the expression of popular impulses but of the president as the people's tribune.

Seventy-five years later Walter Bagehot was to distinguish between the dignified and efficient elements of the English constitution. The former, he wrote, rested with the monarch, who symbolized the unity and tradition of the nation. Responsibility for policy-making and the conduct of government, the efficient side of the constitution, he found in the prime minister and cabinet, whose authority came from their support by a majority of Parliament.

In the American Constitution powers which Bagehot found separated in England were united in the presidency. To be sure, the president shared "efficient" powers with Congress and "dignity" with the Supreme Court, and it required a great emergency or an advanced state of development to call forth the full potential of presidential dominance. When these conditions came to pass with the Civil War and then more or less permanently in the aftermath of the Great Depression and World War II, it could not truly be said that we had departed from the framers' intent. The convention of 1787 was dominated in the end by those who wanted a single chief executive, presiding with a cabinet strictly of his own choosing, put in office by popular vote, possessing powers of initiation in lawmaking, appointments, and foreign relations and having command over the armed forces. Nowhere on earth would there be an executive with greater constitutional power.

This the framers intended, and this is what we have gotten.

PART III

Development

CHAPTER 5

Chief Executive

The invention of the presidency did not end in 1787. The framers created a living organism. All human creations fashioned after a model are imperfect. In this case the model itself—the idea of the presidency—was itself vague and inexact.[1] After the framers had finished their work, there was much creating left to be done by the succession of presidential incumbents and their assistants, by members of Congress, and by justices of the Supreme Court.

There were, first of all, plain deficiencies in the framers' design, among them the failure to specify the procedure for removing administrators from office and the absence of any provision for identifying presidential candidates. These were critical matters, as it turned out, and recurrently the source of controversy and struggle.

Besides these constitutional gaps, changes in the system's environment caused the presidency to develop in unanticipated ways. As the nation's economy became more interdependent, the federal government took on regulatory functions. The assignment and implementation of these powers had a major effect on the constitutional balances. The sheer size of the government created strains in a system that was designed to encourage confrontation. Gradually pressures for centralized management, planning, and administration overwhelmed the jealousies of the separated branches. Congress even conspired in equipping the president to serve as "chief legislator." Yet the constitutional system proved stubborn and amazingly resilient in the face of these pressures. By the end of Franklin D. Roosevelt's presidency in 1945, the national government was delivering a tremendous range of services and undertaking vast feats of regulation. A huge inverted pyramid of government had come to rest on the pinpoint of the presidency.[2] The weight was straining the promise of self-government to its limits.

In this chapter and the next, we will trace these developments in the presidency and its constitutional environment. We will focus first on domestic aspects and then devote a separate chapter to factors arising from war and the international environment.

ADMINISTRATIVE CONTROL AND THE POWER OF APPOINTMENT

As Congress convened under the newly ratified Constitution, one of its first challenges was to enact organic laws establishing the departments of State, Treasury, and War. Almost immediately, it became apparent that the convention of 1787, which had made the president responsible for executing the laws and given him power to appoint officials for this purpose, had failed to specify a process for removing those who performed unsatisfactorily. The text of the Constitution was ambiguous. It permitted four distinct answers, each of which was, in fact, espoused during that first congressional debate.

Some members of Congress held that appointees were entitled to their positions for life, unless they were impeached. Others argued that the Senate, having joined in the appointment, should concur in the removal as well. Still others believed that inasmuch as the Constitution was unclear about the power of removal, Congress had to settle it by legislation, which might later be amended. Finally, there was the position that the Constitution gave the power of removal directly to the chief executive, so that his responsibility for enforcement of the law might be made clear by his control over administrators.

The framers who served in the First Congress were themselves divided among these camps.* During debate in the House of Representatives James Madison at first seemed unsure about the implications of the Constitution and argued that the ambiguity in the text could best be clarified by legislation. In the course of the debate, however, he admitted that he had changed his mind. He was now convinced that the Constitution itself gave the power of removal directly to the president. He saw that the appointment of officers was inherently an executive function. Under the principle of the separation of powers the legislature might create an office and define its powers, but it ought to have nothing to do with designating a man to fill the office. Madison acknowledged that the Constitution qualified the executive's power of appointment by requiring Senate confirmation, but he urged that this qualification be construed as narrowly as possible. It ought not, he said, become the pretext for senatorial sway over the executive branch. If you made the Senate's consent necessary to the removal of appointees, you would abolish at once the great principle of unity and responsibility in the executive department, by which all officers, from clerks to cabinet secretaries, depend on the president, and the president on the nation.[4]

Prominent on the other side of the debate in the House was the old framer Roger Sherman of Connecticut. In Sherman's view, the Senate was an executive council, sharing by advice and consent in the making of treaties and the appointment of ambassadors, and thus by implication in the conduct of foreign relations, and sharing, too, in the selection of judges and all other officers of the government, including the leaders of executive departments. Sherman, whose stubbornness on behalf of "small states" at the Federal Convention had won many crucial concessions, including equal representation of the states in the Senate, fought hard for the notion that the Senate was a full, if not equal, partner in the executive. (One wonders what might have transpired if Sherman had realized the significance of the removal issue before the adjournment of the Federal Convention.

*Charles Thach suggested that the First Congress was practically a continuation of the Federal Convention, in regard to both agenda and personnel. He pointed out that eight of the original framers had seats in the first House of Representatives, and ten in the Senate, half the membership of that body.[3]

He might have succeeded in adding yet another power to the Senate, citadel of the "small states.")

The Senate, with its equal representation of small and large states, symbolized the continuing vitality of the states in the federal system. It was thus a centrifugal force, counterbalancing the weight of the executive in the direction of centralism. An exchange of correspondence between Sherman and Vice President John Adams in the summer and fall of 1789 brought this consideration to the fore. Adams, who had not himself been a framer, sharply criticized the Constitution's arrangements on appointments for involving the Senate even to the point of confirmation. He predicted that partisan considerations would dominate the Senate's proceedings. Senators, he said, would press the president to appoint their supporters. Sherman did not deny it. The Senate, he said, was the "most important branch in the government." From their knowledge of people in their states, senators would know who was best qualified for office. Their involvement in the process of appointment might lessen the president's responsibility, but the net result would be better public service.

When the debate in the House touched on how a president might actually use his powers of removal, some framers got an early inkling of the political realities of presidential power. At first Madison apparently thought of the "magistracy" (what we now call the administration or the government) as a permanent body. He said he was confident that no president would dismiss a "meritorious and virtuous officer." Indeed, he said, wanton removal of department heads would be grounds for impeachment. Not everyone took this view, however. A Representative from New York, taking note of fears that there would be "a complete revolution throughout the whole executive department" every time a new president came to office, admitted it might be true but contended that a president ought to have that power. Otherwise efforts to provide vigorous administration would be hamstrung.[5]

When the question of removal finally came to a vote, the House, the members of which had no constitutional stake in the outcome, adopted Madison's position—giving the power of removal to the president alone as a matter of constitutional interpretation—by a vote of 29–22. In the Senate, however, the vote was tied, being resolved in favor of the president's power of removal only by the casting vote of Vice President Adams.[6]

A decision as closely balanced as this one, between live political forces, is subject to renegotiation. It was a safe bet that the Senate would find ways to make its presence felt in the ongoing process of building governments.

A politician comes to the Senate by building a powerful organization in a state. He or she has every reason to want to reward supporters with good posts in the federal government. If a president, especially one of the same party, ignores a senator when making an appointment in or from his or her own state, the senator's prestige is bound to suffer. It is even worse when the president appoints one of the senator's political enemies to a high federal post.

Sensitive to these considerations, senators began early to protect one anothers' interests in appointments. There evolved a practice called senatorial courtesy, by which the Senate as a body tends to oppose the nomination of an individual if a senator from the appointee's home state objects to it. The Senate is particularly inclined to honor the objections of a senator of the president's own party. Beyond this negative monitoring, senators of the president's party have developed leverage in promoting their own candidates, especially for appointive offices, administrative and judicial, at the regional level.

Initially the tendency toward senatorial domination of the appointive process was modified by the immense prestige and determination of George Washington and by the force of the precedents he established. Not completely, however; even Washington was forced to withdraw his nominee for a federal post in Georgia when senators from that state strongly objected and asked him to appoint another candidate.[7] In general, though, Washington and his early successors were able to resist the Senate's claim to a monopoly on "advising" the president about federal appointments. Control over administrative appointments was regulated by interplay between presidents and the Senate, within the context of the organic acts of 1789 and the practice of senatorial courtesy.

Almost immediately after the assassination of Lincoln, however, the political balances shifted sufficiently to force a rewriting of the legal framework. Republicans in Congress recognized that President Andrew Johnson's policies posed a threat to their policy for rebuilding the South. They moved to limit his influence. One important device was the Tenure of Office Act, passed over Johnson's veto in March 1867. It provided that no officer whose appointment required Senate confirmation, not even a member of the president's cabinet, could be removed from office without the Senate's concurrence. Johnson asked the Supreme Court to rule on the constitutionality of this act, but the Court refused to offer an advisory opinion.

When President Johnson demanded the resignation of Secretary of War Edwin Stanton and Stanton refused, the president issued an executive order suspending him and appointed General Ulysses S. Grant acting secretary. The Senate refused to concur in the suspension of Stanton. Both Stanton and Grant accepted the Senate's action as binding under the Tenure of Office Act, and Stanton returned to office. Thereupon Johnson dismissed Stanton and appointed "an alcoholic, foppish general," Lorenzo Thomas, in his place as secretary of war.[8] Immediately, that same day, the Senate passed a resolution declaring the removal of Stanton illegal, and a motion for impeachment was introduced into the House. Within three days the House had voted to impeach Johnson and prepare articles of impeachment, centering on the contention that the president had committed "high crimes and misdemeanors" by refusing to obey the Tenure of Office Act. After a brief trial the Senate voted 35–19 in favor of conviction—just one vote short of the two-thirds majority needed to remove the president from office.

Thus, if Madison and his allies were right in 1789 about the intention of the framers, the ambiguity of the constitutional text was partly to blame for the impeachment of Andrew Johnson in 1868. Whether President Johnson's position in that clash—that he had the authority, through his control over the secretary of war, to impede the execution of the Reconstruction Acts—would have been recognized by Madison as a vindication of the framers' wisdom is another question.

At any rate, the Tenure of Office Act continued in force, and in the latter decades of the nineteenth century senators at the heads of great, contending political machines asserted dominion over federal appointments, touching off a series of great patronage battles. A good example is the struggle between Senator Roscoe Conkling of New York and Presidents Rutherford Hayes and James Garfield over the lucrative position of port collector in New York City. In 1878 Hayes asked the incumbent collector, Chester Arthur, to resign for violating an executive order forbidding federal appointees from participating in political campaigns. Arthur ignored the request. Under the Tenure of Office Act Hayes could not fire Arthur, but he did suspend him and sent to the Senate a nominee to replace Arthur. With support from the Democrats Hayes won confirmation for his appointee, thereby disgracing Conkling but leaving the Republican party bitterly divided.

Three years later it was Garfield's turn to battle with Conkling for control of the Republican machine in New York. Once again the prize was the port collectorship. When Garfield nominated an opponent of Conkling's, the senator tried to block confirmation. Despite Conkling's opposition, Garfield's nominee was confirmed, whereupon Conkling and his junior colleague from New York, Thomas Platt, resigned from the Senate and returned to seek reelection in New York. In those days, before the Seventeenth Amendment (ratified in 1913), senators were elected by state legislatures. The division of Republicans into irreconcilable factions led to the defeat of Conkling and Platt in their bid for reelection. But the internecine warfare continued. In 1884 Platt, by then head of the New York Republicans, stood aside during the presidential campaign, thus allowing the Democratic candidate, Grover Cleveland, to win the state, and with it the presidency, by a narrow margin.

The struggle over the port collectorship in New York showed that a determined president could insist upon initiative over appointments, but it also revealed the high cost of controversy over these matters. The exception proved the rule: The constitutional processes for appointments work most smoothly when presidents yield initiative over regional offices to their party's organization, in which senators of their own party are normally leading members.

The Tenure of Office Act remained on the books, in one form or another, until 1926, when the Supreme Court finally declared it unconstitutional in the case of *Myers* v. *United States*. In his opinion in that case Chief Justice William Howard Taft, a former president, basically took James Madison's line. He did, however, add a wrinkle of his own, noting that the Senate's role in confirming appointments required a one-time check into a nominee's qualifications, whereas the question of removal required a continual monitoring of an official's performance.[9] This argument was a little tendentious, though. If the Senate were to share in the president's power of removal, it would not be necessary to check into an official's performance until the president sought to remove him. Senators could then review the charges and confirm the removal only if it found them meritorious. The real issue was control and accountability. For three-quarters of a century after the framing, the prevailing view was that presidential responsibility enhanced popular control by making the president electorally accountable for the execution of the laws. Then, for nearly sixty years (1867 to 1926), Congress forced a qualification of that arrangement, giving the Senate a share in the power of removal. In 1926 the Supreme Court (by a 6–3 majority) reestablished the earlier interpretation.

Even then, however, the issue was not closed. Within a decade the Supreme Court ruled that Congress could create agencies that were not strictly executive in nature and could give, to the commissioners of these regulatory bodies, a tenure that protected them from the president's power of removal.[10] Apart from such exceptional agencies, the evolving practices have distributed to the Senate, and to various state political organizations, the responsibility which Hamilton and Madison and the presidentially oriented framers thought they had focused on the chief executive. In chapter 8, we will examine the effects of these practices on modern government.

THE ELECTORAL PROCESS

Despite the importance of presidential selection to the success of the whole design, the framers failed to provide solutions for several crucial aspects of the problem. They wrote just two fundamental principles indelibly into the constitutional framework: Presidential elections must be held regularly, once every four years; and states, acting through electors, must be the building blocks of presidential support. These provisions were not negligible. They set stubborn limits on reform. But they also left many vital issues for resolution by the political process.

Already by 1800, the year of the second contested election for president, political parties had formed and were offering for the "office" of presidential elector candidates who were firmly pledged to the party's nominees. The result was an election in which the nominees of the Democratic-Republican caucus in Congress, Thomas Jefferson and Aaron Burr, received exactly the same number of electoral votes—votes which, under the Constitution as it then existed, could not be distinguished between those for president and vice president. This threw the election into the House of Representatives, then controlled by the rival Federalists. Enough members of Congress preferred Burr to Jefferson to create a deadlock through thirty-five ballots (a majority of the state delegations in the House was required to elect a president; Jefferson had the votes of eight out of sixteen states). Finally Hamilton, who regarded Jefferson as the lesser of evils, used his influence to swing the election to the Virginian.

It was obvious from this stalemate, which invited blatant corruption in pursuit of high office, that the machinery was defective. Congress moved swiftly to correct it, proposing in 1803 the Twelfth Amendment, which provides that electors cast separate ballots for president and vice president. The amendment was ratified by the necessary three-quarters of the states within a year.

The other flaws in the process were less easy to correct. Ironically, the most definite decision the framers made regarding presidential selection—that it should not come from Congress—was the first to be violated, being nimbly sidestepped by many of the framers themselves during the first seven presidential contests (those resulting in victories for John Adams, Jefferson, Madison, and Monroe). From 1796 until 1824 all the leading presidential candidates were nominated by a congressional caucus. No one seemed to know how else to do it. As the Jeffersonian Republicans became the dominant party, until finally they stood alone in 1820, nomination by congressional caucuses became tantamount to election, mocking the framers' intent. It might even be said that during the first quarter of the nineteenth century the United States became the first nation in the world to use the parliamentary method for choosing its chief executive.*

---

*In England, mother of parliaments, kings chose the prime minister and leading cabinet members at least until the reform of 1832. Before that the government needed parliamentary consent, but the initiative remained with the monarch.

American politicians were not happy with their invention. The election of 1824 vividly displayed its weaknesses. The campaign began in 1821 (long campaigns are not a modern invention!), when John C. Calhoun, then secretary of war, announced his candidacy. In 1822 the Tennessee state legislature, reflecting western regional resentments toward the coastal elite, nominated Senator Andrew Jackson, the first time that a major nomination had been made by a body other than a congressional caucus. Later the Kentucky legislature nominated the leader of its delegation in the House of Representatives, Henry Clay, and a meeting in Boston nominated the secretary of state, John Quincy Adams. Finally, the much-maligned caucus itself met (though only 66 out of the 216 Republican members of Congress attended) and nominated the secretary of the treasury, William Crawford.

The ensuing election produced no majority of electoral votes, so the names of the three leading candidates (in order of the size of their electoral votes: Jackson, Adams, and Crawford) were referred to the House of Representatives for a decision. The votes of the Kentucky delegation in Congress turned out to be critical, and Henry Clay arranged that they be given to Adams, despite the instructions of the Kentucky legislature that they go to Jackson. Charges circulated that Clay had traded his influence for an appointment as secretary of state (ever since Jefferson, up to and including John Quincy Adams, the secretary of state had succeeded directly to the presidency), and when the appointment of Clay as secretary of state, in fact, materialized, no denial by Adams or Clay could lay the rumors to rest. People were convinced that Jackson had been the victim of a "corrupt bargain."

The campaign of 1824 marked the last appearance of the congressional caucus as a presidential nominating device. It was certainly defective from a political standpoint, as the fate of the Federalists had shown. Once their base had shrunk to the point that they had no representation in Congress from large areas of the South and West, their nominations for president more and more reflected their diminishing political base. Thus, even apart from the possibility of corrupt deals between congressmen and presidential nominees over appointments, the system of nomination by congressional caucus did not work very well.

The next election, that of 1828, marked a significant stage in the evolution of the separation of powers. Once more Jackson was nominated by the Tennessee legislature (again three years before the balloting) and conducted his campaign through a personal organization, based outside Congress. Meanwhile, a separate convention of delegates gathered in Harrisburg, Pennsylvania, to nominate the incumbent, John Quincy Adams. The separation of electoral processes for the executive and legislative branches was now complete, except insofar as individual legislators might be active as convention delegates from their states.

The electoral process established in the 1830s—candidates nominated by national party conventions; electors reduced to mere agents of their parties; voters making the ultimate choice—prevailed for well over a century. During this period the campaign for a party's presidential nomination was a relatively closed affair. During the preconvention stage, candidates and their agents made appeals directly to party leaders. Even when candidates made well-publicized speeches to the general public, as Lincoln did at Cooper Union in February 1860 and Wilson in his lectures at Columbia in 1907, their ulterior motive, so to speak, was to impress party leaders who would make the nomination. More typical than oratorical fireworks were the quiet efforts of a man like Mark Hanna or James Farley, on behalf of William McKinley or Franklin Roosevelt, respectively, negotiating with party leaders in Congress and in various states and cities, urging that his man was fit to be president and would govern inoffensively. Participants on both sides always conducted these negotiations with an eye to the ensuing general election. Everybody wanted a winner. Especially party leaders were looking for someone attractive to the general electorate, so that they and their followers might sweep to power on his coattails. Straight party-ticket voting was the norm in America from 1830 until well into the twentieth century.[11] Thus, it mattered greatly to a party leader in Philadelphia, say, whether or not the presidential candidate could run well in that city—not so much whether he would win nationally as whether he would run strongly enough in a given locality to sweep his fellow partisans into the courthouse and city hall.

The system established in the 1830s survived virtually intact through a wave of reforms at the turn of the century. At that time (between 1896 and 1912) several state legislatures replaced a system which depended on parties to prepare "tickets" listing only their own candidates with one in which the government provided a secret ballot listing all certified candidates (the so-called Australian ballot). This reform weakened the parties and eventually encouraged widespread ticket splitting, but it had no direct effect on the constitutional process for choosing presidents.

During this same period of reform a few states adopted a preconvention primary, allowing voters to indicate a preference among various presidential candidates. At first these primary elections had little effect on the actual makeup of conventions, nor were the results binding on the state's delegates. No one regarded them as definitive, inasmuch as many prominent candidates did not enter them, and there were too few to establish a clear favorite across the nation. Again, the basic system for selecting presidents was unaffected.

It was not until the late 1960s that the process for choosing presidents underwent its first fundamental change since 1832. But that is another story, part of the "constitutional revolution" that overtook the presidency at the middle of the twentieth century. We will return to it in chapter 7.

Regarding the removal power and the electoral process, one may fairly speak, I think, of defects in the framers' design. None of them was terribly serious. The political process established by the Constitution was able to devise a series of expedients that enabled the system to function pretty much as the framers intended through its first century and a half.

We turn now to a different sort of challenge to the framers' design of the presidency: those resulting not so much from defects in the design as from unforeseen demands and changes in its environment. These new circumstances required measures and actions never contemplated by the framers. Cumulatively, as the nation moved toward the middle of the twentieth century, they began to bend its system of governance out of shape.

REGULATING A MODERN ECONOMY

Has the Constitution always posed an obstacle to governmental regulation of the economy, or have serious problems arisen only with the advent of modern conditions? One can certainly argue that economic progress in the nineteenth century was partly the result of an absence of governmental regulation. The government encouraged economic development by subsidizing westward migration and helping build an infrastructure of canals, roads, railways, and harbors, but these public enterprises never constituted a major part of the national product and could therefore not be manipulated to regulate the economy. As far as public finance was concerned, the Constitution's principal effect was to reinforce the political opposition to public expenditures for purposes other than the "common defense." President Andrew Jackson in 1830 vetoed a bill authorizing that the federal government buy stock in a corporation that was building a sixty-mile road in Kentucky (the so-called Maysville Road) on grounds that such public works projects served "purely local interests" and encouraged private feeding at the public trough. If federal subsidies for roads and canals were thought desirable, declared Jackson, they should be sanctioned by a constitutional amendment.*

Woodrow Wilson's survey of the national government, called *Congressional Government*, published in 1885, tells how difficult it was for congressmen to decide how to spend the revenues raised from the protectionist tariff. The money had to be spent; keeping it in the Treasury was having a deflationary effect. But prevailing commitments to a strict construction of the government's "enumerated powers" limited the objects for which money could be spent.⁺ Wars with the Indians and finally with the Spanish helped get the money out the door, but the problem was not easy for politicians of the late nineteenth century to solve.

---

*Compare John Quincy Adam's first annual message to Congress, December 6, 1825, a vain attempt to launch the federal government on a career of public improvement.[12]
⁺ For a presidential response to this dilemma, see Grover Cleveland's first annual message to Congress, delivered in December 1885, in which he proposed to close the gap by reducing tariffs. Republicans, committed to protectionism, blocked Cleveland's policy without offering an alternative. The result of the deadlock was deflation and depression.

Toward the end of the nineteenth century the economy began to mature, creating a demand for federal regulation of certain fundamental enterprises.[13] In 1889 Congress raised the Agriculture Department to cabinet status and entrusted the executive with monitoring certain practices in the marketing of animals. But as the title of Wilson's book suggests, this was a period of congressional dominance, and Congress as a body was deeply suspicious of executive power—as the framers had hoped and expected it would be. It was also a time of close balance between the two major parties, which often led to divided political control of the houses of Congress and the White House. During fourteen of the twenty years beginning in 1877 the party that controlled the White House was a minority in Congress. Under these circumstances, Congress was particularly reluctant to grant regulatory powers to the executive branch.

Nevertheless, public pressure to regulate the railroads gradually mounted, and in 1887—the centennial of the Constitution—Congress created the Interstate Commerce Commission, the first so-called independent regulatory commission. For the first time an agency of the federal government combined powers of rule making and administration, which Articles I and II of the Constitution had distributed between Congress and the president, and commissioners were given fixed terms, insulating them from the president's power of removal. Decisions by the Supreme Court soon helped make the ICC a feeble agency, unable to impose discipline on the railroad industry. Constitutionally, however, its creation was a milestone.

When Woodrow Wilson became president, he adopted the concept of the independent regulatory commission in calling for a Federal Reserve Board (known as the Fed and the FRB) to regulate the banking industry and control the supply of credit and money circulating in the system. Board members were appointed by the president, with the advice and consent of the Senate, but their terms were fixed, putting them beyond the president's direct control.

In establishing the Federal Reserve Board, an agency of vast and fundamental powers, Congress and the president postponed the day of reckoning for the Constitution. Modern conditions presented a challenge that could not be dodged: The government had to regulate the supply of money. But the legislative branch could not do it. A legislature acts by laws, but laws are too blunt, and lawmaking is too slow, for this purpose. The executive branch seemed unfit, too. Administrators could certainly act precisely and quickly enough, and the government could hire the requisite expertise; but regulating the supply of money involved an enormous discretionary power. The "unity" of the presidency made it fit for enforcement and administration, but unfit for making policy, which requires more highly articulated representativeness. Also, for reasons of institutional jealousy, Congress was simply unwilling to delegate so much discretion to the president.*

It was a pea-and-shell game. Where was the power to regulate money? Not in Congress: too slow. Not in the executive branch: not representative enough. Not in the courts: inappropriate expertise and accountability. Then the power must lie somewhere in the cracks between Articles I, II, and III of the Constitution. The new creature would owe its existence to legislation, its officers would be appointed by the president, with senatorial consent, but it would be insulated from political accountability by fixed terms. It was a cunning solution—but where was the constitutional warrant?

The problem did not end with the FRB. Once the model of the independent commission had been refined, Congress applied it to a number of other areas: the regulation of unfair commercial practices (Federal Trade Commission, or FTC), the securities industry (Securities and Exchange Commission, or SEC), broadcasting (Federal Communications Commission, or FCC), and labor relations (National Labor Relations Board, or NLRB), among others. In some cases the authority of these agencies overlapped with that of existing departments (the FTC and SEC share responsibilities with the Justice Department, for example), and in all cases Congress had delegated considerable discretion to these commissions or boards. Indeed, that was the point of creating them.

From time to time there have been complaints that one or another of the commissions was too weak in pursuing its regulatory responsibilities, or too much beholden to the industry it was created to regulate, or too responsive to the industry's critics.[15] But apart perhaps from the case of the Federal Reserve Board, there was little

---

*As the framers intended, Congress had "the necessary constitutional means and personal motives" to resist presidential "encroachment."[14]

indication of popular restiveness about these extra-constitutional bodies. Only those who were concerned about constitutional government—about the forms of popular government under the conditions of modernity—had misgivings.

GROWTH OF THE EXECUTIVE ESTABLISHMENT

George Washington, from the temporary capital in New York City, administered a federal government headed by five cabinet officers: the secretaries of state, treasury, and war, the attorney general, and the postmaster general. (A sixth department, Navy, was added in 1798.) The first federal budget ran to about $4 million annually, more than half of it for interest payments on the Revolutionary War debt. Thomas Jefferson, the first president inaugurated in Washington, D.C., oversaw a government that was still spending less than $11 million annually, including interest on the debt. Most modern college presidents lead institutions that spend far more money (even discounting for inflation), and are more complicated administratively, than these early presidents of the United States.*

Growth during the first half of the nineteenth century was slow. James K. Polk's *Diaries* reveal that it was still possible in the 1840s for a president personally to monitor the performance of every bureau in the capital. Lincoln found that the Union effort in the Civil War required a tremendous administrative apparatus; but as soon as the war was over, the armies melted away, and so did the administrative support system. Laying aside interest on the war debt, the government administered by Ulysses Grant spent an average of about $270 million annually during his eight years in office.

In fact, not until the twentieth century did any appreciable permanent growth in the federal bureaucracy occur. The capital's architecture nicely reflects the development. Until World War II the headquarters of the major administrative departments—Treasury, State, War, and Navy—flanked the White House. By midcentury

---

*President Benno Schmidt of Yale, for example, administers an institution that spent $434 million in 1985 and had seventy-one separate departments (thirty-six of them academic, the rest administrative).

the main offices of the Treasury Department were still in the building to the east of the White House, but the others had left the building to the west of the White House. The State Department moved to an enormous complex in a section of the capital called Foggy Bottom, and the War and Navy departments, which in 1949 were unified into a single Department of Defense, are now housed in the Pentagon, one of the largest buildings in the world, situated across the Potomac River in Arlington, Virginia. The magnificent French Renaissance Revival building that used to house "State, War, and Navy" is now called the Old Executive Office Building and shelters about half of the Executive Office of the President. Most of the rest is across Pennsylvania Avenue, in the New Executive Office Building and in other buildings around Lafayette Park.

There are other ways to indicate the scope of changes, such as the fact that the Commerce Department alone now employs more people (39,689 in 1981) than lived in New York City, which, with a population of about 33,000, was the nation's largest city in 1790.

Growth in the administrative establishment has not been steady. The first big push came during the Progressive Era, near the turn of the twentieth century. A demand for regulation of the marketplace produced a proliferation of agencies during this period, some of them in new independent bodies, but many of them taking their places in the old departments of Justice and Treasury and in the newer departments of Agriculture, Commerce, and Labor.

The Great Depression and the New Deal stimulated a new kind of demand. Whereas earlier regulative activities had been aimed at particular sectors of the economy, the new need was for policies and programs that applied to the whole economic system or could relieve the suffering of those who were unable to benefit from the national economy. For example, a new understanding of agricultural economics produced a plan for controls over production of farm products, established and administered by the federal government. The Social Security system provided insurance for retired workers and their survivors. At the behest of President Franklin D. Roosevelt, Congress, recognizing that private capital was unable to provide electrical power in remote rural areas, authorized the creation of the Tennessee Valley Authority (TVA) and the Rural Electrification Administration (REA) to provide this essential component of development. To cope with unemployment, the federal government during the Great Depression became an employer of last resort, putting men and women to work building parks, digging harbors, decorating post offices, and producing theatrical works.

Each of these programs, even those which were eventually implemented by local governments and those whose benefits went automatically to certain recipients, required bureaucratic control in Washington and the regional offices of the federal government. Thus, a constitutional system the genius of which lay in carefully checked power, in sensitivity toward constituent opinion, and in virtually unlimited access for pressure groups was being called upon in the twentieth century to administer policies and programs of enormous complexity and scope. It was the responsibility of one person to see that these laws were "faithfully executed."

The Budget and Accounting Act of 1921 marked the recognition of two modern facts: that the federal government needed a comprehensive budget and that budgeting was essentially an executive function. Note that the establishment of the Bureau of the Budget in the Treasury Department was not the achievement of a determined president, wrung from a reluctant Congress. It came while Warren G. Harding sat in the White House, longing—between catnaps and card games—for a "return to normalcy," and it was imposed, not granted, by Congress, in hopes of bringing a measure of discipline to the sprawling executive branch.

Another landmark came during Franklin Roosevelt's second term. In 1936 he created the Committee on Administrative Management, under the chairmanship of Louis Brownlow. After a careful review of federal programs and the government's means for implementing them, Brownlow's committee issued the famous finding that "the President needs help" and recommended some sweeping changes. First, it called for the creation of the Executive Office of the President, including a limited number of White House aides ("probably not exceeding six"), who would serve as the president's eyes and ears, monitoring the performance of executive branch personnel and making sure that his orders produced a quick and appropriate response. These aides, warned Brownlow, must have "a passion for anonymity." They must recognize that their authority in this constitutional republic derived from the president's. They must not seek to make a personal impression. They must serve the president in his policy-making role and not interfere with the administrative work of the departmental secretaries. In addition, Brownlow's committee recommended that the Bureau of the Budget be moved to the White House, so that budget making could help give the president more direct control over the sprawling executive branch.

Brownlow's recommendations were partially implemented by the Reorganization Act of 1939. The Bureau of the Budget (renamed the Office of Management and Budget in 1970) came to the White House, and the president's staff was augmented. However, the legislation did not clarify the division of responsibility between the president's aides and his cabinet secretaries, nor was the bureaucracy insulated from the pressures of the legislative branch. Thus, the constitutional system entered the last half of the twentieth century without adjusting to the demands of modern administration. It was still proceeding on the assumption that a single elected leader could impart vigor and a sense of direction to nearly 3 million civil servants. In chapters 9 and 10, we will examine the effects of faith in this constitutional system.

EMERGENCE OF THE PRESIDENT AS "CHIEF LEGISLATOR"

Perhaps the most remarkable shift in the distribution of constitutional power—the one that marks the most dramatic departure from the spirit of the framers' design—came with the gradual emergence of the president as chief legislator.

In tracing this development, James Sundquist of the Brookings Institution has noted a series of "firsts."[16] William H. Taft was the first modern president to present draft legislation to Congress. Taft's initiative aroused a good deal of resentment in Congress. His successor, Woodrow Wilson, was the first president to gain acceptance as legislative leader of a national political party, and he instituted the practice of presenting bills to Congress in person. The press, for the first time, began to speak of the "administration's bills" in Congress. President Warren Harding attempted to take the matter another significant step when he addressed the Senate from the vice president's chair, urging defeat of a pending bill on soldiers' bonuses. He accomplished his immediate purpose when the bill was recommitted, but an angry debate broke out over his allegedly "unconstitutional" appearance. Senator Robert M. La Follette insisted that the framers had been "careful" to withhold from the president "any express or implied authority to oppose legislation in the making or to participate in the deliberations and debate of either house on a pending measure."[17] In 1932 President Herbert Hoover addressed the Senate on a pending revenue bill, and he, too, stirred up a partisan hornets' nest, partly over the constitutional issue. Since then no president has addressed either house of Congress on an immediately pending piece of legislation.[18]

With the coming of Franklin Delano Roosevelt the modern presidency entered its second period of major legislative influence (the first was under Wilson), and this time the pattern proved durable. Major portions of the New Deal program were drafted at the White House or in administrative agencies, sometimes with participation by congressmen, but on the executive's turf. Democratic leaders in Congress acted as the president's lieutenants. Soon the president's role was institutionalized, through the assignment of a White House aide (Judge Samuel Rosenman in Roosevelt's case) to draft legislative messages. Under Harry Truman came the first full-time congressional liaison specialists, a function that was upgraded by Dwight Eisenhower and tied by John Kennedy into a system of departmental legislative liaisons.

As the habit of presidential initiative in legislative policy became ingrained, Congress began to provide the presidency with institutional mechanisms to discharge the responsibility. Most fundamental was the Bureau of the Budget, which by Truman's time was coordinating the submission of administration bills to Congress and presenting the administration's position on pending legislation.[19] The Employment Act of 1946 established the Council of Economic Advisers. This body was originally intended by congressional conservatives as a restraint on liberal presidents, who seemed oblivious of the harsh truths of the "dismal science." The availability of economists who would tell the president what he wanted to hear soon made it possible to convert the CEA into a tool for presidential policy-making.[20] In 1947 Congress created the National Security Council (NSC) to assist the president in the formulation and coordination of defense and foreign policy. The trend continued with the legislative mandate in 1962 for a Manpower Report and with the establishment in 1970 of the Council on Environmental Quality and the Domestic Council.

Thus, by the 1970s the expectation that presidents would take the lead in proposing national policy in virtually all fields was fixed and well implemented. Congress joined in looking to the president for leadership in fashioning national policy and in equipping him to perform this role. The president became chief legislator, not by usurpation, not even by congressional neglect or passive acquiescence, but by positive congressional delegation.

Why did Congress do it? There were two reasons. First, Congress lacks the capacity to act quickly and secretly, a serious deficiency in the fields of economic management and national security. Modern conditions often seem to demand such action. It was a Democratic Congress that gave Republican President Nixon the authority to impose wage and price controls whenever he deemed them necessary to control inflation. It gave a succession of presidents, of both parties, broad latitude to use military force to protect American interests in Europe, the Middle East, Latin America, the Far East, and Southeast Asia. Thus, even when partisan considerations should have sharpened the countervailing ambitions upon which the framers relied to preserve the system's balances, Congress joined in making the president an initiator of important national policies.

The unique contribution of Congress to the constitutional system lies in deliberation. Its bicameral structure and the practice of careful consideration by committees ensure that Congress will not act hastily or without consulting interested parties. It came to be seen as part of the genius of the constitutional system that when action had to be taken quickly, the president was there to do it. In a modern economy and in a world full of adversaries controlled by dictatorships, it seemed a blessing and a sign of the framers' prescience that the government had a president capable of decisive, energetic, and secret action, thereby allowing Congress to maintain its traditional virtues of openness and deliberation.

The other perceived deficiency of Congress from the standpoint of modern leadership is its inability to integrate the elements of policy into a national program. Again, this weakness was the other side of a peculiar strength of Congress—namely, its ability to devote attention, through its committee system, to particular areas of policy. In some parliamentary regimes, bills are assigned to legislative committees randomly. This helps bring a general perspective to bear on proposed policies but reinforces the committees' amateur standing, so to speak, as far as the substance of policy is concerned. By contrast, an American legislative committee, as its members and staff gain seniority, becomes a formidable influence in a particular area of policy. When members of Congress devote themselves to a particular subject, however, they diminish their involvement in other areas, partly because of time constraints and partly in deference to their colleagues. No one in Congress devotes much time to developing a general perspective.

There have been repeated attempts to organize Congress for a more integrated approach to policy-making, either by strengthening the partisan steering committees[21] or by appointing ad hoc committees to draft legislation for a multifaceted problem such as energy or welfare reform. Despite these efforts, however, there has been "no fundamental improvement in the integrative capacity of the Congress, with the single—though major—exception of the budget process."[22] Even there the costs have been high, and the results mixed, at best. Places of great power have been robbed of their traditional roles. The appropriations subcommittees, as well as the standing authorizing committees, suffered diminution. Overall there is little in the primary incentive system—what has been called the "electoral connection"[23]—to encourage congressmen to wield personal leverage over the policy-making process. Not many voters are interested in what a congressman has done to preserve the checks and balances of the constitutional system.

There are other factors besides the inability of Congress to act quickly or to aggregate policies into a program that help account for its loss of weight in the constitutional balances. Congress, composed of members of various wings of both major parties, reaches its decisions through bargaining. It is difficult for anyone to give principled reasons for its decisions. There is bickering in the executive branch on the way to decisions, too, but it usually takes place behind closed doors, sometimes under the protection of executive privilege. Once the decision has been made, the president can announce it himself, giving the appearance of unity, decision, and vigor. No wonder people look to the president, rather than Congress, for "leadership."

Thus, the reasons for the shift of legislative influence in the direction of the presidency are obvious, but so are the costs, from the standpoint of the framers' design. Initiative has shifted from a representative assembly to a single individual and his dependents. In the process, popular government has shifted its weight in the direction of a plebiscitary presidency.

For most of the nineteenth century the Constitution worked more or less according to the American doctrine of separation of powers. Congress by its lawmaking powers took the initiative in policy-making; most presidents had a fair measure of control over the enforcement of the law and the administration of the government. If the record gave cause for dismay from the framers' standpoint, it would have been in the weakness and dependence of the executive during the period of presidential nomination by congressional caucus (1796–1824) and in the corruption that resulted from congressional dominance for much of the period from the end of the Civil War to the end of the century, especially 1869 to 1892.

By the middle of the twentieth century, however, this pattern was beginning to change. Congress continued to play a major role. It was still the strongest, most independent legislature in the world. When it was aroused, it could exact high tribute from other elements of the system, forcing them to take its judgment and desires into account.

Nevertheless, modernity has disturbed the constitutional balances. Congress rarely took the initiative anymore. Most of the time it let the president define the agenda, then reacted to his proposals. Moreover, it equipped him for leadership by giving him councils and policy-planning bureaus.

Through the 1930s the developments traced in this chapter did not all contribute to an "enlargement of the presidency."[24] Some did. The establishment of the president's role as chief legislator certainly added weight to the executive side of the constitutional balance. So did presidential ascendancy in the field of war powers, which we will examine in detail in the next chapter. But many aspects of modernity weighed against the presidential side in the constitutional balance of power. As the size and power of the federal government waxed, Congress found ways to deny to the president its full political advantages. The development of the civil service system circumscribed the power of presidential patronage. The establishment of independent regulatory commissions put a great deal of regulatory power beyond the reach of presidential guidance and responsibility. President Hoover had more appointments to make than President Washington, but he was also chief executive of a government over which he had far less control than his eighteenth-century predecessor.

By midcentury the institutional character of the framers' design was still doggedly persistent, but modernity was forcing the president to assume responsibility for domestic policy-making which the framers intended for the legislature to exercise. As these changes pursued their course through the tumultuous events of the 1960s and 1970s, their fateful significance for constitutional democracy was steadily revealed. We will return to that story after we have reviewed the impact of foreign relations and war on the framers' system.

CHAPTER 6

Commander in Chief

The Constitution supposes, what the history of all governments demonstrates, that the executive is the branch of power most interested in war, and most prone to it. It has accordingly with studied care vested the question of war in the legislature.

> James Madison to Thomas Jefferson
> (letter, April 2, 1798)

We have placed a shocking amount of military power in the president's keeping, but where else, we may ask, could it possibly have been placed?

> Clinton Rossiter,
> The American Presidency[1]

After World War II, as the United States assumed the role of world power, Walter Millis wrote that in matters of foreign policy and war, those who govern in a democracy, as in any other political system, are "condemned to be dictators."[2] Why "condemned"? Because presidents are politicians with a broad range of purposes. To accomplish them, they need to husband their power. The work of being commander in chief squanders power. It forces presidents to deceive and overwhelm their fellow politicians on Capitol Hill, to devote the nation's resources to massive nonproductive and disruptive expenditures, and to neglect other parts of their program. Lyndon Johnson's career is the most poignant example, but Truman's, too, illustrates the problem.[3]

When a president acts as commander in chief, he tends to operate autocratically. When war approaches, his responsibilities as commander in chief loom larger, and his impact on the nation's affairs increases enormously. Thus, war transforms the American president into an autocrat.

In the past, periods of what Clinton Rossiter has called "constitutional dictatorship" have been relatively brief: Lincoln from 1861 to 1865; Wilson in 1917 and 1918; FDR for a few months in 1933. During the 1940s, however, the United States was thrust into the world environment and reacted by accepting a large share of responsibility for the security of non-Communist nations. This decision, which was made gradually and not without reluctance, was eventually affirmed by almost everyone in the country.* It had the effect of placing the nation on a permanent wartime footing, thereby casting the president in the role of autocrat over a substantial part of the public life of the American people.

In the pages that follow, we will review the clauses in the Constitution bearing on the president's responsibilities as commander in chief. Then, to prevent the error of believing that the modern situation is unique, we will look at the performance of earlier commanders in chief. We will then be in a position to isolate the factors which "condemn" modern presidents to be dictators so much of the time and over so much of the nation's public life.

In the field of national defense the Constitution's provisions are brief and full of leeway. Congress is given the power "to raise and support armies," "to provide and maintain a navy," to make rules

---

*Lest it be imagined that the notion that the United States was responsible for the security of the "free world" was a trick perpetrated by James Forrestal, Dean Acheson, and John Foster Dulles, a speech delivered by Adlai Stevenson at Harvard (1954) is worth recalling. "It has fallen to America's lot," said Stevenson, "to organize and lead that portion of the world which adheres to the principle of consent in the ordering of human affairs. It is an assignment we undertook not by choice but by necessity. . . . [T]he quest for peace and security," he added, "is not a day's or a decade's work. For us it may be everlasting."[4]

for calling the state militias into federal service, and to establish military codes. The appropriation of money for the support of the army is limited by the Constitution to two years.*

Congress is also empowered "to declare war." The verb here is crucial. It originally read "to *make* war," apparently giving Congress the power of command as well as initiation. But when the president was made "commander in chief," the legislative responsibility was narrowed. Article I also states that "no state shall, without the consent of the Congress, . . . engage in war, unless actually invaded, or in such imminent danger as will not admit of delay." It was thus recognized as possible to "engage" in war even if it was not declared, and states were explicitly entitled to do so under certain circumstances. It would seem to follow that presidents, like governors, may likewise "engage" in war without a declaration, when the nation's territory is invaded or in "imminent danger."+

Article I begins, "All legislative powers *herein granted* shall be vested in a Congress. . . ." Article II begins, "The executive power shall be vested in a President. . . ." Thus, at the threshold the president's writ is broader. Section 2 of Article II begins the definition of the president's powers: "The president shall be commander in chief of the army and navy. . . ." It goes on to give him power, with the advice and consent of the Senate, to appoint and commission all officers of the armed forces.

That is all. The power to provide national security rests on those spare clauses. Basically they give Congress the power of supply and the president the power of command.

How many soldiers and sailors should be kept in uniform? How many guns and ships should be available? Should we maintain more or fewer bases at home? What kinds of agreements, if any, should we make for bases abroad? Where should the forces be stationed?

---

*The appropriation of money for any purpose other than the military may be for longer than two years. The limitation on military appropriations bears witness to the desire of the framers to keep a short tether on both Congress and the president in the field of national defense.

+ This interpretation is confirmed by the Militia Acts of 1795 and 1807, which authorize the president, without a prior declaration of war, to call state militias into federal service to repel invasions or suppress insurrections.

Should our navy sail where there is danger of hostilities? Should our marines be sent to protect American diplomats or commercial properties abroad? Under the Constitution, there have always been two parts to each of these questions: What should be done, and who should decide? When the Barbary pirates began in 1801 to prey on American commercial ships in the Mediterranean for failure to pay adequate tribute, Jefferson dispatched a small fleet of warships to retaliate. Always fastidious about constitutional form and the precedents he was creating, he confined his ships to defensive actions until Congress could set a policy. In 1802 Congress passed an act authorizing the president to protect American commerce and seamen against the pirates, to capture ships belonging to Tripoli, and to take "all other acts of precaution and hostility as in a state of war." There was nothing in the Constitution that required this legislation. Jefferson did depend on Congress to appropriate money for ships and sailors. If Congress had been hostile to him (and the Supreme Court sympathetic to Congress), the legislators might have made trouble through their power to "make rules concerning captures on land and water." But where Congress and the president were in general accord (as here, and as regards the military exercises and shows of force in Central America and East Asia later), no provision of the Constitution required specific legislation to authorize the action that Jefferson took.

The opposite boundary of presidential discretion was explored by President James Polk. When he sent the army into disputed territory in Texas, which provoked the Mexican War of 1846–1848, Congress had no choice but to "recognize" that a state of war existed and make appropriations accordingly. Many in Congress wanted to express disapproval of the president's conduct; sixty-seven Whigs, constituting more than one-quarter of the House of Representatives, voted against the first appropriation for military expenditures. As the war drew to a close, a rider was added to the House version of the resolution honoring General Zachary Taylor, asserting that the war had been initiated by the president "unnecessarily and unconstitutionally." But that did not alter the fact that 1,721 men had died of wounds, and more than 11,000 of disease; that $97 million had been spent on military and naval expenditures; and that 1,193,061 square miles had been added to American territory by the treaty (ratified, 38–14,* by the Senate) that ended the war.

What sense does it make to call Polk's action "unconstitutional"? Should not he as commander in chief deploy troops in threatened territory he regarded as belonging to the United States? Of course, by its power to "make rules for the government and regulation of the land and naval forces," Congress might have directed that they not be used where Polk wanted to use them. Or it might have used its political leverage, threatening to cut military appropriations or to frustrate other parts of the presidential program unless the Mexican adventure was stopped. But Polk's action violated no constitutional provision.

Jefferson and Polk represent polar interpretations of the commander in chief clause. In Jefferson's theory, Congress makes policy.† The president's job is to see that the laws are "faithfully executed." The commander in chief has no will of his own, except to execute the judgment of Congress, framed in laws, treaties, and resolutions. In case of emergency, as when the pirates attacked American vessels in the Mediterranean, the commander in chief might have to act before the will of Congress could be enacted. But he is under solemn obligation to perform only the minimum actions necessary to protect American lives and property and to be scrupulous not to commit the nation to policies on his own initiative.

Polk's actions suggest another interpretation. In this view, the president recommends and Congress enacts measures to provide men and matériel for national defense. But it is the president's responsibility to deploy and command the armed forces, once they have been raised, in accordance with his understanding of the national interest. Congress can, by positive enactment, restrain the president, but members of Congress, having narrower constituencies and lacking access to the secret materials upon which the president's policy is

---

* The opposition came mostly from senators who wanted to annex the whole of Mexico.

† Jefferson as president was often ready to ignore this theory when circumstances seemed to require it. The purchase and occupation of Louisiana, for which no hint of constitutional warrant exists, are the most dazzling example, but his early actions against Tripoli also illustrate it.

based, are normally hesitant to interfere with the commander in chief's performance of his duties.

As between the Jeffersonian and Polkian conceptions of the president's responsibilities, it is vain to argue that one is constitutional and the other not. The Constitution's phrases bearing on this function are, as Napoleon recommended, "short and obscure." Command over the armed forces is lodged with the president, so that military power may be kept under political control (an individual being more likely to maintain control, and better able to be held accountable, than an assembly). Control over military appropriations lies with Congress, to inhibit presidents from embarking on grandiose adventures. The powers of supply and command are separated, so that either political branch can thwart adventurism (Congress by refusing to appropriate support; the president by refusing to move troops toward battle). The ultimate power, of course, lies with the people, who elect congressmen and presidents. In the short run this power often seems like a fiction, but wise politicians pay it careful heed.

Since it was born in violence just over two centuries ago, the United States has declared war on five occasions, has waged a grave civil war, and used armed forces abroad in eight other "major actions." In addition, according to a report prepared for the House Committee on Foreign Affairs in 1970, there were 165 instances of the use of U.S. armed forces abroad between 1798 and 1970.

Correlating this list with the terms of presidents, it appears that William Henry Harrison (who was president for one month), James Garfield (president for six months), Rutherford B. Hayes, and Herbert Hoover were the only presidents who served without commanding the armed forces in engagements abroad. Since 1970 we would have to add Jimmy Carter to this list.

Nor is modern guerrilla warfare as unique in kind as we sometimes think. In a book on military history, two soldiers, Colonel R. Ernest Dupuy and Major General William H. Baumer, demonstrate that "by 1950 [that is, prior to the Korean and Vietnam wars] the U.S. government and its armed forces had been exposed to a century and a half of limited little wars on both hemispheres, and in a wide variety of climate, terrain, and international relationships."[5]

On the Caribbean and Mediterranean seas, in the jungles of the Philippines and the frozen tundra of Siberia, alongside allies in the diplomatic quarter of "Peking" and on horseback among the revolutionaries in Mexico, American forces have fought in all kinds of wars. In each of these episodes the president—whatever his training or capacity for military command, whether in temperament as martial as Andrew Jackson or as mild as Franklin Pierce—exercised ultimate authority.

The first job of the commander in chief is to keep armed forces ready at the level he deems necessary to cope with the contingencies. On this point, of course, he must persuade Congress to accept his judgment. Occasionally the president may wish to increase the armed forces simply to deter foreign powers. Although John Adams, for example, was determined to avoid war with France in 1798, he persuaded Congress to create a Navy Department and approve a federal budget (in 1799) that devoted 55 percent of the $9.7 million total to current military expenditures (compared, for example, with the budget for 1797, which allocated 23 percent of the $6.1 million total to the military).

More often, however, presidents have sought to trim their diplomacy to the available armed forces. Sometimes a president finds himself caught between military advisers pleading inadequate preparation and a Congress and public opinion bristling for battle. That was James Madison's predicament in 1812, when he sent Congress a chilling assessment of what it would cost to wage war against Great Britain. The president's report grounded the "war hawks" briefly, but soon they began to soar again, pushing Madison and the army toward a war for which the nation was ill prepared. In more recent times the lack of military capacity under Hoover provided an unanswerable objection to the pressure of Henry Stimson and others for a firm stand against Japanese aggression in Manchuria in 1932.[6]

The work of preparing defenses is a perpetual responsibility of even the most pacific of presidents. He must choose generals of the army and admirals of the navy. He must maintain academies for the training of officers. He must operate bases for training infantrymen and sailors, and he must try to avoid wasting money on bases the nation no longer needs. He must procure clothing, food, shelter, vehicles, ships, weapons, roads, maps, and other supplies. In short, the outfitting and mounting of an army are a major feat of planning, procurement, and engineering. It has nevertheless fallen to such philosophic souls as Madison and Wilson as well as to dedicated administrators such as Polk and William McKinley.

When war becomes imminent, critical responsibilities pile in on the commander in chief. First and most fundamentally, he must provide the authoritative definition of the cause and aims of the war. This is often a delicate task. Before 1941 the United States never engaged in a foreign war the purpose of which was clear and simple. Presidents are always subject to strong cross pressures in defining the aims of war. Even in the case of the Civil War, though its immediate cause was clear enough, the statement of aims gave Lincoln continual difficulty. In his famous letter of August 22, 1862, to Horace Greeley, he gave a blunt statement of the basic purpose of the Union effort—"My paramount object in this struggle is to save the union and is not either to save or to destroy slavery"—though the Emacipation Proclamation and his later refusal to negotiate the reenslavement of the blacks suggest at least that he was trying to draw the nation toward a broader sense of purpose about the war. For Madison in the War of 1812 and McKinley in the Spanish-American War, the claim on statesmanship was to restrain a voracious public appetite for territorial conquest. As it turned out, McKinley was less successful than Madison on this score. The annexation of Puerto Rico and the Philippines was not a deliberate war aim,* but events outran the president's control. As Ernest May has observed, "McKinley's aim was to check, subdue, or master an irrational movement in domestic opinion. The real enemy to him was not the Spaniard but the Democrat, and the true measure of his strategy came, not at Manila Bay or off Santiago or on San Juan Hill, but in November, 1898, when the electorate gave his party majorities in both the House and Senate and in November, 1900, when he was

---

*By the so-called Teller Amendment to the declaration of war in 1898, Congress disclaimed any intention of exercising sovereignty over Cuba, asserting that control over the island would be left to its people. In 1901, in negotiating for the withdrawal of American troops, the United States insisted that Cuba incorporate into its new constitution a clause authorizing the United States to intervene whenever necessary to preserve Cuban independence and maintain law and order, which made Cuba virtually a protectorate of the United States.

re-elected by nearly 900,000 votes"[7] McKinley's performance shows that placing a politician in command of the armed forces does not always lead to restraint, even when the man himself has deep misgivings, as McKinley did, about the plans proposed by his military aides.

Another aspect of the commander in chief's responsibility, once war has begun, is to designate theaters of combat. Often, of course, the choice is forced by the enemy—Madison did not choose the White House lawn as a combat zone—or by overzealous field commanders—Pierce did not authorize the assaults on Nicaragua in 1855. Sometimes domestic political considerations become a factor. Polk's strategy during the war with Mexico, for example, was influenced by his assessment of the political ambitions, as well as military situation and capacity, of his field commanders.

But to the extent that American power and political realities permit, it is the president's job to decide where the war should be fought and to assign priorities to possible theaters. It was Wilson's job to decide whether American troops should join in the Allied attempt to maintain the Russian front against Germany after the Bolshevik Revolution. The problem involved a mixture of military, political, and diplomatic considerations. It fell quite appropriately to the politician in the White House.

The prosecution of the war itself belongs mostly to field and supply commanders and to soldiers, sailors, and marines. The president is never far from the action, however. Often he must intervene directly in the management of the war effort. Presidents vary in their appetite for close personal involvement in the war effort. Polk tried to oversee every detail of the war, partly because he did not trust his Whig commanders* and partly because of the incompetence of his secretary of war, William ("To the victor belong the spoils") Marcy. Polk once discovered that his order to the army to make certain purchases in New Orleans was being ignored because the money was not available. Conducting a personal investigation, he found that a transfer of $2 million from New York to New Orleans had been

---

*To get a Democratic general, he wanted to appoint Senator Thomas Hart Benton. Despite the canons of senatorial courtesy, Benton's fellow legislators balked, and the proposal died.

entrusted to a bonding firm, which had delivered most of it but withheld $400,000 for private investments. Polk decided to keep an even tighter rein on administrative details, driving himself to exhaustion but demonstrating that under the conditions prevailing in the 1840s, "a president could run a war."[8]

Finding the right generals and admirals for particular assignments is a task that persists throughout most wars. Lincoln's trials on this score are well known. Madison's difficulty in replacing the aged relics of the Revolution who still held command in 1812 caused him great embarrassment in the Canadian campaigns early in his war. He had better success with the navy, which was a newer service, but not until he appointed Jacob Brown in the Niagara sector and sent Jackson to New Orleans could it be said that he had secured vigorous leadership for the land forces.

The president's responsibility here is particularly difficult to execute. The military is almost invariably a conservative institution, even in the most liberal states[9] and even (or perhaps especially) when technology is forcing radical alterations in the modes of combat. Thus, the military is unlikely to recognize the need for changes in command and nearly incapable of making them. So it falls to the amateur in the White House, with the help of all available (and usually conflicting) advice, to make the necessary changes.

Depending on the severity of the war, the president must also enforce appropriate domestic discipline. During the War of 1812, waged against an enemy that bore us little ill will and that was in any case preoccupied with the war against Napoleon, Madison tolerated domestic political activity that was plainly treasonous. He tolerated it because he could not rally public opinion against it without inviting civil war. What was required of the president in this case was patience and self-effacement, two qualities Madison had in abundance.

Lincoln's challenge was quite the opposite. The Civil War was the ultimate constitutional crisis. Lincoln's actions during his first four months in office provide a classic illustration of crisis government under the United States Constitution. As soon as the rebels fired on Fort Sumter (April 12, 1861), Lincoln discerned the gravity of the crisis and resolved to meet it. His boldest decision was his first, announced in the proclamation of April 15, two days after the fall of Sumter: to postpone the convening of Congress until the Fourth of July, giving him three months to act without having to justify himself to a divided legislature. He may have thought that he could quell the rebellion during that time. At any rate, he determined that the oath he had taken to defend the Constitution could not be fulfilled unless he took into his own hands all the powers of government which political tradition and the framers of the Constitution had so carefully distributed.

In the same proclamation Lincoln declared the existence of an "insurrection" and called the state militias into federal service. A week later he declared a blockade on the seceded states, a measure hitherto regarded, in both American constitutional law and the law of nations, as contingent upon the existence of war, which Congress alone could declare. The next day he advanced $2 million of unappropriated funds to three private citizens and directed them to use it to meet requisitions "necessary for the defense and support of the government." A week later he authorized the commanding general of the army to suspend the writ of habeas corpus along the rail line between Philadelphia and Washington—despite almost unanimous opinion at the time that the power to suspend the writ of habeas corpus belonged to Congress alone. And on May 3 the president passed beyond even the most latitudinarian construction of his powers under the Constitution: He called for 42,034 volunteers to serve for three years and enlarged the regular army by 23,000 men and the navy by 18,000.

In a special message to Congress on July 4, 1861, Lincoln asserted the legality of calling out the state militias, establishing the blockade, and suspending the writ of habeas corpus. Regarding the appropriation of funds and the raising of military forces, however, he offered a different justification. "These measures, whether strictly legal or not, were ventured upon under what appeared to be a popular demand and a public necessity, trusting then, as now, that Congress would readily ratify them." In other words, in circumstances of "public necessity," when the president is supported by public opinion, the "war powers" of the Constitution pass completely into his hands.

Lincoln's action came before the Supreme Court in the Prize Cases of 1863. The question was whether ships which had violated the blockade, proclaimed by the president before Congress convened, had been lawfully condemned. It was acknowledged by everyone that the condemnation was lawful only if the blockade itself was legal and that the legality of the blockade depended upon the existence of war. What separated the justices was whether the president could lead the nation in war without a congressional declaration.

The four dissenters insisted that in the legal sense of the term (which mattered here, since the issue before the Court concerned the lawful disposition of property), war did not exist until Congress, on July 13, 1861, authorized the President to interdict all trade between inhabitants of the states in insurrection and the rest of the United States. Although this act was not an explicit declaration of war, it was an act of war, since it made a categorical distinction between insurrectionists and loyal citizens. Before the passage of this act, argued the dissenters, the president under the Militia Acts of 1795 and 1807 might lawfully resist attack or put down insurrection, but he could not declare war, and he could not undertake actions which were tantamount to or dependent upon war.

The opinion of the Court, endorsed by a bare majority of five, rejected this approach as legalistic. It was vain, they held, to insist that the nation was not at war. The insurrection amounted to civil war by virtue of its "accidents"—the number, power, and organization of the rebels. When it broke out, "the President was bound to meet it in the shape in which it presented itself, without waiting for Congress to baptize it with a name. . . ." It was the president's responsibility as commander in chief to determine whether the "accidents" of the uprising compelled him to resort to acts of war in response. The Court could not second-guess his judgment.

As a war's drain on domestic resources increases, the president's dominance over society and economy increases apace. Of the four declared wars before 1940, three (1812, Mexican, and Spanish-American) were "limited wars," causing relatively little disturbance of social and economic routines. The Civil War (never "declared," of course, but certainly a major war) demanded all available energies, indeed, stimulated the discovery and development of productive capacities hitherto unsuspected. Lincoln and Wilson, president during World War I, were accordingly "condemned to be dictators," to give firm direction to Congress and to the nation mobilizing for the war. Wilson's powers were set forth in the Lever Food and Fuel

Control Act, which authorized the president "to requisition foods, feeds, and fuels; to take over and operate factories, packinghouses, pipelines, mines or other plants; to fix a minimum price for wheat; to limit, regulate or prohibit the use of food materials in the production of alcoholic beverages; and to fix the price of coal and coke and to regulate the production, sale and distribution thereof."[10] In an age when the Supreme Court was accused by its "great dissenter," Oliver Wendell Holmes, Jr. of trying to enact "Mr. Herbert Spencer's Social Statics," and when the court declared a child labor law unconstitutional on the ground that it regulated local labor conditions rather than interstate commerce, the Lever Act was a spectacular grant of power to the president.

The complexities of coordinating American military efforts with those of allies were hinted at before 1938 but hardly experienced. During the relief of the seige of the legations in China in 1900, for example, the United States was a junior partner in the operation, but the strategy of the Western powers was simple and required only a minimum of interallied coordination. The United States' role in the First World War, on the other hand, was full of delicacy. Entering late, the Americans teamed up with forces led by proud old men. The situation was further complicated by Wilson's driving idealism, toward which Europeans reacted with profound ambivalence. From the start Wilson determined to remain aloof from political maneuvering during the war, to save his authority and options for postwar diplomacy. He insisted that the United States be called an "associated power" rather than an "ally." Yet he deferred wherever possible to European military judgment, even to the point of risking the wrath of his own prickly commander, General John Pershing.

Despite these efforts, Wilson's dreams were frustrated. He may have been a virtual dictator while the nation was at war, but after the war Congress quickly regained its leverage, forcing the pace of demobilizing by drastic cuts in military appropriations, thereby depriving the president's diplomacy of any realistic sanction.

The pattern during the first century and a half under the Constitution (1788–1938) was that when war was over, power drained quickly out of the president's hands. Sometimes, as in 1865 and 1918, subdued areas had to be occupied. Or, as in 1848 and 1898, conquered territories had to be absorbed. Inevitably presidents have had administrative oversight of these operations. Nevertheless, during the postwar period the initiative on policy has moved back toward Congress. The public, weary of the expense of war, has been eager to return to peacetime pursuits, a mood reflected in the rapid withdrawal of appropriations for the military.

Invariably presidents have deplored the haste of demobilization. Even Madison, who knew all the arguments against "standing armies," proposed a "peacetime military establishment" of 20,000 men, but Congress cut his request in half and ordered that the navy's gunboat flotilla be put up for sale. Thus did the erstwhile "war hawks" deal with the counsel of their commander in chief after the war was over.

Hitherto we have been using examples drawn from the first century and a half of constitutional history to illustrate the responsibilities of the president as commander in chief. The point of this focus has been to show that presidential Caesarism is not a recent departure, that it has been not only inherent in the presidential office from the beginning but actually exhibited, and necessarily so, whenever the nation perceived itself to be severely threatened. We turn now to more recent events, specifically the altered context in which presidents—especially those who have served since the close of World War II—have performed as commander in chief.

After the end of the Second World War John McCloy, assistant secretary of war (1941–1945), wrote an article[11] focusing on the half dozen or so strategic decisions which shaped America's role in the war. Prominent in his short list was the selection of a commander for the cross-Channel invasion at Normandy in June 1944. The question of the timing of the invasion had divided Allied leaders for many months. The Russians, in the absence of a second front on the European continent, had been absorbing terrible punishment from the Germans since the summer of 1941. Throughout 1942 and 1943 they had insisted, with increasing bitterness, that the United States and Great Britain relieve the pressure by beginning an invasion from the west straightway. The Americans were sensitive to this pressure and were impatient themselves to smash into the German heartland. But for Churchill, writes McCloy, the invasion through France "held the menace of untold casualties. He seems to have had before him always the dread prospect of a repetition of 1916 and 1917 when such a vital element of the young manhood of England was lost in the prolonged slaughter on the Somme and at Passchendaele." To avoid a repetition of this catastrophe, Churchill urged that Germany's hold on the French beaches be weakened by assaults on the "soft underbelly" of the continent (Italy and the Balkans).

The deadlock was broken at Teheran. Stalin, furious because of broken promises and determined to push the Western Allies off dead center, demanded that a commander for the cross-Channel invasion be named. Churchill had tentatively promised the assignment to Field Marshal Alan Brooke, but "the force of circumstances was too great to allow this," says McCloy. The United States would furnish most of the men and supplies for the assault. In addition, "its military leaders, backed by the full vigor of a youthful nation, were less impressed by the difficulties of a European conquest" than those whose memories had steeped in the bloodbaths of World War I. And so an American, Dwight D. Eisenhower, was chosen to lead the Western Allies against the Nazis.

The Allies' choice of Eisenhower was significant, not only for the war but for American constitutional development as well. It signaled the assumption, by the United States, of responsibility for the security of the Western world. The implications of this new responsibility were not immediately grasped. The nation did sense, in the words of President Truman's first postwar speech on "reconversion," that we had "an immediate obligation to bear a share, commensurate with our national standing, in safeguarding the future security of all peace-loving nations." But what this share was, and to what extent it would require modifications in constitutional structure and political traditions, no one knew. For five years after the war the nation was to struggle in great confusion to answer these questions. But by 1950 patterns were set that involved a substantial revision in fundamental values and were profoundly to influence the nation's political life as long as it accepted the role of "leader of the free world."

Two factors changed the constitutional position of the commander in chief in the years following World War II: the creation of a massive, permanent military establishment and the negotiation and ratification of a network of treaties making explicit the responsibility of the United States for security around the world. Both these factors were rooted in a consensus: that the freedom of nations was threatened by communism, that the might of the Soviet Union (and, later, the population of China) made communism menacing, and that the United States was primarily responsible for "containing" the Soviet Union and thus defending the independence of non-Communist nations. This consensus was affirmed almost universally in the American political culture, by powerful majorities in the public, the press, Congress, and the executive branch[12] In this sense, the expansion of presidential power since World War II was not the result of a deliberate decision to strengthen the presidency but an inescapable consequence of the decision to make the United States the garrison of liberty.

The decision to create a permanent military establishment was a painful one, at odds with a profound tradition. As Hamilton once remarked, the abhorrence of standing armies was virtually a hereditary trait of the American people. It was not the danger of imperialism so much as the domestic repercussions of such an establishment that impressed the Americans: the tendency for troops to eat out the substance of the civilian population, the aggrandizement of the central government and the patronage available to the executive, and the distraction from more productive pursuits. This attitude, plus the sense of security arising from geographical circumstances, gave the American democracy the qualities which De Tocqueville noticed: the reluctance to go to war; the desire, once in, to win quickly and decisively; and the determination, when peace came, to demobilize abruptly. Consistent with this tradition, Congress especially, which held the purse strings, stood vigilant against the policy of preparedness during peacetime and against a continuation of mobilization in the aftermath of war. America's experience during and after World War I strongly reinforced this animus. Many Americans during the 1930s thought that Wilson had made a mistake in entangling the United States in Europe's conflicts.

Thus, when Roosevelt saw the nation threatened by the Nazis and by Japanese ambitions, he faced monumental opposition to a candid policy of rearmament. As war in Europe began to break out, he tried to prepare the country for the contingencies. While Congress spun a web of neutrality acts and enthused about the Ludlow

Resolution (which would have required that a declaration of war be affirmed by a national referendum before it could take effect), Roosevelt pushed in 1938 for his billion-dollar naval building program, called for the production of 50,000 planes a year (just after Munich, also in 1938), and replaced the isolationist Harry H. Woodring with Henry Stimson as secretary of war in July 1940. Stimson immediately moved for a military draft, the first peacetime program of compulsory military service in United States history, which was approved in September 1940. It provided for the registration of all men between twenty-one and thirty-five and for the training of 1.2 million troops and 800,000 reserves in the first year. A year later the act was renewed for eighteen months. The vote in the House of Representatives was 203–202—less than four months before Pearl Harbor.

Simultaneously Roosevelt moved to bolster the Allies. Although Congress sought to guard against direct involvement, the nation's sympathies were clearly with the Allies. Roosevelt's quarantine speech of October 1937 met stiff resistance from isolationists, but it was nevertheless "the true guide to United States policy" in the prewar period.[13] By the destroyer deal in September 1940, the president "exchanged" fifty overage United States destroyers with Britain for the right to lease bases in (that is, to defend) Newfoundland, Bermuda, British Guiana, and several Caribbean islands. By the lend-lease agreement in March 1941, he provided arms and supplies to countries whose defense he deemed vital to the United States. The initial appropriation was for $7 billion, most of which went to Great Britain but $1 billion to the Soviet Union. By bolstering friendly nations and by presenting an impressive display of America's capacity for military production, Roosevelt hoped to intimidate the enemy and to bring about its defeat without direct involvement of United States forces.

General George Marshall, army chief of staff, noted that Roosevelt's policy at this stage was "contrary to the considered judgment" of his military advisers. Marshall believed that the president had "surrendered to a momentary whim" when he ordered the production of "planes—now—and lots of them." In Marshall's opinion, this allocation of resources unbalanced the nation's military posture and prevented the proper development of ground forces.[14] Roosevelt's first priority was to avoid war, not to prepare for it. From the military viewpoint this was madness. Thus, when disaster fell on an unprepared nation at the end of 1941, military men were appalled but not surprised. It took two years of intensive effort following Pearl Harbor to get the United States ready for war. Fortunately, during those two years the Russians and the British were able to absorb Hitler's pounding, and Japan concentrated on Southeast Asia and China, rather than Hawaii and San Diego. No wonder military leaders later argued that with the United States assuming the first line of defense, events were not likely to permit such a leisurely response to danger.*

Once mobilized, the United States showed a stupendous capacity for war. At the height of mobilization in 1944 and 1945, there were 12 million men in arms, more than 50 percent of the males between eighteen and forty. In 1945 the military machine consumed $82.9 billion, more than 89 percent of the federal budget and almost 40 percent of the gross national product.

As the war moved to its climax, thoughts turned to planning for the future. Roosevelt was determined that the United States not be committed to a role in postwar European politics. American public opinion, he believed, would not support it, any more than it had in 1920. Preparing the American position for the conferences at Cairo and Teheran with Churchill and Stalin, he warned the Joint Chiefs that the United States "should not get roped into accepting any European sphere of influence." At Teheran he told Stalin that any future American intervention in Europe would be limited to planes and ships, not ground forces.[16]

Truman knew the patterns of American history as well as Roosevelt, and as a sensitive politician he knew that he would feel the hot breath of popular demand for demobilization. But he also read the lessons of Wilson's tragedy differently from Roosevelt. Rather than trim his diplomacy to fit the nation's traditions, Truman was determined to alter those traditions. He began to speak about "our

---

*In his message to Congress on October 23, 1945, recommending universal military training, Truman argued that "the latent strength of our untrained citizenry was no longer sufficient protection and that if attack should come again, as it did at Pearl Harbor, we could never again count on the luxury of time with which to arm ourselves and strike back. Our geographical security was forever gone—gone with the advent of the atomic bomb, the rocket, and modern airborne armies."[15]

new obligations in the world" and to warn that an accelerated demobilization ("disintegration" he called it) of our armed forces "threatened to jeopardize our strategic position in the midst of the post-war tensions that were building up around the world."[17]

Despite these presidential misgivings, the political pressure, focused in Congress, was overwhelming. Truman's pet project was a universal military training (UMT) program. It would have provided one year of military training for all eighteen-year-olds, with no exemption except for total physical disqualification, after which the citizen-soldiers would become members of a general reserve. The reserves would have no obligation to serve at home or abroad unless called to service by an act of Congress. In his memoirs, Truman's reasons for promoting this measure are candidly stated: "I am morally certain that if Congress had gone into the [UMT] program thoroughly in 1945, when I first recommended it, we would have had a pool of basically trained men which would have made the Soviets hesitate in their program of expansion in certain strategic parts of the world."[18] But universal military training was never adopted. Congress and the public were clamoring for lower taxes and the return of the "boys." The public mood forced the pace of demobilization.

The United States had accepted responsibility for a zone in Germany and had insisted on having complete charge over the occupation of Japan. These demands absorbed the available military forces. But trouble, meanwhile, brewed over Trieste, the Berlin corridor, Greece and Turkey, the Mideast, and China. The Pentagon kept pointing out that Truman's firm words in these disputes were based on bluff (unless, of course, the president actually meant to use the atomic bomb).* Truman knew they were right, that there was great risk in the American position. But he also knew the political realities. The people deplored Soviet pressure, but they were unwilling to sustain a posture of preparedness for war. Thus, public opinion,

---

*The question was discussed at a meeting in September 1948 between Marshall, Robert Lovett, Charles Bohlen, James Forrestal, and several leading journalists. Forrestal noted "unanimous agreement that in the event of war the American people would not only have no question as to the propriety of the use of the atomic bomb, but would in fact expect it to be used." Forrestal also reported John Foster Dulles's remark to Marshall, that "the American people would execute you if you did not use the bomb in the event of war."[19]

reflected in executive budgets and legislative appropriations, limited the military force available to the commander in chief. Instead of Mars, fully clad for war, Truman became an overmatched light heavyweight, whose corner men alternately told him not to take any guff from the bully and warned him that he would get whipped if the bully ever started to punch.

In June 1950 the bear finally swung. Once more the United States was caught unprepared, and the president was forced to go to Congress with a crash program of rearmament.

The Korean War was a watershed. During World War II responsibility for the security of non-Communist nations had passed to the United States. Dimly the nation sensed its new situation, but until the North Korean armies swarmed across the thirty-eighth parallel, the implications of its role were avoided, in deference to tradition and habit.

Why hadn't the atomic bomb deterred the Communists? American policy had relied on this weapon to deter aggressors. Should it now be used? Truman told a press conference on November 30, 1950, that "active consideration" was being given to the use of the weapon in Korea.* But it was apparent within the government that the bomb could not be used to retaliate for aggression by the North Koreans, not even against the Chinese when they entered the war. The risk of suicidal global warfare was too great. Our allies would abandon us. The American people themselves would recoil.

Instead, Truman asked Congress to reverse the five-year downward trend in military appropriations, and he was candid about his intentions. Not only would we meet the aggression in Korea, but we would also station troops in Europe in fulfillment of the North Atlantic Treaty and prepare military forces to meet the threat of Communist aggression wherever it might occur.

The full cost of America's new role began to be understood dur-

---

*The British government reacted to this pronouncement with shock. The use of the bomb, it pointed out, would affect all the peoples of the world. Before the United States, in the name of the United Nations, invoked this fate, the British argued, it ought to consult its allies. Truman immediately agreed to a summit meeting with Prime Minister Clement Attlee and, in the ensuing discussions, assured him privately that the Americans had no intention of using the bomb in Korea.[20]

ing the so-called great debate in the winter and spring of 1951. Former ambassador Joseph Kennedy and Herbert Hoover helped spark the exchange, criticizing the commitment of American forces to Korea and urging that the United States concentrate its military expenditures on air and naval defenses for the Western Hemisphere. The biggest guns in the bipartisan security establishment (Thomas Dewey, Dean Acheson, John Foster Dulles) sprang to reply, characterizing the opposition as unrealistic and criticizing it for offering the same counsel that had given opportunity and encouragement to Hitler, Mussolini, and the Japanese militarists.

The debate came to focus on a resolution offered by Senate Republicans, to the effect that American troops ought not to be sent to Europe until Congress explicitly endorsed such deployment.* Senator Robert Taft of Ohio, the chief spokesman for the congressional Republicans, insisted that the president had no power to send troops abroad since war would automatically result from an attack on those troops by the Soviet Union. Such deployment, argued Taft, rendered the congressional power to declare war nugatory.

Taft was right, but Truman's action was not unprecedented. It was perfectly comparable to Polk's. Like Polk, Truman (through the North Atlantic Treaty) had established a basis for regarding alien territory as equivalent to our own, and as commander in chief he decided to deploy troops to defend that territory. During the debate over the ratification of the treaty, the opposition had made several efforts to attach reservations which would have forbidden a response to Soviet aggression without congressional approval. In the end it was a political argument, rather than a constitutional or legal objection, to say that the president had no right to expose American forces to such dangers. Taft simply lacked the political muscle in 1951 to make his position stick.

As the "great debate" fizzled out, Truman's requests for military appropriations of $61 billion (compared with $13.3 billion for defense, in a total federal budget of $42.4 billion, the previous year) came to a vote. The House by a margin of 342–2 approved $56.1 billion; the

---

*The administration held that, under the North Atlantic Treaty (1949), the United States was pledged to regard an attack on Western Europe as an attack on U.S. territory and that the commander in chief should deploy troops accordingly.

Senate by 79–0 voted $59.5 billion; and the conferees compromised on $56.9 billion.

This was the turning point. (See Table I.) After the Korean War there would be no general demobilization. Force levels would never again fall below 2 million men on active duty. Congress would never again fail to meet or approximate the president's estimate of what was needed, in terms of weapons or other matériel, to provide for the "national defense." Henceforth the commander in chief would have a powerful standing army at his disposal.

TABLE I
POSTWAR LEVELS OF DEMOBILIZATION

PEAK WARTIME MOBILIZATION		PREWAR LEVEL		POSTWAR LOW		
Year	Men in Active Service	Year	Men in Active Service	Year	Men in Active Service	Postwar Low as Percent of Mobilization
1814	46,858	1811	11,528	1822	9,863	21%
1848	60,308	1845	20,726	1851	20,699	34%
1865	1,062,848	1860	27,958	1877	34,094	3%
1898	235,785	1897	43,656	1899	100,166	42%
1918	2,897,167	1916	179,376	1923	247,011	8%
1945	12,123,455	1939	334,473	1948	1,445,910	11%
1952	3,635,912	1950	1,460,261	1957	2,795,798	76%

SOURCE: U.S. Bureau of Census, *Historical Statistics of the U.S., Colonial Times to 1957*, pp. 736–37.

As commander in chief the president is primarily responsible for defending the territory of the United States from attack. Decisions made during the cold war were to show how elastic this concept could be.

Americans had been slow to take alarm from Hitler's aggression in Europe and Japan's in Asia, but in 1948 the connection between the Communist coup in Czechoslovakia and the security of North America seemed obvious to almost everyone. The general public was uncertain how to respond, but Democratic Undersecretary of State Robert Lovett and Republican Senator Arthur Vandenberg of Michigan developed a plan. In the Senate Vandenberg offered a resolution calling for the United States to join in regional collective security arrangements to resist Communist aggression. It passed the Senate on June 11, 1948, by 64–4. Meanwhile, Dean Acheson, who had become secretary of state in January 1950, took the lead in negotiating the North Atlantic Treaty, the twelve signatory nations of which agreed to regard an attack on any one of them as an attack on them all. Article II of the treaty stipulated that its provisions were to be "carried out by the parties in accordance with their respective constitutional processes." In the ratification debates in the Senate this language was subjected to close scrutiny, particularly by conservative Republicans. In an effort to quiet concern, the report of the Foreign Relations Committee asked rhetorically whether the United States would be obligated to react to an attack on Paris or Copenhagen in the same way it would react to an attack on New York City and whether, in such an event, the treaty gave the president the power to take any action, without specific congressional authorization, which he could not take in the absence of the treaty. The answer to both questions, it said, was "No."[21] In light of this

TABLE II

MAJOR COLD WAR TREATIES AND RESOLUTIONS

	Senate Vote	House Vote †
Multilateral Defense Treaties		
Rio Pact (1947)	72–1	
NATO (1949)	82–13	
ANZUS (1952)	Voice vote*	
SEATO (1955)	82–1	
Bilateral Defense Treaties		
Philippines (1952)	Voice vote*	
South Korea (1954)	81–6	
China (Taiwan, 1955)	65–6	
Japan (1960)	90–2	
Congressional Resolutions		
Formosa (January 29, 1955)	85–3	410–3
Middle East (March 9, 1957)	72–19	355–61
Cuban (October 3, 1962)	86–1	384–7
Berlin (October 10, 1962)	Voice vote	312–0
Tonkin (August 10, 1964)	88–2	414–0

*Earlier that day the Senate ratified a mutual defense treaty with Japan, 58–9, after rejecting (22–45) a "reservation" that would have required congressional approval of any administrative agreement regarding the disposition of United States forces.

† The House does not vote on treaties.

understanding, the North Atlantic Treaty was ratified by the Senate, 82–13, in July 1949.

It soon became obvious that the Senate had been misled by its Committee on Foreign Relations. The president was not *obligated* to respond to an attack on Paris; but as commander in chief he was certainly free to, and the North Atlantic Treaty strongly reinforced the likelihood that he would. Vandenberg's support of Thomas Dewey's position during the 1948 campaign offered better guidance to the meaning of the treaty. Vandenberg commended Dewey for his "nice distinction between the 'commitment' of troops and the 'deployment' of troops when once committed." The deployment, he added, was "necessarily a prerogative of the commander in chief." By ratifying the North Atlantic Treaty, the Senate was making a commitment to defend Europe and Canada. In this sense the treaty gave the president power to take action, without specific congressional authorization, which he would not have dared take if conservative legislators had had enough political weight to pass their qualifying provisos to the ratification. As it was, Truman was soon committing American troops to NATO without congressional authorization. Several senators raised a protest, much of it appealing to constitutional considerations, but they were not able to stop the deployment of forces which they had put at the disposal of the commander in chief.

In addition to the North Atlantic Treaty, the United States during the 1950s entered into a number of other treaties and agreements with European and Asian nations. The Southeast Asia Collective Defense Treaty (which created the Southeast Asia Treaty Organization, or SEATO), hailed by Dulles as an "Asiatic Monroe Doctrine," came into force in 1955. It bound the United States to Australia, France, New Zealand, Pakistan, the Philippines, Thailand, and Great Britain. In a separate protocol, the treaty's protection was extended also to South Vietnam, Cambodia, and Laos, which had been barred by the Geneva Agreements from joining any military alliance.* Unlike the North Atlantic Treaty, which identified foreign territory as

---

*Cambodia and Laos have officially rejected the protection of SEATO, and France and Pakistan have become "inactive" members.

equivalent to our own for purposes of national defense (the so-called automatic trigger), SEATO affirmed that aggression on any member state constituted a danger to them all and promised that in the event of aggression each state would "act to meet the common danger in accordance with its constitutional processes."*

The ANZUS Pact (1952), linking Australia, New Zealand, and the United States, stated that "an armed attack in the Pacific area on any of the parties would be dangerous to its own peace and safety"; each promised to "act to meet the common danger in accordance with its constitutional processes." Similar language was included in bilateral treaties between the United States and the Philippines (1952), South Korea (1954), Taiwan (1955), and Japan (1960).

One other treaty should be mentioned in this connection, although its provisions understate the American stake. The Rio Pact of 1947 bound the United States to eighteen Latin American nations, but its terms were guarded. The principal effect of the treaty was to make the Monroe Doctrine reciprocal. The Monroe Doctrine (1823) declared that the United States would consider it dangerous to American peace and security if a European power attempted to extend its system to any point in the Western Hemisphere. The Rio Pact asserted that "an attack by any state against an American state shall be considered as an attack against all the American states" and promised that collective measures would be taken to meet the attack, such measures to be determined by an "organ of consultation."

Such vague and cautious language gives only a hint of the attitude that recent American presidents have taken toward subversion and disorder in Latin America. Kennedy's dramatic reaction to the Cuban missile crisis in 1962, Johnson's occupation of the Dominican Republic in 1965, and Reagan's aid to the government in El Salvador and the rebels in Nicaragua and his invasion of Grenada are better illustrations of the continuing vitality of American concern.

In addition to the treaties, commitments have taken other forms. In times of crisis presidents have gone to Congress and obtained resolutions proclaiming a determination to resist aggression in a

---

*The United States has stipulated that its obligation under SEATO is limited to cases in which aggression in Southeast Asia comes from Communist sources.

threatened area. Thus, in 1955 the Eisenhower administration responded to military activity in the Formosa Strait by asking Congress to adopt a resolution that the United States would resist any armed attack on Formosa and the Pescadores Islands with its own forces. In requesting this resolution, Eisenhower pointed out that as commander in chief he had inherent authority to take "emergency action . . . to protect the rights and security of the United States," but he added that a joint resolution would inform the Communists unmistakably that the United States stood united in opposition to any attempt to "liberate" Formosa.

In the wake of the Suez crisis in 1956 the Eisenhower administration feared that the Soviets would move into the vacuum created by the withdrawal of Britain and France. Appearing before a joint session of Congress in January 1957, the president asked for a resolution proclaiming legislative support for the Eisenhower Doctrine, which he explained as follows:

> In the situation now existing, the greatest risk, as is often the case, is that ambitious despots may miscalculate. If power-hungry Communists should either falsely or correctly estimate that the Middle East is inadequately defended, they might be tempted to use open measures of armed attack. If so, that would start a chain of circumstances which would almost surely involve the United States in military action. I am convinced that the best insurance against this dangerous contingency is to make clear now our readiness to cooperate fully and freely with our friends of the Middle East in ways consonant with the purposes and principles of the United Nations.

To this end, the president asked, among other things, that he be authorized to use the armed forces of the United States "as he deems necessary" to protect the Middle East (defined as the area between Libya and Pakistan, Turkey and the Sudan) against "overt armed aggression from any nation controlled by international communism."

The president's request provoked some hostile responses. Dulles insisted that unless the United States declared its intentions promptly, "this area is very likely to be lost." When Majority Leader Lyndon

Johnson complained that the administration's case rested on generalities, Dulles replied, "If Congress is not willing to trust the President to the extent he asks, we can't win this battle." Adlai Stevenson and a few senators (Wayne Morse of Oregon, William Lander of North Dakota and several southerners) complained that the president was asking for a "blank check." But most of the criticism came from the opposite direction. Democrats, anxious to vindicate Truman's response to aggression in Korea, pointed out that the Formosa and Middle East resolutions were merely declaratory. To strengthen the Middle East resolution, Senator J. William Fulbright of Arkansas led a successful effort to include language declaring that whenever the president "determined the necessity," the United States would use armed forces against aggression from any country controlled by international communism.[22]

The Eisenhower Doctrine provided the basis for landing United States marines in Lebanon in 1958. It was reaffirmed by President Johnson, in 1967, in a speech that "firmly committed" the United States to support the political independence and territorial integrity of all nations in the Middle East. The United States did not, however, intervene in the Six-Day War, which broke out less than two weeks later and which resulted in Israeli occupation of large parts of Egypt and Jordan. To borrow a phrase from Charles Evans Hughes, America's commitments mean what the commander in chief says they mean.

Pursuant to these treaties and resolutions, presidents stationed American troops in bases around the world, then declared that the United States would bring its power to bear if the countries in which those forces were stationed were assulted. According to a congressional report in 1970, there were 2,200 U.S. bases in thirty-four foreign countries around the world. Major bases were located in the Azores (Portugal), Canada, Guantánamo (Cuba), West Germany, Greece, Greenland, Iceland, Italy, Japan, Libya, Okinawa, the Philippines, South Korea, Spain, Taiwan, Thailand, Turkey, South Vietnam, the United Kingdom, and the West Indies.[23] As of 1968, the United States had about 1 million men in uniform in the Pacific area, including 500,000 in Vietnam, 50,000 in South Korea, and 40,000 on Okinawa. In addition, there were 315,000 Americans stationed with NATO in Europe, mostly in West Germany, Great Britain, and Spain. Another 290,000 men were with the Atlantic fleet, many of them in the Mediterranean.*

As presidents and their spokesmen have repeatedly pointed out, these troops guarantee the nation's commitments. Thus, Eisenhower assured President Carlos García of the Philippines in June 1960 that since any attack on his country would involve danger to the American troops stationed there, it would be "instantly repelled" by U.S. forces. Similarly, Vice President Hubert Humphrey stated in Korea that "As long as there is one American soldier on the line of the border, . . . the entire power of the United States of America is committed to the security and defense of Korea." Korea, he added, was "as strong as the United States and Korea put together."[26]

It is almost impossible to set any territorial bounds on the responsibilities assumed by recent commanders in chief. In this sense, it is misleading to analyze the cold war treaties too closely. As Undersecretary of State Nicholas Katzenbach told the Senate Foreign Relations Committee in 1967, "nobody has a hunting license" in territories not covered by formal treaties. As a matter of fact, in the leading instances of the uses of American armed forces since World War II (Korea, Lebanon, Cuba, Dominican Republic, Vietnam, Grenada, Libya), American action was traceable more to the underlying spirit of our foreign policy than to the letter of treaties or congressional resolution.

Before World War II presidents were restrained in the exercise of their powers as commander in chief by the lack of readily available armed forces and by a deep tradition against entanglements in controversies between foreign powers. Few presidents rankled under these restraints. After all, presidents arose out of the same political culture which chose members of Congress and formed public opinion. But if ever a president did glimpse a design that seemed to require massive armed force, he soon ran up against these external limits. If there were policies that could be pursued without a large military

---

*Apart from the absence of troops in Vietnam, these figures have not changed much since 1968. In 1985 there were American military bases in forty foreign countries[24] and about 500,000 troops stationed abroad.[25]

establishment, as in Latin America or in the Orient, presidents were free, and often impelled by popular expectations, to pursue them. For policies which might require the sustained application of military force abroad, however, they simply lacked the troops.

Since 1950 these restraints are off. The commander in chief is served by the largest and most powerful permanent military establishment in human history. In addition, the president's aides serve at his pleasure. None of them has a truly independent constituency or base of power. Congress, once it provides the tools of security policy, has little practical leverage. So long as the president operates within the broad consensus regarding America's posture in the world and until his policies bring profound, widespread disturbance in the domestic scene, he has virtually unlimited power to direct the use of the nation's armed forces abroad.

As the framers recognized, the command of the military is an executive function. It must be centralized and capable of secrecy and dispatch. The larger the military function looms, the more dominant the executive becomes. It is not a matter of congressional abdication or executive usurpation.

During the cold war period the commander in chief had virtually plenary power over the deployment and use of armed forces. When the nation decided that the Soviet Union was bent on the expansion of its empire and that it was the United States's responsibility to defend the "free world" against this design, power shifted irresistibly to the executive. This undertaking was not lightly entered into. There were powerful voices counseling against it. On the left Henry Wallace urged "peaceful competition [between] the Russian world and the American world." On the right Robert Taft admitted that "deterrence" made no sense to him and warned that we would lose our souls if we tried to dominate the whole world. But others were convinced that Soviet policy was expansionist, that it threatened our national interests, and that it must be opposed by firm diplomacy, backed by armed might. Men like Dean Acheson, John Foster Dulles, and George Kennan had firm spirits, clear minds, and strong voices, and they worked at their task with a devotion that was fanatical. In and out of government, at war colleges and on barnstorming lecture tours, in speeches, books, and press conferences, these men sought to educate the people to the view that the Soviet Union had embarked upon a new kind of war and that the United States should prepare its defenses.*

Between 1947 and 1950 cold warriors established their position. The United States was put on a permanent wartime footing. Henceforth, commanders in chief might behave aggressively, as when Truman drastically revised our aims in Korea or Eisenhower dispatched the marines to Lebanon or Kennedy "quarantined" Cuba or Johnson sent troops to the Dominican Republic or Reagan bombed Libya. Or they might behave with restraint, as when Truman refused permission to bomb north of the Yalu River in Korea or Eisenhower withheld support from the Hungarian "freedom fighters" or Johnson reacted calmly to the seizure of the *Pueblo* or Reagan limited himself to bellicose talk when the Soviets shot down a passenger airliner bound for Seoul. The point is that, in all these cases, the decision about the American response belonged to the commander in chief.

---

*Some of these men now have second thoughts about their performance during these years. George Kennan, for example, deplores the militarization of his containment policy. But his work was snatched from the obscurity of State Department files and vigorously promoted by the secretary of defense, who also got him a job as "deputy commandant" at the National War College. Nor did he modify his position much in response to a strong reprimand from Walter Lippmann.

PART IV

Crisis

CHAPTER 7

Winning Elections

Our last two presidents, Carter and Reagan, different in so many ways, shared one fundamental characteristic. They approached the office of the presidency deeply estranged from the government they proposed to lead. Even after four years in office they both were still distant from the government.

Toward the end of his term Carter declared that the nation was suffering from "malaise" and that the American people had lost confidence in their government. At the same time he asked for the resignation of his entire cabinet, then accepted those of his secretary of health, education, and welfare for disloyalty, his secretary of energy for political exhaustion, and his secretary of the treasury for disharmonious relations with other leaders of the administration and with Congress.[1] From the standpoint of governmental effectiveness, it was not a pretty picture.

Reagan's campaign for reelection in 1984 was waged against Walter Mondale, a man who personified the conventional approach to government. Being the incumbent in these circumstances seemed to pose no special awkwardness for Reagan. He still devoted some of his most memorable campaign moments to stories about "waste and fraud" in the federal government.

It tells much about our system that the American people reward such campaigns. We vote for people who criticize the government because we, too, are troubled by its performance. We do not think that it works very well. We want a change. That may not have been so surprising in 1976, after Watergate. But it was still true in 1980 and in 1984. We elected an incumbent in 1984, but he was still promising to rid us of failed policies and broken promises and told us he needed another term to complete his revolution against the bad habits into which we had fallen.

The American people want a change, and every four years the electoral system gives them an opportunity to register that sentiment. Is that not what an electoral system is for: to allow voters to register feelings about their government and choose someone to take charge for the next four years?

That is part of it, but not all. Elections are prospective as well as retrospective. They are, in fact, democracy's most vital ritual. By reelecting a popular incumbent or by throwing the rascals out and giving a fresh mandate to a new leader, we revive the nation's political life.

In recent years presidential elections have failed to produce a durable sense of political renewal. The active, public part of the campaign stretches on for nearly a year, and long before it is over, both the candidates and the public have been exhausted and disgusted by the spectacle. The primaries, once a useful means for informing and checking the judgments of party leaders about the popularity of candidates, have assumed a dominant role in the nominating process, though they are clearly unfit for it. Therefore, few voters participate in them, and the relative influence of states is so capricious that the results are an unreliable guide even to a candidate's popularity, much less his fitness for the nation's most demanding job. Yet because the primaries are dominant, the party conventions, once great festivals of democracy,* have been reduced

---

*One ought not, I suppose, to be too sentimental about the old-style conventions. After the Democratic Convention of 1924, which dragged on for 103 ballots before deciding on its nominee for president, H. L. Mencken wrote, "There is something about a political convention that is as fascinating as a revival or a hanging. It is vulgar, it is ugly, it is stupid, it is tedious . . . yet it is somehow charming. One sits through

to second-rate television entertainment. Most delegates, chosen for their loyalty to particular candidates rather than for their own political skills, are unknown to one another and unsuited to deliberate creatively on their party's nominee, and without this dramatic element the festivities become boring and are virtually devoid of political meaning.

As for the general election, it becomes a contest between two ad hoc organizations with only tenuous connections to political party organizations. Despite strenuous efforts by candidates and campaign organizations, including the preparation and publication of innumerable issue papers and party platforms, and despite earnest work by reporters and commentators—or perhaps *because* of these massive efforts—the public remains confused about the significance of the choice it must make, as far as future policies are concerned. Thus, the mandate is blurred. Candidates for president do not totally ignore their party affiliations. They may seek to quicken partisan loyalties and to use partisan organizations—but only to the extent that they do not interfere with prior commitments and strategic objectives. As a result, party leaders cannot claim any leverage over the candidates on behalf of ongoing organizational commitments, and party labels provide unreliable cues for voters. The absence of loyalty to an ongoing organization obscures the meaning of popular choice, and after the election ordinary citizens become spectators while the winning candidate develops his own interpretation of the "mandate."

What does the Constitution have to do with these failings in the electoral process? To answer that question, we need to consider the electoral system as part of a whole system of government. The first thing to notice is that the Constitution, by separating the executive and legislative branches, allows for a radical separation of the processes of election and governing. It does not require that the two be separated, but it does encourage it. The framers sought to free the president from dependence on Congress by forbidding any legislator

long sessions wishing heartily that all the delegates and alternates were dead and in hell—and then suddenly there comes a show so gaudy and hilarious, so melodramatic and obscene, so unimaginably exhilarating and preposterous that one lives a gorgeous year in an hour."

from serving as a presidential elector. Almost as soon as the government got under way, leading politicians, including many of the framers, frustrated the apparent intent by having party caucuses in Congress assume control over the nominating process. Until the 1820s these congressional caucuses controlled the route to the White House. For most of that period the Republican party of Jefferson, Madison, and Monroe governed the country.

In 1824 that system broke down when the Republicans in Congress were unable to prevent forces outside Congress from launching an effective campaign for the presidency. First state legislatures, then national conventions began to make nominations that produced successful presidential candidates. The process was still controlled by political elites (those who became delegates to the conventions), and some of the leading delegates were men who also served in Congress as senators and representatives. But the nominating bodies were no longer factions in Congress. Andrew Jackson, by his victory over the remnant of the coastal elite that framed the Constitution, deserves a lot of the credit for revitalizing the framers' doctrine of separation of powers.

Since Jackson's time several developments further democratized both the government at large and the presidency specifically. One was the introduction of the secret ballot toward the end of the nineteenth century. Before that voters obtained ballots from party headquarters. Naturally such ballots contained only the names of that party's nominees, which helps account for the virtual absence of ticket splitting during the late nineteenth century. Reformers deplored the use that party leaders made of their control over nominations and the electoral process. They began to demand that the government print ballots, listing all qualified candidates, and that voters cast their ballots secretly.

Another important development, further weakening the ties that bound the regime together, was the ratification of the Seventeenth Amendment to the Constitution, providing for the direct election of senators. Again, the argument for the reform was irresistible. Senators, fortified by their power to confirm presidential appointments and by the custom of senatorial courtesy, controlled a great deal of patronage. Owing election to state legislatures, they were under great temptation to trade official positions for votes—a temptation to which many yielded. Reformers were determined to break this corrupting connection. Naturally the Senate resisted any change. Just when the movement for reform seemed about to succeed in its demand for a constitutional convention (under Article V), the Senate began to cooperate, and by 1913 the Seventeenth Amendment was ratified.

The spirit behind these reforms of the ballot and of senatorial elections was that of direct democracy. It was impatient to sweep aside intermediaries, particularly those who functioned as party leaders.

The same spirit came to bear on the presidency, though initially with less devastating effect. The electoral process for the presidency had already been pretty fully democratized. Electors were no longer taken seriously as political agents, and not since 1825 has an election been resolved by the House of Representatives. The only remaining impediment to direct democracy was the national nominating convention. Reformers took aim at this bastion of party bossism by calling for primary elections, but for several decades they failed to get their way. Early in the twentieth century several states did institute primary elections for presidential candidates, but most did not. The result was a slight modification of the route to the White House, but no fundamental change.

What is most remarkable about these developments, in the context of the revolutionary changes that were engulfing the system's environment, was how little they affected the basic system of governance, particularly the relationship between the president and the rest of the system.

Critics often contend that the electoral system, by imposing a radical separation between winning elections and conducting the government, produces winners who cannot govern effectively. There is truth in this observation, but it is often misapprehended.

Sometimes analysts assume that the ability to conduct a successful campaign is largely irrelevant to the work of governing. It is not. Both require great stamina and intimate knowledge of the nation's geography, culture, and leadership. Both require the ability to lead complex organizations under the pressures of time and imperfect information. And both, preeminently, require highly developed skills of communication. Those who dismissed Reagan as merely an actor were foolish. His experience as an actor was excellent training, both for campaigning and for his efforts in office to rally support for his policies. In fact, under the conditions of modern electronic communications, Reagan's training as an actor was probably as useful to him as Madison's training in comparative politics was to him at the Federal Convention.

The real point about the cost of separating elections from governing is *constitutional*. Modern campaigns do test and prepare a candidate for the conduct of the modern presidency—not perfectly, but well enough. What they do not do is build governments. They never have, at least not since the demise of the congressional caucus in 1824. It is not the campaign process that is faulty. It is the constitutional structure of the presidency. Politicians, journalists, and voters have made a reasonably creative adjustment to the demands of the constitutional framework. We ought not blame them for the fact that it does not produce effective government.

The system's only national electoral process is sharply focused on the selection of an individual to serve as president. Members of Congress, the other leading actors in the national system, are deliberately excluded from the process. The isolation works the other way, too. The Constitution does not forbid presidents from participating in congressional elections, but it virtually guarantees that they will fail if they try and will pay a high price politically for their lack of understanding of how the system works. The best example is Roosevelt's attempt in 1938 to "purge" Democrats who opposed his program in Congress.[2]

Sometimes presidential candidates lend their coattails to fellow partisans running for Congress. Johnson's landslide over Barry Goldwater in 1964 helped produce swollen majorities for the Democrats in Congress, with the result that his legislative program moved impressively through Congress in 1965. Even before that extraordinary two-year term for House members was over, though, the system's centrifugal forces began to reassert themselves. Those who swept in with Johnson knew they would have to run for reelection in 1966. As each congressional district began to register its distinctive reaction to what was going on, members preparing for reelection felt a need to show independence of the White House.* The orgy of

* The Democratic "party unity" score for 1965 was 69 percent, about average for the quarter century since 1960; in 1966 it fell to 61 percent.[3]

enactment ended almost as suddenly as it had begun.

The Constitution's electoral system is well geared to produce the kind of president the framers had in mind. They wanted a president who was vigorous but aloof, a person of Roman virtue—like George Washington and John Adams.

The congressional caucus produced a different kind of president: relaxed, more intimate and personal, apt to wear slippers when entertaining congressional leaders at the White House—behavior that caused the old Roman John Marshall to worry that Jefferson was trying to "embody" the presidency in the House of Representatives.

With the restoration of the separation of powers by the Jacksonian Democrats, presidents once more distanced themselves, though in different ways, from Congress. Old Hickory lacked George Washington's formality, but he was stern in exercising presidential authority over Congress. So were the other successful presidents of the nineteenth and early twentieth centuries: Polk, Lincoln, Hayes, Cleveland, McKinley, Theodore Roosevelt, Wilson.

With Franklin Roosevelt, as we have seen in chapter 5, the federal government assumed both more powers and different kinds of power in American life. A democratized presidency led the way to this "great transformation," then assumed most of the responsibility, politically, for making it work.

As this revolution in governance became routinized after World War II, the electoral process for the presidency underwent a transformation. Its constitutional structure remained the same: regular four-year schedule; formal separation from congressional elections; the electoral college, voting by states. It was the cultural substance of the process that changed, putting new strains on a system that was already failing to deliver on the promise of effectiveness and accountability.

There were three aspects to this cultural transformation: a change in the political character of the people making presidential nominations, the initiation of public financing for presidential campaigns, and the systematic application of new technologies (television, jet transport, and computers) to all phases of the campaign. Interacting, these factors closed the old avenues to executive power and opened new ones, changed the leading actors in the selection process, and altered the roles that each of them played.

THE NEW NOMINATORS

The United States now has "a government of strangers,"[4] a phenomenon deeply rooted in the post-World War II electoral system. The estrangement is pervasive. Delegates to national nominating conventions are no longer linked even by a network of party leaders who are familiar to one another. Most delegates are strangers even to the candidate they support. They know only his television persona. The strangeness extends throughout the election, and beyond. During the campaign local party workers are shoved aside by the candidate's lieutenants, people sent in from distant precincts and states. When presidents first gather their newly appointed cabinets around a table at the White House, the room is full of strangers.

This is a relatively recent phenomenon. Its roots go back to 1952 and Eisenhower, who won the nomination by successfully challenging the regular delegations committed to "Mr. Republican," Senator Robert Taft of Ohio, and then proceeded to conduct his general election campaign through an organization called Citizens for Eisenhower, rather than the Republican National Committee.[5]

The changes did not gather momentum and become permanently institutionalized until the cultural revolution of the 1960s. The civil rights and antiwar movements produced demands that institutions open up to broader participation. Such demands fell heaviest on institutions that were perceived as abusing their authority. The Democratic party, personified by President Johnson, came under heavy attack by the advocates of "participatory democracy" at its 1968 national convention. The convention responded in part by promising that the party would appoint a commission to "reform" the process for choosing delegates to its national convention.

A disarming but astute senator from South Dakota, George McGovern, agreed to chair the commission that inherited this task. Called the Commission on Party Structure and Delegate Selection, it took its mandate from a resolution of the 1968 convention which directed that all Democratic voters be given an opportunity to participate in the selection of delegates to the 1972 convention.

The report of the McGovern Commission, issued in April 1970, had an apocalyptic tone. The Democratic party, it said, offered the only hope for orderly, peaceful change in America. If it failed to reform, people demanding change would have no alternative but to join splinter parties or engage in the "anti-politics of the street." Piecemeal concessions would not suffice. For the party to survive, it would be necessary "to open the door to all Democrats who seek a voice in their party's most important decision: the choice of its presidential nominee."[6] The commission issued guidelines calling on state parties to take "affirmative steps" to encourage the representation of minority groups, young people, and women "in reasonable relationship to the group's presence in the population of the state" (what came to be called quotas); to prohibit ex officio delegates (that is, those who became delegates by virtue of holding office as a governor or senator, or whatever); and to forbid the unit rule as an infringement on the conscience of individual delegates.

In retrospect, it is worth noting that the commission did not require or even urge the adoption of primaries as a means for achieving these ends, although in a brief, concluding section of its final report, summarizing progress to date in responding to its guidelines, the commission saluted several states that had already adopted primaries.[7]

In any case, primaries did proliferate in the ensuing years. According to Howard Reiter, whereas in 1968 fourteen states used them to select or bind delegates to national conventions, by 1976 twenty-seven states did so, and by 1980, thirty-four of them.[8] The consequence was to shift the center of gravity at the conventions. Whereas in 1968 only about one-third of the delegates were chosen or bound by primaries, by 1976 nearly three-quarters were.[9] To shift the onus for complying with the Democratic party's new rules, political leaders in several states had seen to it that voters themselves could choose the delegates in primaries. One motive initially may have been to evade the call for affirmative action. Mayor Richard J. Daley of Chicago, leader of the Illinois Democrats, apparently assumed that slates chosen in a primary would be beyond reproach, even if they fell short of the standard of proportionality. However, the 1972 convention rejected Daley's slate in favor of one that showed the mandated balances, and the United States Supreme Court upheld the party's right to do so.[10]

The main effect of the McGovern Commission guidelines was to change the traditional role and character of presidential primaries. From the beginning of the twentieth century, when primaries were first introduced as checks on the power of bosses to dictate the nomination, they had been few in number, and their influence on the nomination had been informal and special. They gave opportunity to Adlai Stevenson to demonstrate that he could win in the South, to Dwight Eisenhower to prove that his popularity as a war hero had electoral value, and to John Kennedy to show that Bible Belt Protestants would vote for him. Never before the McGovern reforms, however, did a candidate win a nomination solely, or even mainly, by winning a string of primaries. Estes Kefauver tried in 1952 and 1956; but there were not enough of them, and their outcomes were not binding. Kefauver's victories in several primaries failed to convince the party's leaders that he was fit for the presidency; at the 1952 convention they made their choice of Adlai Stevenson over New York's Governor Averell Harriman.

The campaign of 1972 was the first in which a candidate parlayed primary victories into a presidential nomination. The beneficiary—many thought not coincidentally—was George McGovern. The situation was ironic. A process that was intended to allow popular choice to triumph over the dictates of bosses resulted in the nomination of a man who had consistently trailed his rivals in surveys of public opinion. In a January sampling McGovern had the support of only 3 percent of voters who identified themselves as Democrats. Even after his victories in the primaries McGovern had the support of only about 30 percent of the Democrats nationwide.

The ensuing general election showed that the 1972 Democratic Convention had failed to unite the party. McGovern got one of the lowest percentage of votes ever won by a Democratic nominee. Despite the fact that Democrats outnumbered Republicans that year by a 43 to 28 percent margin,[11] McGovern got only 38 percent of the vote to Nixon's 61 percent. The distaste of the electorate for the choice between McGovern and Nixon was indicated by the fact that the turnout of eligible voters outside the South was the lowest since 1824, excepting the elections of 1920 and 1924, the first two in which women were eligible to vote.[12]

Yet for better or worse most of the large states were committed to binding primary elections by the mid-1970s. In fact, when Senator Edward M. Kennedy argued in 1980 that delegates, even those chosen in primaries, should be free at the convention to vote their personal preferences (an interpretation in accord with the McGovern Commission guidelines), the delegates, most of them pledged to support President Carter, said no. Delegates, they said, like federal electors, were not chosen to exercise judgment. They were chosen to carry out the will of the voters.* Thus were primaries controlling the nominating process.

One other aspect of these developments needs to be underlined: the abrupt dismissal of senators from the nominating process, particularly by the Democratic party, and their replacement by "strangers." Between 1952 and 1968 an average of more than 70 percent of incumbent Democratic senators became delegates to their party's national conventions. In 1972 that number was cut in half. In 1976 it was 18 percent, and in 1980, 13.8 percent. Meanwhile, the percentage of delegates attending their first national convention rose from 54 percent in 1964 to 87 percent in 1980.[13]

By the early 1980s these developments in the nominating process were amply satisfying the framers' hope that the presidency would be separated from the rest of the system. The logic of the constitutional system, coupled with the insistence of modern culture on direct democracy, had triumphed almost completely over the impulse of politicians to bind the elements of the system together.

PUBLIC FINANCING

The second recent development that has had a major impact on the politics of presidential selection is the introduction of public financing. The cost of campaigning for the presidency has risen sharply in recent years. In each of Eisenhower's two campaigns (1952 and 1956), he spent less than Governor Alfred Landon had ($8.9 million) in 1936; Stevenson in those same two campaigns spent less than FDR had ($5 million) in 1936. But the 1960 campaign set records for both parties (about $10 million each for Nixon and Kennedy), and in 1968 Nixon spent more than $25 million, while Humphrey was spending $11.6 million.[14]

---

*This rule was changed for 1984, but it made no difference. Delegates still voted for the candidate to whom they had pledged themselves.

The argument for public financing is based on the notion that candidates should be free from having to prostrate themselves before people who can contribute large sums of money to their campaigns. For a long time a distaste for using public money for politics, coupled with a reluctance on the part of incumbents to provide funds for their challengers, blocked the measure.

By the early 1970s the enormous cost of campaigning had added urgency to the idea, especially for presidential elections. The legislation came in two waves. In 1971 Congress established a fund, supported by taxpayer contributions of $1 each year, and authorized that the money be given to the presidential campaign of each major party for their general election campaigns, provided they agreed to accept funds from no other source and limit their spending to the amount provided by the federal fund. The law also required that all contributions and all campaign expenditures in excess of $100 be reported to the comptroller general of the United States.

The presidential campaign of 1972 was a watershed. It was the last campaign supported by private contributions (the public fund, established in 1971, was not available for distribution until 1976). It cost each party more than twice as much as any previous campaign (Nixon raised and spent more than $60 million; McGovern, about $30 million). It was also the best documented, owing in part to the disclosure provisions of the 1971 legislation, which went into effect on April 7, 1972.

Shortly after the 1972 election, provoked by the gathering Watergate scandal, a special Senate committee chaired by Sam Ervin of North Carolina conducted hearings on the extent to which "illegal, improper, or unethical activities" had occurred during the 1972 presidential campaign. The committee's report, more than 1,000 pages of testimony and documents published in June 1974, presented an appalling record of corruption and "dirty tricks." A nation that had always rather tolerantly assumed that those who sat near power could manipulate the government's authority to their own advantage was now told in detail how deeply those arrangements had compromised the conduct of the Nixon administration. Even cynical observers were surprised at its extent.

The story of George Steinbrenner, chairman and chief executive officer of the American Ship Building Company, was typical. Steinbrenner's company was involved in two major controversies with the federal government: a cost overrun on a contract to build an oceanographic survey ship and an antitrust investigation by the Justice Department into the company's purchase of nine cargo ships operating on the Great Lakes. Steinbrenner had a reputation in Washington as a fund-raiser for congressional Democrats. In early 1972 he was approached by Herbert Kalmbach, a fund-raiser for the Committee to Reelect the President (the infamous "CREEP"). Kalmbach told him that the Republicans were "going to win big" in 1972 and that it was time to "get on the right team." Steinbrenner asked what level of contribution would be appropriate. Kalmbach replied that there were various categories, in increments of $25,000, but that if Steinbrenner wanted any "input into the administration," he would have to think in terms of making a very substantial contribution. The committee would be happy, of course, to receive a contribution in any amount, but "if you were in the $25,000 class or . . . the $50,000 class, you would be amongst many, many thousands, and . . . you probably would be lost in the shuffle or wouldn't be remembered."

On April 6, 1972, an official of Steinbrenner's company delivered $100,000 to the offices of the Committee to Reelect the President. Steinbrenner, incidentally, got pretty poor value for his money. The Commerce Department denied his company's petition for a cost overrun subsidy and assessed penalties for late delivery of the ship, and in August 1972 the Justice Department filed an antitrust suit against American Ship Building for the purchase of the cargo ships. The suit was later settled in a way "not altogether beneficial" to Steinbrenner's company. In April 1974 he was indicted for making false statements about his contributions and for obstructing a criminal investigation.[15]

The hearings also revealed links between campaign contributions and presidential appointments. Some of the grossest abuses came in the so-called ambassadorial auction, whereby choice diplomatic appointments were offered in exchange for large contributions. A notorious example involved Dr. Ruth Farkas, a sociologist and director of a department store in New York City. Kalmbach testified before the House Judiciary Committee's impeachment inquiry in 1974 that during the 1972 campaign a White House aide told him to approach Dr. Farkas about making a contribution to Nixon's campaign in exchange for the ambassadorship to Costa Rica. According to Kalmbach, Dr. Farkas replied that she was interested in Europe and added, "Isn't $250,000 an awful lot of money for Costa Rica?" Apparently she made her point. President Nixon appointed her ambassador to Luxembourg in early 1973. At her confirmation hearing before the Senate Foreign Relations Committee she acknowledged that she and her husband had made a $300,000 contribution to the Nixon campaign. She added that she had met with Maurice Stans, a Nixon campaign aide, who explained that it was illegal to contribute more than $5,000 to any single committee but that he could provide her with a list of committees to which the contributions could be made. Dr. Farkas and her husband wrote seventy-six separate checks to thirty-one different committees.[16]

President Nixon's apologists used to annoy his accusers by insisting that what he did was not fundamentally different from his predecessors. They may be right. What was different was that never before had such practices gotten a broad public laundering. Inevitably there arose a demand for remedial legislation. Congress responded with the Federal Election Campaign Act of 1974, which established a bipartisan Federal Election Commission; set limits on the amount that any organization or individual, including the candidates themselves, could contribute to a campaign; and provided public financing for both primary and general election campaigns for the presidency. Funding for the general election campaign was contingent on the candidate's undertaking not to accept money from private sources. To qualify for public financing during the primary season, candidates had to raise at least $5,000, in small contributions, in at least twenty different states. Once a candidate qualified, the public treasury would match up to $5 million in contributions.

Several features of this legislation were challenged in court. The Supreme Court in *Buckley* v. *Valeo*[17] ruled that a limit on the amount of money an individual could spend on his or her own campaign for Congress violated the First Amendment and that spending limits were acceptable only for candidates who took public financing.

By 1976 the public financing provisions were effectively in place. They made vast sums of money available for a presidential candidate in both the primary and the general election campaigns, provided he had a large, geographically dispersed campaign organization. The money came directly to the candidate, not to a political party or its leaders. It came in stages through the campaign season, beginning with the early primaries and mounting through the later primaries and on into the general election, provided his personal organization could keep his campaign rolling.

NEW TECHNOLOGIES

The third new factor in modern presidential campaigning is the availability of new technologies, which have made candidates even more independent of party leaders and preexisting political machinery.

Jet airplanes have been one source of liberation. FDR and Truman traveled around the country on railroads, but Carter and Kennedy, Reagan and Bush, Mondale, Gary Hart, and Jesse Jackson conducted their rivalries at jet speed, sometimes coast to coast and from the Great Lakes to the Rio Grande on a single day. It was like magic, the way a candidate would drop from heaven for a brief appearance, then be whisked away to some other, far distant target of opportunity.

Even more revolutionary was the computer. Roosevelt relied on James Farley's legendary memory, but modern candidates rely on computers—and on people who know how to use them. Computers keep lists of voters, arranged according to their reliability on election day, as ascertained by telephone surveys. Computers enable a candidate to solicit funds by sending out mail that looks like a personal letter from the candidate, although an aide manufactured it by pushing a single key on a computer board. Campaign managers use computers to analyze voting and survey data, so that candidates can target particular appeals on counties and precincts where they will do the most good. No candidate for president whose organization is not highly sophisticated in the use of computer technology has a chance of winning, whatever his or her other virtues may be.

Television is, of course, the other wonder of technology that is absolutely essential for modern campaigning. Unless a candidate is attractive over television and adroit in using it, he cannot win. Television enables him to appeal directly to the voters and (if his advisers are astute) to dramatize his appeal in memorable ways. Who that saw it will ever forget the image of Ronald Reagan, with the Statue of Liberty in the background, appealing for the ethnic vote? And millions did see it, because of television.

Television has become virtually a substitute for party organization. The candidate who can afford to advertise on television hardly needs to come to terms with his party's national organization at all. He must raise a great deal of money, meaning that virtually all his gatherings must be fund-raisers, and to do that, he must have a substantial personal organization. But he can dispense with the party organization.

Television is not a neutral medium. Certain types of personality—those that are "cool" and informal and look relaxed—seem to be appealing over television, whereas those who are energetic and vivid in person often appear harsh, strident, shrill on television. Politicians, most of whom are amateurs in these matters, often express amazement at television's alchemy, which not only turns personal dross into political gold but can work the other way as well.

What is not clear is whether television helps the electorate identify individuals who are best qualified for presidential leadership. In the age of television it is not irrelevant for a president to be a skillful communicator over this medium, as Ronald Reagan has so masterfully demonstrated. But if skills with television are highly useful for a modern leader, they are not sufficient, as the case of Jimmy Carter demonstrates, and it may be that reliance on television as a medium of evaluation causes the electorate to ignore or slight other relevant factors.

It is easy to exaggerate the influence of television on the constitutional system. There is a tendency to assume that given its huge impact on modern culture generally, television has revolutionized not only campaigning but the whole political process. I hope this chapter makes clear that this has not been the case. Television has indeed helped free candidates from dependence on party organizations; but that process began long before the invention of television, and it has been abetted by many other factors, cultural and technological. What television has done is to strengthen the inherent logic of the constitutional system. It is the framers, not the networks, who created the separated presidency. It is their system, coupled with the drive of American culture for direct democracy, that has made such eager use of television's potential for direct communication between a leader and the nation's popular mass.

Ever since the founding, a determination to democratize the selection of presidents gradually cast aside every impediment. The notion that independent electors should choose the president was the first to go. The Jacksonian movement eliminated the congressional caucus. In the name of democracy many states adopted a binding preconvention primary. In the name of equality the process opened up to women, minorities, and other categories of citizens who had traditionally been underrepresented in the nominating conventions. In the name of equity Congress made public financing available to any candidate whose organization was large and sophisticated enough to raise seed money in several states. Now candidates are using modern technology to circumvent the last barrier to direct democratic choice: party leaders.

None of the reforms of the past century was adopted in the interest of enhancing a successful candidate's capacity to govern. In fact, reformers have almost always stressed the importance of reinforcing a candidate's *independence* from those whose cooperation would be essential for effective government. And they have left us with a process unrecommended by success in any previous system, anywhere in the world. No other nation in the world, none ever, anywhere, has chosen its candidates for leader of the government by a direct popular election.

The changes were not adopted as a system. They were added piecemeal, some (the financing provisions) through federal law, some (the increased use of primaries) through party rules and state statutes, some in response to technological imperatives. Yet their cumulative effect has been a radical revision in the method of choosing presidents, more radical than anyone intended or would have dared propose explicitly.

We return finally to our central question: Is the Constitution responsible for the defects in our current method of choosing the president? The short answer is yes, at least partly. It is the Constitution that sends political energies into channels that frustrate responsible political leadership and cause reform efforts to be misdirected.

The drive to democratize the government by streamlining presidential elections had impatiently swept aside all barriers—except the apathy and cynicism produced by a system that promises more, in terms of democratic control, than it can possibly deliver. To achieve true democratic control, we need, first of all, to broaden accountability by encouraging competing teams of political leaders, rather than individual candidates, to run for office. Only teams can govern, particularly in a system of separated powers. Secondly, we need an electoral system that offers elections at times of real political decision, rather than at intervals dictated by the calendar. Such a system would shorten campaigns, curb costs, and produce campaigns that yield true popular mandates.

As it stands, the constitutional system blocks evolution in this direction. It encourages the illusion that a single individual, through a campaign for the presidency, can elicit a popular mandate and impose it on the rest of the system. In so doing, it fragments political leadership and frustrates the development of an effective, national political will.

CHAPTER 8

Building
a Government

At every presidential election the stakes are tremendous, larger even than most voters are aware. Everyone knows that the winning candidate will have tremendous influence over the nation's domestic and foreign policies, that he will have awesome weapons at his command and will lead us in case of war. Everyone knows that he will bring his own aides into the White House and appoint his own cabinet. Most also know that a president may appoint one or more Supreme Court justices.

What fewer people realize is that the choice of a president determines the fate of thousands of public officials, from the top reaches of the federal bureaucracy in Washington down to countless regional offices around the country. The opportunity to rebuild the government and to satisfy partisan appetites for patronage is particularly great for a president-elect whose party is different from the incumbent's. Once inaugurated, his administration will have an opportunity to fill such positions as U.S. marshal in Honolulu, Hawaii, and administrator of the St. Lawrence Seaway Development Corporation in Massena, New York, and hundreds of others (the vast majority of which, unlike these two, require an appointee to move to Washington while serving). And even if, like President Carter, he never gets an opportunity to name a Supreme Court justice, he can expect to name more than 100 federal judges to the lower courts.*

The Constitution provides that the president, with the advice and consent of the Senate, shall appoint ambassadors, Supreme Court justices, and "all other officers of the United States," unless Congress by law establishes another mode of appointment. The Constitution put the president at the center of the appointment process basically for two reasons: so that a single, firm will might stand behind the enforcement of federal law and the administration of federal programs and so that everyone would know who was responsible for the appointments. It involved the Senate in the process also for two basic reasons: so that by their advice senators might broaden the field of recruitment and so that, by withholding their consent, they could prevent the appointment of unqualified people.

In writing of these arrangements in *The Federalist*, Alexander Hamilton anticipated that the role of the Senate would be passive. Senators, if they disapproved, might defeat the president's choice and oblige him to make another, "but they cannot themselves *choose*— they can only ratify or reject the choice he may have made."[1] Hamilton's interpretation proved misleading. The president does indeed shape the process of appointment in important ways, but senators, by aggressive use of their constitutional powers and by adroit exploitation of the instinct for accommodation and political survival, have seized a good share even of the president's formal powers of initiation.

The president's power to initiate appointments is nevertheless a formidable weapon in his arsenal of persuasion. As the size of the federal establishment has grown, apprehension that it would destroy the equilibrium of the Constitution has arisen. Responding to this danger, Congress in 1883 created the civil service system. The idea was that many federal jobs required expertise, but most were policy-neutral, and that the public interest would be served if the officials in these positions were not replaced wholesale every time the White

---

*During his single term Carter named 202 appointees to the district court bench and 56 to the circuit courts of appeals. In his first term Reagan named 129 and 31, respectively, as well as one justice—Sandra Day O'Connor, the first woman—to the Supreme Court. Midway into Reagan's second term Chief Justice Warren Burger resigned, giving the president an opportunity to elevate William Rehnquist to chief justice and name Antonin Scalia to the vacancy.

House changed hands. The system did not change overnight. By 1900 more than 60 percent of federal employees were still in patronage positions. After the turn of the century, however, coverage expanded fairly rapidly. Just prior to our entry into World War I nearly 70 percent of the 480,000 people employed by the federal government were integrated into the system.[2] Currently more than 90 percent of all federal jobs are covered by some sort of merit system.

Thus, in the modern era, when we speak of a president's opportunity to mold the government by exercising his powers of appointment, we are not referring to the nearly 3 million people who have their jobs in the federal government by virtue of their performances on competitive examinations. Nor are we referring to the many thousands of military and diplomatic officers whose positions call for presidential nomination and senatorial confirmation but who are not normally subject to political screening either at the White House or on Capitol Hill. We are talking about the positions, perhaps 3,000 or 4,000 in number,[3] in which the nation's political leadership takes special interest.*

Of these, perhaps 100 are clearly presidential: positions in the cabinet and in the Executive Office of the President (including such officials as the national security adviser, members of the Council of Economic Advisers, and the director of the Office of Management and Budget), heads of the leading boards and councils (such as the Joint Chiefs of Staff, the Federal Reserve Board, and the Nuclear Regulatory Commission), and members of the Supreme Court. These positions are national in scope and highly visible to the general public, and they are handled as one might assume from the text of the Constitution. The president gathers advice from many sources and makes nominations for which he alone is held responsible. Then the

---

*It is devilishly difficult to estimate the number of important appointments which a new president must make. One careful student concludes that it "usually numbers in the vicinity of five hundred or six hundred, about half of which require Senate confirmation."[4] Another estimates that of the nearly 3,000 officials in the executive branch who owe their appointments to presidential nomination, roughly 700 are "political executives at or near the top of government agencies."[5] I have used a slightly higher figure because my interest is in appointments that lie in the zone that is contested between the White House and the Senate.

Senate, through committee hearings and by floor debate, examines the nominees' qualifications. Once in a while, as with two of President Nixon's appointees to the Supreme Court, the Senate deems the nominee unfit for the office and withholds confirmation. Normally, however, the president gets his way, even if a majority of the Senate is ideologically distant from him.

Sometimes the confirmation process provides an occasion for criticism of the president's policy. When President Reagan named Kenneth Adelman to be director of the Arms Control and Disarmament Agency in January 1983, for example, senators subjected the nominee to a close grilling on the administration's intentions regarding arms control agreements. Almost always, however, the president gets the nominee he wants for these visible positions—to the point that critics sometimes complain that the Senate's consideration of these nominees amounts to little more than a rubber stamp.*

These top-level appointments, however, constitute only a small percentage of the president's patronage. Presidents are also responsible, under the Constitution, for nominating people to serve in subordinate positions in the bureaucracy in Washington and as administrators in regional offices of federal programs around the country. They must nominate people to fill vacancies on regulatory commissions and judges to serve on federal district and circuit courts. For these appointments, they are under enormous pressure to share their patronage, with senators and with other party leaders.

Politics inescapably involves conflict. Presidents and senators battle all the time to advance their policies and cultivate their political roots. They have every incentive to develop a system for managing the politics of appointments so as to reduce potential conflicts. A politician comes to the Senate by building a powerful organization in his own state. He naturally wants to reward his supporters with good posts in the federal government. If a president of his own party ignores him when appointing someone from his own state, the senator's prestige is bound to suffer.

---

*After studying the confirmation process during President Carter's first year in office, Bruce Adams concluded that "Presidential nominees are hastily considered in an extremely comfortable atmosphere without the benefit of a full record or tough scrutiny. No clear standards have been established by which Senators judge whether or not to confirm nominees."[6]

All senators understand this. Thus, even a maverick like Senator Lowell Weicker, Republican of Connecticut, can expect support from his fellow Republicans and from his colleagues on the Democratic side in defending himself from any presidential impulse to appoint his political enemies to federal positions in Connecticut. In this way political reality conditions the opportunities of a conservative administration, such as Ronald Reagan's, to shape the regional administration of federal programs. On the other hand, in accordance with the Constitution all appointments must come, at least formally, from the president, and that gives the White House considerable leverage. Senator Weicker must negotiate with the White House about these positions, and the result is likely to be a compromise, whereby certain positions are allocated to the senator and his allies while others go to Reagan Republicans in Connecticut, and each group gets a veto on the other's choices, which must, however, be exercised with restraint.

What this means is that when we elect a president, we are determining which *party* will dominate the process of building the federal government for four years. No matter which party controls the Senate, if a Republican wins the presidency, Republican senators gain an opportunity to make certain federal appointments for their states, including judgeships, while Democratic senators take a backseat. By the same token, Republican candidates for these appointive positions gain a distinct, nearly insuperable advantage over their Democratic rivals. To the victors go the spoils. Parties may have lost their efficacy in other areas, but for staffing the federal administration and the federal judiciary, partisan loyalties still remain a powerful determinant of an individual's chances.

The instinct for political survival and accommodation at both ends of the bargaining process often produces curious results. When Richard Nixon was president, both senators from California, Alan Cranston and John Tunney, were liberal Democrats. A deal was reportedly struck whereby one-third of the appointments in California went to the senators. President Nixon ended up appointing many liberal Democrats to positions in the state he himself had once represented in the Senate.[7]

Senators often strike such deals, with presidents and with one another. For many years New York's two senators have had an agreement to share the appointments there. These arrangements are no secret. The *New York Times* reported a compact between Senator Daniel Patrick Moynihan, a Democrat, and his Republican colleague, Senator Alfonse M. D'Amato, providing that three out of every four federal judicial appointments in New York would go to the senator whose party was in the White House. The occasion for the publicity was a report that the Reagan White House was stalling on one of Senator Moynihan's nominees for the bench, a man who had served as a lawyer for the Legal Aid Society. Another nomination, submitted by Senator D'Amato at the same time, had been cleared and the candidate nominated, confirmed, and sworn in without any difficulty, but Senator Moynihan's nominee was stuck. The White House was apparently unwilling to reject it outright but had consigned it to limbo. Senator Moynihan was outraged. "In the seven and a half years I've been here," he said, "this is the first occasion where there has been any such delay in the approval by the White House and the Justice Department." Senator D'Amato, through a spokesman, said that although he did not see eye to eye with Moynihan's nominee on political ideology, he was "absolutely committed to support the nomination."[8] Despite this backing, the administration never did appoint Senator Moynihan's original nominee. A year later, after President Reagan's reelection, Moynihan submitted a new nominee, who was finally confirmed in 1986.[9]

Between the extremes of the cabinet and the Supreme Court, on the one hand, and regional offices and district courts, on the other, lie the middle-level administrators, regulatory commissioners, and appellate court judges. In these middle zones there is less certainty about the standing of various participants in the bargaining process. In recruiting potential appointees, White House and cabinet officials negotiate with senators, but they also listen to representatives, other party leaders, and private citizens with a special interest in particular appointments. In appointing an undersecretary of commerce for international trade, for example, a president can expect "advice" from the ranking members of his own party who serve on the various congressional committees that deal with foreign trade. In appointing an administrator for the National Oceanic and Atmospheric Administration, the White House might get suggestions from a senator or representative with special interest in environmental matters and certainly from interest groups active in that area. Despite these importunings, however, a determined president can usually have his own way with these appointments if he is willing to pay the political price. President Reagan, for example, was heavily criticized by environmentalists when he appointed James Watt to be secretary of the interior. Watt had been head of the Mountain States Legal Foundation, an organization that had challenged, in a series of lawsuits, the very laws which he would now be expected to administer. But the president stuck by his guns, believing that he had, in Watt, a man who shared his views about the nation's resources, and the Senate confirmed the appointment by a vote of 83 to 12.

Judgeships on the twelve circuit courts of appeals, the next to top level of the federal judiciary, are another potential area of discord, offering both opportunity and danger for the president. Unlike the eighty-nine district court jurisdictions, all of which fall within state boundaries, each judicial circuit (except the one for the District of Columbia) encompasses several states. Thus, when a vacancy occurs in, say, the Seventh Circuit, which covers Illinois, Indiana, and Wisconsin, each senator of the president's party from that region has an interest in the appointment. Often senators make deals to rotate the vacancies. Even in that situation, though, a strong and astute president can sometimes find opportunity to advance his own political goals.[10] When there are no senators from the president's party in a given state or circuit, party leaders from the region will expect to be consulted, to offer recommendations, and to have those recommendations treated with respect.

If a president chooses, he can try to buck the system. In the days when the South was solidly Democratic, Republican state party organizations existed more to dispense federal patronage than to win elections. In 1928, however, Herbert Hoover carried several southern states, and in office he was eager to help build a stronger Republican party in the South. Shortly after his inauguration he announced that he would no longer give carte blanche to Republican party leaders in the South, whose recommendations in many cases had been scandalously bad. The Florida organization defiantly continued to forward nominees of the usual poor caliber and sought to marshal opposition to Hoover's own nominees for district attorney in Florida. Hoover stood firm. In a sharply worded letter to the secretary of the Florida Republican organization, he reminded his correspondent that the "appointive responsibility rests in the President, not in any [party] organization." He noted that for seven months the Department of Justice had investigated "first one candidate and then another" proposed by the Florida organization but had not found that it could "conscientiously recommend to me any one of the names presented."[11]

By making it a high priority, Hoover did make some progress in raising the quality of federal officials in the South. When he tried to bring the same principles to bear in Minnesota, Kansas, Pennsylvania, and other parts of the country where there were powerful Republican organizations, however, he was quickly frustrated. In Pennsylvania Republican Senator David A. Reed recommended a candidate for a district court judgeship. After investigations had revealed opposition by the Republican governor of Pennsylvania, by leading members of the bar, and by the senior judge of the circuit court of appeals, among many others, Hoover's attorney general decided not to forward the nomination to the Senate for confirmation. Senator Reed went to the White House and told President Hoover that unless he submitted Reed's candidate for confirmation, he would get no further support from the Pennsylvania delegation in Congress. Hoover capitulated. When the nomination came before the Senate, many senators of both parties vigorously opposed it, partly on the ground that the nomination had been engineered by the head of the Republican party organization in Pennsylvania, who was also president of the Pennsylvania Railroad, a frequent litigant in federal courts. The vote in the Senate was 53 to 22, in favor of confirmation.[12] If there was one refreshing note in this sordid clash, it was Reed's candid statement—not contradicted by the White House—that he, not the president, had made the choice.

President Carter also made strenuous, and politically costly, efforts to reform the process for appointing federal judges. However high-minded this attempt may have been, his difficulties suggest that what he was trying to do ran counter to the nature of the Constitution.

President Carter committed himself to two basic goals: selecting on the basis of merit and appointing a larger proportion of women, blacks, and Hispanics. These goals were in tension but not necessarily in conflict—any more than the practice of giving preference to Democrats or Republicans is incompatible with a concern for merit. If his staff members looked carefully, the president was convinced they would find meritorious female Democrats.

Soon after President Carter took office, Congress passed a bill creating 117 new district court and 35 circuit court judgeships, increasing the size of the federal judiciary by about one-third. These positions, along with normal vacancies caused by resignations and deaths, gave the new president an opportunity to make an unusually large number of judicial appointments.

In the legislation creating these judgeships, Congress bade the president to propose guidelines for selection based on merit and "to give due consideration to qualified women, blacks, Hispanics and other minority individuals in making nominations." The emphasis on minorities and women was, of course, in line with Carter's own preferences. He chose to interpret the call for guidelines as an invitation to promulgate his idea for screening commissions.

Many senators reacted sharply against this snatch at prerogatives which they had come to regard as their own. In the ensuing negotiations it was settled that President Carter by executive order would establish commissions for the circuit court positions, but that senators would set up panels for the district court positions only if they deemed them personally useful. While Carter was president, senators in thirty states established commissions to generate judicial recommendations.*

President Carter established a nominating commission in each of the federal circuits and directed it to recommend five persons for each vacancy, from whom he would select one to forward to the

---

*Senator Edward Kennedy, who served as chairman of the Senate Judiciary Committee from 1979 to 1980, made several significant reforms of his own in the judicial selection process. He directed the committee staff to make independent inquiries into each nominee's background and ended the practice of refusing to call hearings on nominees simply because a senator from the state where the judge was to sit failed to return the "blue slip" (a form sent to a senator to ask his or her opinion about judicial nominees). In the past the Judiciary Committee had usually refused to schedule a confirmation hearing, even if the senator who failed to return the slip was not a member of the president's political party.

Senate for confirmation. Under deft prodding by the Justice Department, these commissions engaged in energetic recruitment of minorities and women. Carter appointed more women (forty), more blacks (thirty-eight), and more Hispanics (sixteen) to the federal bench than all previous presidents combined, and the overall level of qualifications of his nominees, as measured by the American Bar Association's Standing Committee on the Federal Judiciary, was at least as high as during any administration since 1945.[13]

But the political cost was high, too, despite the president's respect for the unwritten rule that he favor members of his own party.[14] President Carter had a notoriously difficult time working with Congress. His willingness to clash with senators over judicial appointments was symptomatic of his preference for rectitude over success in advancing his programs. Compare Lincoln, who coolly instructed an aide to trade three patronage appointments for votes in Congress on the admission of Nevada, which he deemed essential for the adoption of the Fourteenth Amendment and a successful conclusion to the Civil War.[15] Whereas some presidents (Hoover, Carter) have expended large amounts of political capital in efforts to reform the appointment process, presidents with a more positive orientation toward policy goals have tended to accept the system as it has evolved within the constitutional framework. These presidents, focusing on broader issues, eschew procedural reforms and learn to live with the system that has evolved out of the constitutional framework.

It is, in fact, the natural tendency of the constitutional system to encourage politicians in the White House and Congress to manipulate the appointment process in service of other goals. In 1975 and 1976, at the end of a Republican administration, Congress, controlled by the Democrats, held up a bill to create a large number of new judicial positions, in hopes that the patronage windfall would come to them through a Democratic victory in 1976. During the delay the judicial process bogged down all over the country. In the Middle District of Florida, for example, all action on civil cases had to be suspended. Judges there were handling an average of 700 cases each, 300 more than the limit recommended by the Judicial Conference (a board of directors for the federal judiciary, headed by the chief justice and composed of twenty-four other judges).[16] Never mind. Democrats in Congress would not be hurried. Justice would wait a few months to see if a Democrat could win the presidency— and then a few months longer while senators tried to persuade the new president that his scheme for recruitment by commissions must not be made mandatory.

It happened again four years later. Toward the end of Carter's term Senate Republicans named a three-member panel, consisting of Mark Hatfield of Oregon, Ted Stevens of Alaska, and John Tower of Texas, to review all appointments that the president submitted for confirmation and to flag those that involved important considerations of policy, so that they might be delayed, pending the outcome of the election. The point of emphasizing policy was to deflect the charge that they were merely saving patronage for themselves. Among the appointments sidetracked and eventually defeated by this tactic were five to the board of the Legal Services Corporation, four to the Public Broadcasting Corporation board, and seventeen judgeships. When the Republicans won not only the presidency but a majority in the Senate as well, thus capturing control of the Senate committees, they quickly shed the nagging procedural reforms of the preceding four years and proceeded to harvest a windfall of patronage.

One vacancy slipped through the net, however. The story is worth recounting because it illustrates rather vividly how presidents and senators, even those who are reform-minded, manipulate the appointment process for political purposes. In November 1978 the *New York Times* carried a report that the new First Circuit judgeship had been promised to Massachusetts and that Senator Edward Kennedy (not the president) had chosen Archibald Cox, Harvard Law School professor and former Watergate prosecutor, for the vacancy. In the same announcement Kennedy named four people for federal district court vacancies in Massachusetts, appointments which President Carter meekly, though warmly, praised. The "leak" on the circuit court judgeship infuriated President Carter because it threatened to undermine the integrity of his new commissions and create a precedent for short-circuiting the process. So when the First Circuit Commission later forwarded its list of approved candidates for the vacancy, including Cox's name, the administration refused to appoint Cox, saying that he was too old for the post.

By this time Senator Kennedy was openly moving toward challenging President Carter's renomination, and further action was suspended. President Carter knew that it would be an empty gesture to submit another name from the list without Senator Kennedy's concurrence. When Carter beat Kennedy for the Democratic presidential nomination, he began negotiating for Kennedy's endorsement. One of the senator's conditions was a promise that the First Circuit nomination go to Stephen Breyer, a Harvard Law School professor on leave, serving as chief counsel to the Senate Judiciary Committee. Back in the Senate Kennedy obtained a promise from Senator Strom Thurmond, the ranking Republican on the Judiciary Committee, that the Republicans would not block the nomination (annoying Senator Gordon Humphrey, Republican of New Hampshire, who had hoped to have a say with President-elect Reagan on filling this post). After the election Carter fulfilled his promise, forwarding the nomination of Breyer. With the cooperation of Senate Republicans, Breyer became the last Carter appointee to the federal courts confirmed by the Senate.[17]

By the end of his second term Ronald Reagan will likely have appointed a majority of the judges serving on the federal district and circuit courts. That is not an unusually high proportion for an eight-year period. President Eisenhower named more than 56 percent. Presidents Kennedy and Johnson appointed about 70 percent, Nixon and Ford, more than 58 percent, and Carter, in a single term, just over 40 percent.[18] An analysis of Reagan's appointments during his first term shows that the proportion of women was down to 8 percent, from Carter's 15.5 percent, though it was much higher than any administration previous to Carter's. He appointed eight Hispanics; Carter had appointed twice as many. And he named just two blacks; Carter had named thirty-seven. Commenting on the latter figure, one of President Reagan's judicial recruiters explained that it was extraordinarily difficult to find qualified blacks who shared the president's philosophy and were willing to serve on the federal bench. Also noteworthy was the partisan background of Reagan's appointees. More than 97 percent were Republicans. That was the highest figure for partisanship of any administration during the past half century. One had to go back to the Harding administration to find another president who appointed not a single member of the opposition party to the circuit court bench.

There were indications, though, that the president's drive carried

a political price. In an attempt to gain confirmation for Daniel Manion, whose qualifications for a judgeship were widely questioned,
the White House promised Slade Gorton, Republican of Washington, to clear the nomination of the senator's candidate for a district
court judgeship in western Washington, even though Gorton's man
was obnoxious to conservative Republicans. Gorton later admitted
that he had cast his affirmative vote for Manion despite his opinion
that the qualifications of the president's man were "no more than
marginal." Gorton was up for reelection in 1986 (he lost), and his
Democratic opponent made capital of these injudicious confessions.

Reagan's judicial appointments were not surprising, considering
the ideological character of his presidency. Perhaps not since Franklin D. Roosevelt had we had a president whose principles of government were so distinct, and marked such a radical break, from those
of the preceding administration. Inasmuch as the president's party
controlled the Senate for the first six years of his presidency, there
was little that the Democrats could do to block the conservative swing
of the judiciary. From the standpoint of presidential accountability
and effectiveness, however, Reagan's judicial appointments left little
room for complaint. He had campaigned candidly about his intentions in this area, and despite the criticisms of his opponents, his
personal performance continued to have strong support from the
public.

It is clear from the foregoing record that the Constitution does
not deliver the benefits it would seem to promise: clear presidential
responsibility for the quality of federal appointments, unified executive control over the administration of federal programs, and careful scrutiny of the fitness of the president's nominees by the Senate.
Instead, what we get is a very complicated process, by which presidents and senators seek to minimize conflict and share the benefits
of federal patronage. Reagan's decision to nominate Senator Gorton's man, in effect trading a district court judgeship for a vote in
support of a circuit court nominee, shows that even the most ideologically determined chief executive cannot escape from the forces
set in motion by the Constitution.

The central promise of the separation of powers is that it reduces
corruption. The framers believed that if they separated the power of

appointment from the power to create and finance public functions, they would break the connection that had given rise, in eighteenth-century England, to vast patronage machines. Despite their efforts, political parties quickly arose in America and sought to bridge the separation, and the irony is that they succeeded best in the area of patronage distribution. The Constitution has indeed deterred parties from committing themselves to coherent platforms, primarily by encouraging regional tendencies to find representation in Congress. But by centralizing the power of initiating appointments in the presidency, it established the framework for a national two-party system, and by placing the power of confirmation in the Senate, it incorporated Congress into the system. If the two major parties existed for no other reason, they would still serve as the principal channels of recruitment for federal appointments.

Thus, the framers' leading purpose in separating the executive branch from the legislative has been frustrated. The arrangement serves other purposes, of course, and no one proposes now to fuse these branches. Nevertheless, it is important to recognize that the constitutional provisions for appointments have not worked as the framers intended. The Constitution seeks to focus responsibility for appointments on an individual who can be held accountable for them and to empower an independent body to see that this authority is not abused. These provisions are not compatible. If the Senate can withhold confirmation, the president must share his powers of appointment. Therefore, he is not solely responsible for those who administer the laws or for the quality of his judicial appointments.

There is one further implication of this argument: If a modification of the framers' design led to closer, more candid cooperation between the president and Congress in making appointments, it would represent a departure from the strict doctrine of the separation of powers—but not from the practical effects of the framework that emerged from the convention of 1787.

CHAPTER 9

Enforcing the Laws

The Constitution established a system of "separated institutions, sharing powers." Thus, the executive and legislative branches share in making the laws, and they share, too, in staffing the administration. But the executive's responsibility to the laws, once enacted, is clear. He is to "take care" that they are "faithfully executed." This doubly emphatic phrase* stands out in a text that is otherwise—apart perhaps from its preamble—unrhetorical. The framers wanted to erect the firmest possible barrier against prerogative, that ancient claim of monarchs to act without lawful warrant, or even against it, in the event of emergency.[1] The American chief executive was to obey the laws strictly and faithfully, carrying out their mandate with zeal and without reservation or reluctance.

The principal reason for separating the executive from the legislature was to encourage vigorous and evenhanded administration of the laws.[2] The devices for sharing powers (the executive veto, senatorial confirmation of appointments, close congressional control over the purse strings) were designed to enable the branches to monitor each other and to defend themselves in the exercise of their assigned

---

*The Constitution could have said, "The President shall see that the laws are executed."

functions. The arrangement had the further effect of requiring a broad range of officials, serving different constituencies, to reach agreement before the government could embark on a new policy. This made the government inherently conservative. It also provided an incentive for negotiation and cooperation.

As modern conditions gave rise to demands for more positive government, Congress was often compelled to delegate discretion to the president and his appointees. It did so reluctantly, because separation made Congress jealous and suspicious of executive power. To avoid giving power directly to the president, it introduced the concept of a merit-based civil service, it created commissions whose members were insulated from the president's removal power, and it invented the legislative veto.

These tactics, some of which were at least dubious from a constitutional standpoint, helped curb the power of the executive, but they did not solve the problem. In many areas of governance it was impossible for Congress to avoid granting discretion to the president. In others Congress delegated power to the president because it was unable to make up its own mind or because it wanted to embarrass him politically. On the president's side, sometimes he used his discretion in service of the lawmakers' intent; other times he deliberately subverted it.

In this chapter we will examine several contemporary cases of presidential policy-making, to see how the constitutional separation of powers operates under modern conditions. We will see how the demands of modern governance tend to efface the line between lawmaking and implementation, and we will analyze the judiciary's attempt to enforce the constitutional separation of powers. Throughout, we will bear in mind the question of whether or not some modification of the separation of powers might reduce the cost of conflict between the branches and strengthen the incentive for cooperation in pursuit of public objectives.

In December 1980, one month after his crushing defeat by Ronald Reagan, President Jimmy Carter announced a spectacular triumph of his own. He was signing into law a bill that doubled the size of the nation's park and wildlife refuge systems and tripled the wilderness areas, setting aside for permanent preservation a total of 104 million acres in Alaska, an area larger than the state of California. It was no exaggeration when he called it "one of the most important pieces of conservation legislation in the history of our country."[3] It was, in fact, an extraordinary achievement, particularly for a lame-duck administration.

One of the areas protected by the legislation was a remote, mountainous island called St. Matthew, situated in the Bering Sea about halfway between Alaska and Siberia. Fog blankets its high coastline cliffs for most of the summer, and eighty mile-per-hour winds sweep the island throughout the winter. The *Encyclopaedia Britannica* calls it "uninhabited."[4] On the contrary, it supports one of the richest seabird-nesting colonies in the world. It is an important stopping place for migratory birds. Sea lions, seals, walruses, and whales, including seven endangered species of whale, swim in the waters off its coast. Polar bears and arctic foxes roam its tundra.

Because of its harsh conditions and remote location, St. Matthew Island has been inhospitable to man. In the nineteenth century fur trappers hunted there. Scientists have visited briefly to study the wildlife. During World War II the United States Coast Guard stationed a few men there for two years. Otherwise, there is no record of any human being's staying on the island for as long as a year. It is isolated from airplane and shipping routes.

In 1970, by act of Congress, it was designated a wilderness area, which meant that there could be "no commercial enterprise and no permanent road" on the island without congressional consent.[5] It is, as the Department of the Interior stated in a 1982 publication, "as close to pure wilderness as can be found in the United States today."[6]

There is one other fact about St. Matthew Island which turned out to be nearly as crucial to its fate as those pertaining to its natural history. It is the closest point of land to the Navarin Basin, a seabed west of the island where the Interior Department announced that it would lease tracts for oil exploration and development, starting in 1984. When a major oil refining company in 1981 expressed interest in using St. Matthew Island for an air base and tanker port, the Interior Department replied that the Wilderness Act of 1970 and the Alaska Lands Act of 1980 apparently prohibited the proposed development. Nevertheless, the department suggested that the company explore the possibility of a "land exchange."

It has been customary in legislation intended to promote the conservation of resources in Alaska to include a provision allowing the secretary of the interior to obtain private holdings located within federal sites by exchanging them for lands "of equal value" elsewhere in the state. Accordingly the 1980 legislation included a provision authorizing the secretary to exchange protected lands with corporations organized by native groups, "notwithstanding any other provision of law." Exchanges were to be on the basis of equal value, "except that if the parties agree to an exchange and the secretary determines it is in the public interest, such exchanges may be made for other than equal value."[7]

The oil company already had lease arrangements on the mainland with a native group called the Cook Inlet Region, Inc. (CIRI), based near the city of Anchorage. It enlisted CIRI's assistance in obtaining rights on St. Matthew Island. On August 20, 1981, CIRI approached the Interior Department to propose an exchange. Negotiations ensued. Two years later Secretary of the Interior James G. Watt announced that an agreement had been reached. The Interior Department would convey about 4,000 acres on the southern end of St. Matthew Island to CIRI and associated native corporations. In return, the natives would relinquish their rights to parcels on the mainland totaling more than 6,000 acres and to an easement affecting 8,000 acres along Kokechik Bay. The agreement was to last fifty years, or until the land was no longer needed to support oil production activities in the Navarin Basin. CIRI's lessees would be permitted to dredge a deepwater seaport on the island and to build a jetport, a helicopter base, and lodging for 250 people. The agreement also allowed CIRI to use the island as a port for domestic and foreign fishing vessels.

CIRI's lessee was, of course, the refining company. By the time the agreement between CIRI and the Interior Department was signed, the oil company had developed plans to construct an air base with two runways, each more than a mile long, to be built by mining 400,000 cubic yards of gravel from sites on the island. Also planned were a base to house eighty people, roads, generators, fuel tanks, and other facilities, including a freshwater reservoir created by damming a creek. When the base came into operation, plans called for an average of one Boeing 737 flight in and out each day, plus three helicopters arriving and taking off each day. The flight path was to have been along the cliffs where the seabirds nest. The proposed port for ocean barges and other boats was to have required dredging 4.5 million cubic yards of material from the ocean floor to build a channel 1,000 feet long and 40 feet deep.

The Interior Department justified the agreement by pointing out that it called for the permanent acquisition of many thousand acres of native claims. (Department assessors valued these mainland properties at around $2.5 million; they set the value of the land on St. Matthew Island at $19 million.) In addition, the department noted, the agreement provided for the "ultimate clean-up, restoration and return forever" of the island parcel to the refuge system; it gave native people an opportunity to benefit economically from "the inevitable outer-continental-shelf exploration off their shores"; and it contained safeguards for human safety during the oil operations.[8]

Environmental groups reacted sharply to Secretary Watt's announcement. Russell Peterson, president of the National Audubon Society, declaring that his group would file a lawsuit against the exchange, said, "If Watt's ploy succeeds none of the lands that Congress [set aside] in the state of Alaska will be safe from development. Watt will have a free hand to give away the crown jewels of our nation." Former Senator Gaylord Nelson, chairman of the Wilderness Society, added that "exchanges should not be taking place administratively . . . , with Congress and the public left in the dark."

The suit brought by National Audubon Society was resolved in November 1984 in favor of the conservationists. The federal district court in Alaska voided the agreement, ruling that the secretary of the interior's "Public Interest Determination" for the exchange "suffered from serious errors of judgment and misapplications of law, leading to a clear error of judgment."[9]

What happened between 1980, when environmentalists hailed new legislation to protect the Alaskan wilderness, and 1983, when the same people brought suit against the implementation of the very same law? The answer, of course, is a change of administrations. The same provision which was designed to give flexibility to someone like Secretary Cecil Andrus to promote conservation was used by Secretary Watt to encourage development. There can be little doubt what would have happened if the oil company had approached the Interior Department under Secretary Andrus with its proposition for St. Matthew Island. Yet Secretary Watt's department expedited the inquiry and sought to guide it toward a successful outcome. In the end, because a determined and well-organized private group made skillful use of the judicial process, a federal court intervened to stay the hand of the executive.

One's orientation toward the issue of environmental protection versus development inevitably affects one's outlook on this case. There is, however, a deeper issue at stake: whether ours is a government of laws or a government of men.

The rule of law tends to make government objective. In one respect at least, it encourages an egalitarian spirit. It reduces the importance of being personally and politically close to those in power. As the St. Matthew Island case shows, the existence of a statute does not guarantee the rule of law. Under this statute, with its broad discretionary language, it made a great deal of difference whether the executive favored conservation or development. Representative John Seiberling, Democrat of Ohio, chairman of the House subcommittee on public lands and national parks, claimed that the exchange provision was designed to help the Interior Department eliminate private holdings in wildlife ranges, not to substitute one private holding for another. On the other hand, an aide to Senator Ted Stevens, Republican of Alaska, pointed out that "We [in the Senate] wrote a little of that law, too," and it was hard to contradict him when he added that "it was written to allow exactly what's being done here."[10] Indeed, the vagueness of the law may well have reflected the close balance of opposing political forces in December 1980. In any case, it gave an opening for the exercise of discretion—initially by administrators in the Interior Department and ultimately by a federal judge.

The case of St. Matthew Island shows how the same statute can be put to different purposes by administrations with contrasting political ideologies. The Economic Stabilization Act of 1970 is an example of another kind of abuse into which we are led by the way our Constitution separates the political branches. It was a case of government by executive edict, but the blame must be shared by all the players.

In 1970, at least partly to create a political issue, Congress, controlled by the opposition Democrats, gave President Nixon the power to "stabilize prices, rents, wages, and salaries" by issuing "such orders and regulations as he may deem appropriate." The president was authorized to "delegate the performance of any function under this title to such officers, departments, and agencies of the United States as he may deem appropriate." The statute also set a maximum penalty of $5,000 for the violation of regulations. That was it. This statute, authorizing a program that would affect the income and adjust the property values of every American, occupied about fifteen lines in the U.S. Code. When the bill was presented for President Nixon's signature, he indicated that he did not believe in economic controls and would not use these powers, but because it had been incorporated in the Defense Authorization Act, which he favored, the president signed it into law.

A statute as flaccid as this one raises an important point about the character of law. In specifying the powers granted by Congress to the president, laws can be more or less specific. They may direct the president, in certain circumstances, to take specific action. Or they may permit the president, in pursuit of broadly defined purposes, to take such action as he deems appropriate. Technically both are statutes and adhere in form to the requirement that government be "by law." But in substance they are radically different. One reflects control by Congress over the policy-making process: specific definition of a problem and a clear choice of remedies. The other legitimizes virtually anything the president chooses to do in a broadly defined area of governance.

Clearly the Economic Stabilization Act was of the latter type. As soon as President Nixon signed it, Democrats in the Senate, several of whom were planning to run for president in 1972, began to taunt him for failing to use powers Congress had given him. He could solve the problem of inflation, they said, by the stroke of a pen. When, a year later, the supple politician in the White House finally did move, his critics were completely disarmed. The legislation had given him complete authority to discern the need for action and had left it to him to decide what orders to issue and how to constitute the agencies for their implementation and enforcement. Congressmen were now in no position to complain. They might quibble about the timing and details of implementation, but they had totally mortgaged their authority to argue that the president was exercising legislative powers.

The permissiveness of the original Economic Stabilization Act reflects the machinations of party politicians, but the periodic renewals of the act cannot be explained this way. What was revealed here was a pathology of a different kind: legislators daunted by a complicated, controversial issue and a constitutional system that permitted them to legislate irresponsibly.

The fiasco that took place in April 1973 illustrates the derangement. Driven by the impending expiration of the president's authority to impose controls, the House Banking and Currency Committee quickly framed a bill the main feature of which was a rollback of prices to the level of January 10, 1973. It was soon apparent that such a proposal had no chance on the House floor. The Democratic leadership thereupon put together a substitute bill, a hodgepodge of regulations and exceptions pasted together in a desperate attempt to satisfy enough different interests to ensure passage. But the need here was not for logrolling. Inflation cannot be controlled by the same process that is used to write tax codes or tariff schedules or to distribute public works. What was needed, if anything, were a few simple rules and some clear guidelines for imposing or lifting them. Disciplined support could not be secured, however, either for the leaders' exercise in logrolling or for the more responsible versions proposed on the House floor by individual representatives. Republicans stood firm against any fetters on the president's discretion, and enough Democrats deserted each proposed rule to ensure defeat. At the end of a mortifying day the House passed a simple one-year renewal of the president's authority, the Senate followed suit, and the president signed his own blank check. Thus, the nation embarked on another year of economic policy by executive fiat.

In the cases of St. Matthew Island and the wage-price programs of the early 1970s, problems developed from the vagueness of the enabling legislation. In other cases, executive control over the activities of the government stems not from the dereliction of Congress but from the fact that the implementation and enforcement of the law inescapably involve discretionary judgments, such as how to deploy scarce administrative resources and whether to prosecute a suspected violation of the law or to seek compliance by persuasion. In the making of such judgments, it is the executive that determines what the government will require of its citizens.

Antitrust policy is a case in point. The law forbids the formation of companies that are large enough to subvert competition and holds the Justice Department responsible for administering this policy.* The Antitrust Division of the Justice Department has limited staff and time. It must decide where to concentrate its resources. It is under intense pressure from people who supported the president's campaign or those close to the attorney general to direct attention elsewhere. There is also the factor of presidential commitment. If the president regards the formation of monopolies as a serious problem, his staff makes antitrust activities a priority and carefully monitors the government's performance in this area, and the people at the Antitrust Division tend to be of higher quality, show higher morale, and get better funding. As the functions of government grow, the impact of this kind of discretion spreads as well.

Sometimes statutory language is left loose because Congress hates to choose between desirable programs and prefers to trust administrators to "do the right thing." Should limited antipoverty money go for improved schools, better housing, good nutrition, or a job-training program? Whatever decision is made, many constituents will be disappointed. So Congress appropriates the funds and directs that administrators spend the money for purposes "including, but not limited to," those included on a long wish list in the statute. The administrators then have to make the hard choices, and if the program fails or disappoints anyone, members of Congress can take the posture of agreeing with the aggrieved. This is obviously a recipe for weak administration, and a government weakly administered, as Hamilton pointed out, "whatever it may be in theory, must be, in practice, a bad government."[11]

The performance of the Reagan administration in the field of civil rights illustrates another kind of problem that arises when the exec-

---

*The problem is further complicated by the fact that the Federal Trade Commission is also authorized to prevent corporate mergers which substantially lessen competition or tend toward monopoly.

utive assumes a broad measure of discretion. Late on Friday afternoon, January 8, 1982, the White House announced that the Treasury Department was changing the rule denying tax exemption to certain colleges and academies that allegedly practiced racial discrimination. Furthermore, said the announcement, the Justice Department was withdrawing from a suit brought by these schools to challenge the government's policy and would urge the court to vacate it on grounds that the policies in question had been rescinded.

This announcement reversed a policy that three previous administrations, two of them Republican, had enforced. In the 1960s, as pressure mounted from Washington to desegregate the public schools, fundamentalist groups in the South and Midwest had founded private academies, expecting them, as private, church-related institutions, to be exempt from taxes. Civil rights lawyers attacked their tax-exempt status in federal courts and were generally successful. The Department of Health, Education, and Welfare under the Nixon administration urged the Internal Revenue Service to deny exemptions to schools that practiced racial discrimination, and in July 1970 the IRS complied.[12]

Over the ensuing decade, the IRS applied the ruling, not just to the new private academies but to older institutions as well. Bob Jones University in Greenville, South Carolina, admitted a handful of nonwhite students (in 1981–1982, it claimed to have about a dozen "yellow and black" students in a student body of 6,300), but school rules prohibited interracial dating and marriage, on grounds that Scripture forbade it. The IRS decided that this prohibition constituted racial discrimination and withdrew the school's tax exemption. The university then joined the Goldsboro Christian Schools, of Goldsboro, North Carolina, run by Bob Jones alumni, in challenging the IRS ruling as a denial of religious liberty. The Carter administration entered this suit on the side of the IRS. It was this position which the Reagan administration changed by its pronouncement of January 8, 1982, directing the IRS to grant the exemption and to stop its drive against these schools.

Leaders in the black community and many white sympathizers immediately rose in opposition. As the reaction mounted, a White House aide asked the President to listen to an expression of black sentiment. A call went out to two black men who had offices in the

Old Executive Office Building: a domestic affairs adviser on Vice President George Bush's staff and a junior staff member in the White House Office of Policy Development. These aides expressed their own disagreement with the policy and reported strongly emotional reactions they had encountered at black church services over the weekend. The president, we are told, was astonished by their testimony. He sat in silence for a moment or two, then turned to the White House aide and said, "We can't let this stand. We have to do something." He then called Samuel R. Pierce, Jr., his secretary of housing and urban development (HUD) and a black man, and asked him to come to the White House to "talk over the best way to get out of it."[13]

The path chosen was to depict the original White House announcement as a procedural matter, clumsily handled. What the administration really wanted, it was claimed, was to stop the practice of policy-making by regulatory fiat. According to this line of explanation, the IRS had been promoting social change without legislative warrant. The administration would ask Congress to pass appropriate legislation as soon as possible. In the meantime, Bob Jones University and the Goldsboro schools would temporarily get their tax exemptions, but the IRS would be directed to suspend further rulings until Congress acted.

Unfortunately for the Reagan administration, Congress and the federal courts refused to cooperate with this strategy. The circuit court of appeals in Washington quickly ruled that the administration could not restore the tax exemptions until the pending case had been settled, and the hastily drawn Reagan bill died without being reported out of committee in either house of Congress. In May 1983 the Supreme Court issued its decision in the Bob Jones-Goldsboro cases, vindicating, by a vote of 8 to 1, the IRS denial of tax exemption on grounds of racial discrimination. (Justice Rehnquist, incidentally, was the lone dissenter.)

There was much speculation in the press about how this damaging episode had come to pass. White House aides, anxious to defend the president against charges of bigotry or insensitivity, insisted that it was a product of poor staff work. Of the three top staff members at the White House, it was said that two had known nothing about it until the day before the announcement and that the president himself had not been informed until the morning of the announcement. Even then, said these aides, he had simply been given the information, without an adequate briefing.

The difficulty with these explanations was that they ignored at least one crucial step the president had taken about two months before the announcement in question. Congressman Trent Lott of Mississippi, second-ranking leader of Republicans in the House of Representatives, wrote to the president in October about pending cases relating to the tax-exempt status of church schools. There were several schools in Lott's state that had a stake in the issue. Reagan's staff included a summary of Lott's letter in the "Presidential Log of Selected House Mail," which the president receives regularly. The summary noted that the Supreme Court "has now agreed to review the case of 'Bob Jones University v. United States,' and [Lott] urges you to intervene in this particular case." In the margin next to this entry the president wrote, "I think we should."

An aide in the White House office of legislative liaison sent a photocopy of the page to Lott, who had been cochairman of the Platform Committee at the Republican National Convention in 1980. The platform on which Reagan ran had promised that the GOP would stand "shoulder to shoulder with black Americans" in combating the "vestiges" of racism, but it had also carried solace for those among Reagan's supporters who regarded the question of tax exemption for religious schools as a crucial test of Reagan's willingness to stop the intrusion of the federal government into the affairs of private citizens. Specifically it promised to "halt the unconstitutional regulatory vendetta launched by Mr. Carter's IRS Commissioner against independent schools."[14] Armed with this language from the platform and reinforced by the president's notation on the log, Lott pressed the Treasury and Justice departments for action. At the end of December 1981 White House Counselor Edwin Meese was told that the decision was ready. There was no further discussion of it until two days before the announcement.

At a news conference following the announcement President Reagan acknowledged that he had been the "originator of the whole thing." He insisted, "No one put anything over on me." It was true, he said, that the reaction had surprised him. "We were dealing with a procedural matter," he said, but the press had interpreted it "as a policy matter, reflecting a change in policy." He repeated that his main concern had been to prevent the IRS "from determining national social policy all by itself." That this last comment was at least partly disingenuous was suggested by a letter to the president from James E. Wheeler, a professor of accounting at the University of Michigan, who drew the president's attention to an IRS ruling, in effect since 1941, which excludes Social Security benefits from taxation. The exemption, which has no explicit statutory authorization, costs the federal government $140 billion each year, enough to offset most of the federal deficit. President Reagan ignored Professor Wheeler's suggestion.[15]

The approach of the federal government toward civil rights has varied from administration to administration. President Eisenhower made little effort to disguise his distaste for the duty, but he did enforce the court order to integrate the schools of Little Rock, Arkansas, "at the point of bayonet,"* and he cooperated with congressional leaders in enacting the first important piece of modern civil rights legislation, the Civil Rights Act of 1957, which established the Civil Rights Division in the Justice Department and authorized it to sue for denials of voting rights. President Kennedy dramatized his commitment to civil rights by sending government lawyers and troops to assist in the integration of the University of Mississippi. President Johnson lent every available resource to the enactment of the epochal Civil Rights Act of 1964, which prohibited discrimination in public accommodations and employment, and in a dramatic speech at Howard University affirming his support for the goals of the civil rights movement, he shouted to an ecstatic audience the words of the great anthem of the movement, "We shall overcome!" President Nixon, who espoused a "southern strategy" in politics, nevertheless developed the so-called Philadelphia Plan, which required companies doing construction work under a federal contract to hire black laborers. President Ford did not have much time in office to show his racial views in action, but no one doubted his commitment to enforce civil rights laws vigorously. President Carter, a deep southerner, displayed his attitude toward racial discrimina-

---

*This is Reagan's term, often repeated by him, to describe Eisenhower's action at Little Rock.[16]

tion most dramatically by his close personal relationship with Andrew Young, an intimate of the late Dr. Martin Luther King, Jr., and by appointing unprecedented numbers of blacks to high-level administrative positions and to the federal judiciary.

Of presidents since Eisenhower, Reagan seemed most ambivalent about civil rights as that term had come to be understood since the 1960s. Those who knew him personally insisted that he was a compassionate man devoid of bigotry, but he seemed to have little interest in responding to the concerns of the civil rights movement. He drew vital political support from the religious right, many of whom opposed racial integration. His difficulties stemmed from ideology as well as politics. His conservative principles included a fierce animus against big, active government (except in the field of national defense), whereas most blacks, particularly those who were politically active, believed that vigorous efforts by the federal government were required to overcome the legacy of slavery. There were no blacks in the Reagan entourage, and none in leadership positions at the White House or at the leading departments of the executive branch, except for Secretary Pierce at HUD. Thus, on a question like tax exemption the administration made policy without consulting any blacks.

The 1980 Republican platform contained the basic tenet of the administration's outlook of race: It promised to eradicate the "vestiges" of racism. William Bradford Reynolds, head of the Civil Rights Division in Reagan's Justice Department, in a speech to the Delaware Bar Association in February 1982, noted that there was a "consensus, in Congress and in the country as a whole, that racial discrimination is wrong and should not be tolerated in any form."[17] To eradicate the "vestiges" of racism, to deal with pockets of resistance to the national "consensus," Reynolds said he preferred to use persuasion rather than litigation, and when litigation was unavoidable, he intended to proceed on a case-by-case basis and to seek remedies that would reduce disruptions to a minimum. One result of this approach was the virtual elimination of class action suits in race-related cases. Another was a refusal to ask courts to use busing to overcome residential segregation. Reynolds argued that busing heightened racial tension and led to violence in neighborhoods. Race, he insisted, should not be taken into account in fashioning remedies for past discrimination. The Supreme Court, however, had consistently decided otherwise. In 1971, in upholding a busing plan in Charlotte, North Carolina, the Court held that if there had been no history of discrimination, it might be best to assign pupils to schools nearest their homes. "But . . . in a system that has been deliberately constructed and maintained to enforce racial segregation," the government had to adopt other strategies. In doing so, it need not hesitate to deal with the problem forthrightly. "Just as the race of students must be considered in determining whether a constitutional violation has occurred, so also must race be considered in formulating a remedy," wrote Chief Justice Warren E. Burger for a unanimous Court.[18]

Two actions taken by the Reagan administration illustrate the effect that a change in the approach of the executive branch can have. In a move that abandoned a policy established for more than twenty years, the Office of Federal Contract Compliance in the Labor Department, which monitors the employment practices of companies that work for the federal government, announced the intention to reduce drastically the number of companies that would be required to file affirmative action plans for increasing minority representation in their work forces.[19] Prior to the proposed new policy, companies with 50 or more employees and $50,000 or more in contracts had to file such reports. By setting those trigger figures at 250 employees and $1 million in contracts, the office intended to exempt several thousand companies from the filing requirement.*

The other situation involved Central Prison, a maximum security facility in Raleigh, North Carolina. Officials of the state government in North Carolina admitted that the prison was segregated, as well as illegally crowded, and promised to end these conditions as soon as a new state prison was completed. The deadline for building the new facility, however, repeatedly slipped. Staff lawyers in the Civil Rights Division of the Justice Department pressed to bring suit against the state, in order to negotiate a judicially enforceable timetable for correcting the violations, but Reynolds refused, saying that he pre-

---

*The proposed new regulations were published for comment in the *Federal Register* on August 25, 1981, and again on April 23, 1982. As of this writing, they have not yet been formally issued.

ferred to seek voluntary compliance. When staff attorneys went to Raleigh to discuss the situation, state officials reminded them that Senator Jesse Helms, Republican of North Carolina, had good contacts in Washington. They were not frightened, they said, by threats of litigation.*

Thus, the change of administration in 1981 brought about a distinct shift in the federal government's approach toward civil rights, without changing a word in the statute books. The courts continued on the previous course. Congress, despite mixed signals from the administration, enacted a twenty-five-year extension of the Voting Rights Act. But in areas where rights depended upon stiff regulations, aggressive enforcement, and a willingness to prosecute cases against those who sought to perpetuate the old patterns of discrimination, the government operated differently from the way it had under President Carter.

Sometimes it is the nature of the problem that makes it difficult to frame precise statutory language. In 1970 Congress decided to get tough about air pollution. Rather than delegate discretion to officials who might not be able to stand up to pressure, Congress enacted a statute requiring automakers, by 1975, to install devices in their cars that would reduce emissions to a specific standard. The administrator of the Environmental Protection Agency (EPA) was given power to postpone compliance only if he or she determined that the companies had made every possible effort to meet the deadline.

This legislation was noteworthy because it mandated the use, by a certain date, of a technology that did not exist when the statute was enacted. As the deadline approached, automakers complained that they were losing ground to foreign competition and insisted that it was technologically impossible to meet the deadline. Only the latter argument had any weight under the law, but it was difficult to determine if the companies had made a real effort to comply before filing their applications for deferral. In the end, after months of acrimonious public debate and intense pressure on the EPA, the admin-

---

*In December 1982 the Justice Department did finally file the suit, and the facility has now been built.

istrator granted a delay, a decision which was supported by most objective observers.

In this case a difficult objective was eventually achieved, though at considerable cost. Congress was willing to confront a major industry like automaking because it was confident of broad and deep public support. Usually it prefers a more flexible, ongoing process, one more open to the usual give-and-take of political influence. The problem is that the political process then continues long into the implementation stage, and the way is left open for the executive to bring an independent will to bear on the policy.

Congress, jealous of its constitutional responsibility to enact the government's will in statutes but mindful also of the need for flexibility in applying policy to rapidly changing circumstances and regional variations, has sought ways to retain control without tying the hands of the government. One device it developed over the past half century to meet this need was the legislative veto. The theory was that if Congress reserved the right to overrule administrative decisions that violated the intent of a statute, it might be possible to delegate discretion without abandoning responsibility for the nation's policy. But the device led to abuses. It allowed majorities in Congress, or in one house of Congress, or even in a single committee, to protect favored clients. Government by law is supposed to give citizens a dependable basis for planning and to discourage the practice of influence by powerful interest groups. The legislative veto undermined these values, prolonging the uncertainties of the policy-making process and giving an advantage to powerful and well-organized interests.

The abuses encouraged by the legislative veto may be seen in the field of environmental protection. In 1976 Congress enacted the Federal Land Policy and Management Act, which authorized the secretary of the interior to lease to private companies the right to extract minerals from national forestland. The act also empowered the secretary to withdraw land from leasing if either he or the House Interior or Senate Energy Committee determined that an emergency required that the land be protected from development. In 1978 Interior Secretary Cecil Andrus used the emergency provision to withdraw 110 million acres of land from development, after Congress had failed to pass legislation to protect them.[20] Thus did the Carter administration substitute its judgement for that of Congress.

The election of 1980 brought a different administration to Washington. The laws remained substantially the same: tilted toward environmental protection but conferring wide discretion on administrators and on certain congressional committees. In May 1981 the new interior secretary had before him some 343 applications from oil companies that wanted to drill in a national forest area located just south of Glacier National Park, in Montana. Fearing what Watt might do, the House Interior Committee adopted a resolution ordering him to withdraw the entire 1.5 million acres from mineral leasing. Watt considered challenging the constitutionality of the committee's order; instead, he issued the order withdrawing the lands from leasing. Thereupon the Mountain States Legal Foundation, which he had headed before his appointment as interior secretary, challenged his action in court, giving rise to charges of collusion between the secretary and his former colleagues. In December 1981 a federal district court judge sustained the House committee's order. In subsequent maneuvers the committee agreed to rescind its order in return for an undertaking by Watt not to authorize leasing in the Montana national forest, at least until after the 1982 congressional elections.

Partly to end such maneuvering, the Supreme Court in 1983 declared the legislative veto unconstitutional. The Court ruled that the Constitution authorized only one procedure for lawmaking: passage of a bill by Congress, followed by the president's signature or by enactment by two-thirds majorities of both houses of Congress over the president's veto. A scheme that violated this procedure was impermissible under the Constitution.

The Court's ruling affected more than 200 laws that contained the legislative veto, but its impact on the relative power of Congress and the president seemed to vary from case to case. Where the courts found that Congress was using the veto to interfere in matters that were essentially administrative, they blocked the veto but let the executive's power stand. Where judges deemed that a statute gave the executive a power which was inherently legislative and which Congress would not have delegated without believing that it retained control in its own hands, they struck down the executive's authority, as well as the legislative veto. Such was one court's ruling in a case involving President Reagan's decision not to spend more than $5 billion appropriated for housing and other assistance to low-income individuals, in order to reduce the deficit. The president had acted under the Impoundment Control Act of 1974, which gave him power to impound funds, subject to the condition that he notify Congress and release the funds if Congress passed a resolution disapproving his impoundment. The Supreme Court's 1983 ruling against the legislative veto voided the latter provision, but President Reagan assumed that he retained the impoundment power without the legislative veto. The effect would have been to give him an item veto. But the court ruled against him, holding that the purpose of the impoundment-control statute was not to empower the president to spend or not as he saw fit but the opposite. If the legislative veto fell, so must the president's authority to impound funds. The court ordered the funds released, in accordance with the appropriations.[21]

Thus, the prohibition of the legislative veto, which was seen initially as a blow to congressional pretensions, apparently affects the powers of the executive as well. It was indeed, as the Supreme Court argued in 1983, a perversion of the institutions and processes ordained in 1787, and it was subject to abuse. But it also represented an attempt to adapt an eighteenth-century frame of government to twentieth-century realities—specifically, the need in a modern nation to delegate broad powers to the executive, without sacrificing the control that rightfully belongs to the representative assembly.

Ironically, the separation of powers has plunged us into personal government. Congress passes loosely worded statutes.* The pressures of time and other business cause the habit of vague statute writing to spread to areas where circumstances are not compelling. Implementation rests with an executive chosen by a distinct political process. Because of the disengagement of legislative and executive

---

*Louis Fisher argues that the need for flexibility in timing (allowing the president to take action in the event that certain circumstances come to pass) and for fact-finding (permitting variations in standards, such as minimum wages, in different regions) necessitates the delegation of discretion to the president.[22]

power, the course of policy sometimes does an about-face with the change of administration, even though there has been no material change in the law or in public opinion relating to the law.

There is, of course, something to be said for personal government. Leaders only loosely bound by law can act energetically, flexibly, quickly to meet situations as they present themselves. Despite these advantages, though, the tradition of liberty to which America subscribes prefers government based on law. It is less exciting but more broadly accountable. It is slower and more cumbersome; but by its stability and continuity it gives a sound basis for planning, and by its universal application it takes away the advantage that some citizens might gain by having friends in high places.

In the American tradition the notion of separated powers has always been closely linked to the promise of the rule of law.* We would avoid corruption by confining the exercise of discretion to lawmakers and to a highly visible and electorally accountable chief executive. Clearly worded laws and incorruptible courts would discourage appointed officials from abusing the public trust. Yet our adherence to the forms of separation seems not to have saved us from the abuse of power by those in high places. We have become almost inured to the idea that legislators and their staff members, high-ranking members of the administration, and influential people in the private sector will interact together in determining the pace of enforcement and the flow of disbursements. Hardly anyone is surprised, or much troubled, when a former White House aide, now set up in the lobbying business, trades on his friendship with erstwhile associates to win favorable treatment for well-heeled clients—sometimes even for a foreign government. It is the kind of thing that the framers regarded as characteristic of monarchical governments. Now it has become endemic under the Constitution as well.

What is ultimately at stake here is popular control over policy. In

---

* The Massachusetts Constitution of 1780, drafted by John Adams and now the world's oldest written constitution still in force, links the separation of powers directly to the notion of a government of laws: "In the government of the Commonwealth, the legislative department shall never exercise the executive and judicial powers, or either of them; the executive shall never exercise the legislative and judicial powers, or either of them; the judicial shall never exercise the legislative and executive powers, or either of them; to the end it may be a government of laws and not of men."[23]

this chapter we have reviewed several cases centering on the issue of the environment versus development. Public opinion supports environmental protection, even at the cost of obstructing the exploitation of new sources of energy.[24] The laws framed during the 1970s reflect this opinion. On the other hand, a fair reading of Ronald Reagan's record, opinions, and political associates shows that he has consistently favored a more vigorous exploration for oil and less regulation of business, and Reagan won the last two elections decisively, over men who placed high value on environmental protection.

In view of these facts, how should the laws on the environment be administered? For guidance, we can turn to *The Federalist*, Number 71, in which Hamilton argues that the "deliberate sense of the community" should control the government's actions. Because the public mind can sometimes be swept away by a "sudden breeze of passion," the president's term must be long, to fortify his courage to resist these transient popular moods. The legislature can also develop "humors" that cause it to forget the public good; the executive must resist these pressures, too. "It is one thing to be subordinate to the laws, and another to be dependent on the legislative body," says Hamilton. Note that he is not contending that the executive should be free to ignore the law. Whatever he personally might have thought of such an argument, it would not have served the cause of ratification in 1788. For the founding generation, the voice of the legislature, speaking through constitutional statutes, expressed the will of the regime. Presidential strength and independence were needed, not to resist or bend the laws but to see that they were applied firmly and without favor.

Modern conditions have unavoidably expanded the executive's discretion. The separation of powers places that discretion in the hands of a person whose electoral arrangements were designed partly to insulate him from accountability for particular actions, so that he would be free from whimsical public opinion and the pressure of legislators. The result is that a substantial part of the government's authority has started to drift away from popular accountability. Meanwhile, the Supreme Court, responding to indications that congressional attempts to recover a role in policy-making have led to growing abuses, has begun to insist that the Constitution be interpreted more strictly.

We are at an impasse. Unless we can find ways to induce closer cooperation between executive authority and the representative assembly, we must sacrifice either the effectiveness of our government or its accountability.

CHAPTER 10

Managing the Economy

To a very large extent a president's reputation, and thus his ability to govern effectively, are based on the performance of the nation's economy. Perhaps the leading factor in changing a close and uncertain race into a decisive victory for Ronald Reagan over Jimmy Carter in 1980 was the devastating question he put at the close of their final debate, when he asked voters to consider whether they were "better off" than they had been when Carter took office four years earlier. On the basis of that simple question many who had been undecided seemed to conclude that it was time for new leadership. Two years later a feeling that President Reagan's policies were responsible for unemployment and continuing high interest rates led to sharp losses for his party's candidates in that year's congressional races. In 1984 a sense of brightening economic prospects helped reelect the president by a handsome margin.

The popular feeling that the president is responsible for the state of the economy is also reflected in law. The Employment Act of 1946 makes it "the responsibility of the federal government . . . to promote maximum employment, production, and purchasing power" for all those willing and able to work and singles out the president as the official who is "to foster and promote free competitive enterprise, to avoid economic fluctuations or to diminish the effects thereof, and to maintain employment, production, and purchasing power." To accomplish these ends, the president is called upon to propose "a program for carrying out [this] policy . . . , together with such recommendations for legislation as he may deem necessary or desirable."[1]

The president's responsibility, in public opinion and in law, is clear, but his powers are not commensurate. To begin with, he has very little control over a number of factors bearing on economic performance—such things as the price of fuel, the climate, and the policies of foreign governments on interest rates, the repayment of debt, and the stimulation of competitive industries. If his own economic doctrines are clear, a president may seek to persuade other people to act sympathetically, but in the end, if they choose to respond to other imperatives, his powers of coercion are limited.

These exogenous factors are a constraint, but they leave plenty of room for the policies of the federal government to influence the performance of the economy. The expenditures of the federal government now account for about one-quarter of the gross national product; federal receipts (taxes and social insurance contributions) are the equivalent of just under one-fifth.* The policies that shape these figures are made by the interaction of the executive and legislative branches. In addition, monetary policies (the amount of money in the system, the supply of credit, and interest rates) are set primarily by the Federal Reserve Board, the authority of which rests on law and the members of which are appointed by the president, subject to confirmation by the Senate. Thus, the interactions of the political branches have a major impact on the performance of the nation's economy.

Yet our political system mocks the promise of accountability. Instinctively we hold the president responsible for economic policies and their impact, and the laws confirm this instinct; but the president's powers are severely limited. Effective economic management requires close cooperation not only between the president and Congress but with countless other authorities as well, some of which are independent of presidential control. The system inhibits control,

---

*In 1983 federal expenditures totaled 24.8 percent, while receipts stood at 19.4 percent, according to Commerce Department figures.[2]

makes it impossible to assign responsibility for the course of the economy, and prevents the electorate from rendering an intelligent verdict.

In 1981 economist Lester Thurow announced that the United States had fallen to tenth among all nations in per capita gross national product. A year earlier, he wrote, it had been fifth. It was not difficult, he added, to devise a policy to reverse this slide. "The problem is political. . . . Every group has the ability to veto anything it does not like; no group or even coalition of groups has the ability to act positively."*

By the mid-1980s there were some signs of improvement in the nation's economy. Inflation and interest rates were down, prices on the stock exchanges rose to record levels, and consumer confidence was strong. Yet serious weaknesses persisted. Growth in the national product was sluggish. Unemployment stuck at around 7 percent of the work force and was even higher in the manufacturing sector; according to government statistics, the number of people working in factories declined by nearly 400,000 between 1984 and 1986.[5] Agriculture was no longer a profitable enterprise; since 1979 a negative gap had developed between the cost of farming and the prices farmers received for their products. Meanwhile, the average hourly earnings of nonfarm workers, which had been growing at a diminishing rate for the three decades before 1980, now began actually to decline.[6]

Several factors contributed to this decline; some of them (like the increasing competitiveness of foreign industries) were not the fault of public policies. But everyone recognized that the persistent inability of the federal government to live within its means was a drag on economic recovery. In 1985 the federal government spent $212 bil-

---

*Thurow concluded his analysis by arguing that "America must alter its structure of government. The men of 1776 [sic] may have designed a set of checks and balances that succeeded for the nation's first 200 hundred years, but they did not anticipate the dilemmas of the 1980s."[3] In mitigation of Thurow's alarming statistic, it should be noted that five of the countries that ranked above the United States in GNP per capita were oil-exporting states: Qatar, United Arab Emirates, Brunei, Kuwait, and Saudi Arabia. Thurow was not alone, however, in suggesting that America seemed to be heading for a decline reminiscent of Great Britain's, which ranked twenty-third on a list of 142 nations in GNP per capita in 1982.[4]

lion more than it raised. In 1986, defying the administration's initially rosy estimates, the deficit remained well above $200 billion, which brought the cumulative federal debt above the $2 trillion mark. (It took two centuries to amass a federal debt of $1 trillion. In just six years that figure had doubled. The result is that until budget surpluses make it possible to reduce the debt, interest payments at rates of 10 percent will consume at least the first $200 billion of revenues each year.)

The opposition party always deplores deficits. No one was more adept at charging Democrats with "fiscal irresponsibility" than Ronald Reagan before he moved into the White House. Between 1981 and 1987, Republicans controlled both the White House and the Senate, and it was primarily the Democrats who raged that the administration was piling up huge debts which would constitute the first claim, probably a preemptive one, on future revenues.

Even apart from these partisan quarrels, however, a deficit of current proportions poses profound dangers for the nation. First, a large deficit draws resources from other sectors of the economy. Because revenues are insufficient to cover expenditures, the Treasury must borrow huge sums of money to pay the government's bills, forcing up interest rates, crowding out private borrowers, undermining industries that depend on credit (such as housing, automobiles, and agriculture), and preempting capital investments in industrial plants and public works (roads, bridges, airports, harbors).

A second danger arises from the fact that domestic sources of credit can no longer meet the demand for borrowing. In 1983 the American economy needed $280 billion in new funds to cover the public and private debt. Net domestic savings available for borrowing totaled only $250 billion. The difference of $30 billion had to be obtained from foreign sources. The year 1982 was the first in more than six decades in which foreigners invested more in the United States than American companies, banks, and individuals invested or lent abroad—$8.3 billion more. In 1983 this negative balance grew to $32.3 billion, and in 1984 it was estimated to exceed $80 billion. Martin Feldstein, then chairman of Reagan's Council of Economic Advisers, noted that in 1985 Americans would, for the first time since we became a modern, developed nation, owe more to foreign creditors than they to us.[7]

In that situation national independence depends upon the ability of the government to raise enough taxes to meet its interest payments, plus any scheduled retirements of principal, or to arrange new loans. It was New York City's difficulty along these lines in 1975 that led to its having to accept the dictates of bankers concerning its spending priorities and level of indebtedness. Poland in the early 1980s had to restructure its budget before creditors would grant new loans. Mexico and Brazil, among other developing nations, are currently at the mercy of their creditors in similar ways.

The American national economy is not yet in a condition of vulnerability comparable to New York City's in 1975 or Poland's in 1982. If the trend in deficits continues, however, American taxpayers will soon owe the first fruits of their labors to foreign creditors.

These considerations led a bipartisan group of senators in 1985 to frame a novel strategy for bringing the federal deficit under control. Named for its sponsors, Phil Gramm, Republican of Texas, Warren Rudman, Republican of New Hampshire, and Ernest Hollings, Democrat of South Carolina, the act required that the annual deficit in the federal budget be reduced to zero in large annual installments over a five-year period, beginning in 1986. Because Congress and the president had been unable to agree on taxes and cuts to achieve this goal, the senators proposed an automatic procedure. If government economists projected that the budget adopted for a given year would fail to reach the targeted reduction, proportional cuts would be applied automatically, across the board (with certain exemptions).

The Gramm-Rudman-Hollings bill was enacted and signed into law late in 1985, amid howls of anguish and a hail of challenges to its constitutionality. It was a desperate measure, a "mindless" constraint on the political process, made necessary by deadlock between a president and Congress who were unable to balance revenues and appropriations by normal constitutional processes. The new law exempted many of the most expensive items in the budget from the automatic cuts, including Social Security (which consumes nearly 20 percent of the federal budget), health benefits (just over 11 percent), payments for interest on the debt (almost 14 percent), and about half of the money devoted to national defense (about 13 percent).[8] That meant that the mandated reductions would have to come

from the remaining 40 percent of the budget, much of which supports programs that are supported by a wide consensus in and out
of government. Most observers thought that the target for reductions in the first year could be met without too much distress but
that the pain would increase dramatically in subsequent years, particularly if the president stuck by his pledges to continue the defense
buildup, to exempt Social Security and Medicare from cuts, and not
to raise taxes.

The deepest concerns raised by the new procedure, however, were
constitutional. One aspect—the one presented to the courts—was
fairly technical. It had to do with the procedure for implementing
the automatic cuts. In enacting the law, Congress confronted an old
dilemma. For both institutional and partisan reasons lawmakers were
unwilling to trust the president to determine whether the projected
deficit for the coming year justified automatic cuts, and if so, at what
level. Their concern was fed by the confessions of David Stockman,
whose book, significantly entitled *The Triumph of Politics*, told how
he, as director of the Office of Management and Budget for five
years, had cynically adjusted the figures in his budgetary presenta-
tions to Congress to suit the administration's purposes. To escape
from such manipulations, Gramm-Rudman-Hollings entrusted the
responsibility for projecting the deficit jointly to the OMB and the
Congressional Budget Office (CBO) and, in the event of disagreement between these two, empowered the comptroller general to make
the final determination. The question for the courts was whether the
role of the comptroller general met constitutional standards. The
Constitution vests the president with power to execute the laws.
The president appoints the comptroller general, but (unlike most
political appointees of the president) he is subject to removal by joint
resolution, which must be passed by both houses of Congress, then
signed or vetoed by the president, and, if vetoed, passed again by
two-thirds majorities in both houses.* Historically the General
Accounting Office, which the comptroller general heads, takes most
of its assignments for conducting audits of government programs
from Congress and is normally considered an agency of the legisla-

---

*This, by the way, is a greater majority than is required for impeachment, making
the comptroller general one of the most secure officials in the government.

tive branch. It is so listed, for example, in the official *United States Government Manual*. On July 7, 1986, the Supreme Court ruled that the comptroller general's assignment did indeed violate the Constitution.

Beyond this limited question, however, lay a more fundamental and far-reaching constitutional issue: whether the exigencies of economic management justified such elaborate efforts to insulate the process from the modes of political accountability envisioned by the framers of the Constitution. Technically Congress and the president were responsible for this law and could repeal or amend it anytime they thought better of it. By enacting it, they had declared that the restraint of spending* was the overriding necessity. At the same time, however, they admitted that they could not achieve it if they had to consider each item in the budget on its merits. The passage of the act thus signaled a breakdown of the constitutional system. After five years of deadlock between president and Congress over budget priorities, they had resorted to an automatic mechanism for determining the level of appropriations, and because Congress did not trust the president to administer the law objectively, both had in desperation skirted the procedures established in the first and second articles of the Constitution.

To understand how we came to this impasse, it will be useful briefly to review the course of economic policy-making during the past two decades. It is a story of conflicting policies, set in motion by authorities that have too little incentive to cooperate.

When Ronald Reagan came to power in 1981, the economy was mired in a protracted slump. The president's remedy was an economic policy that combined increased expenditures for national defense, reductions in domestic social programs, and tax cuts. In budgetary terms, the defense increases more than canceled out the savings in domestic social programs. Thus, the commitment to cut taxes seemed to mean large deficits. The administration believed otherwise. Tax cuts would stimulate investment and lead to greater productivity, which would soon have the effect of increasing govern-

---

*Not balancing the budget. The revenue side was left out of the automatic process. Gramm-Rudman-Hollings was a clear victory for the president on this score.

mental revenues, even from lowered rates of taxation.

Members of the Federal Reserve Board, meanwhile, were convinced that the root of the nation's economic problems was inflation and that the way to curb inflation was to reduce the supply of money. By raising the discount rate, the board could slow the growth in the money supply, meaning that less money would be chasing the available goods and services. One effect of this policy was to cause interest rates to rise, as competitive borrowers, including the government, bid up the cost of money. High interest rates made it difficult for young families to purchase houses and cars, and industries that depend on borrowed money (farming, construction, automobiles, banking) started laying off workers or sliding toward bankruptcy.

The effect of the Fed's monetary policy was to counter the president's fiscal policy, by increasing the demand on the government's welfare services and discouraging investment. Did the Reagan administration object to the monetary strategy of the Federal Reserve Board? The evidence—statements by Treasury Secretary Donald Regan, economic adviser Martin Feldstein, OMB Director David Stockman, and other spokesmen—was contradictory.

The biggest problem with the Reagan approach, though, was that the president was unable to push it through Congress. He did score some dramatic tactical victories along the way. By adroitly using the congressional budgeting process and wringing every possible vote out of his fellow Republicans and the conservative Democrats, he gained an apparent commitment to his approach. But to achieve these victories, he had to make damaging concessions to powerful legislators,[9] and before the end of his first year in office there were signs that Congress was beginning to chafe under the disciplines that the president was seeking to impose.

The previous administration had faced many of the same problems but had taken a different path to try to solve them. In terms of budgeting priorities the Carter administration exerted greater discipline on national defense. But the most important difference was the concern for balance of payments. For President Carter and his economists the most threatening factor to the American economy was the drain of money to pay for imported oil, which was igniting inflation and reducing funds for investment at home. To stop this hemorrhaging, the president proposed several measures designed to curb the consumption of oil, such as import quotas and fees, lower speed limits, and removal of price controls on fuel. Carter's party had huge majorities in Congress, but the president was unable to persuade his fellow partisans to adopt his policies. Voters, sensing the disarray, denied Carter a second term in office.

The problem of inflation had been around at least since the late 1960s. It had been caused then by the refusal of the Johnson administration to choose between the Great Society and the war in Vietnam. These enormous demands on the economy, unaccompanied by discipline in the form of increased taxes, touched off sharp increases in wages and prices.

Voters in 1968 punished Johnson's policies by putting Republicans in the White House but left the Democrats in control of Congress. By 1970 the new president, Richard Nixon, who favored a free-market approach, was blaming Congress for excessive spending, while congressional leaders argued that the solution lay in wage-price controls. As we noted earlier, Congress by a broadly worded statute gave Nixon power to impose controls, and the president in 1971 adroitly reversed his stand and implemented a far-reaching program of economic controls.

The details of the policy—what would be controlled and especially who would be responsible for administering the policy—were terribly important, but the Democrats in Congress, having made it all seem so easy, were poorly positioned to criticize what the president was doing. The result was a short-term political gain for Nixon, but in the longer run it became evident that a malfunctioning of the constitutional system had allowed the president to exert virtually autocratic control over the economy for more than a year and postponed for several critical years the time when the nation would confront its basic economic problems.

These brief sketches of economic policy-making lead to an inescapable conclusion: Our constitutional arrangements frustrate sound approaches to economic regulation.* There were other factors con-

---

* Herbert Stein, who was chairman of the Council of Economic Advisers under President Nixon, has reached the same conclusion about recent economic policy-making, although his remedy is to call for stronger political leadership.[10]

tributing to the problem besides the unfitness of the system: the inherent complexity of the issues and the natural tendency of elected officials to seek short-term relief rather than to impose sacrifices in support of fundamental remedies for the long run. But after due allowance for these factors one must recognize that the American economy has been floundering in large part because the Constitution operates to frustrate intelligent consideration and vigorous action by coordinated, responsible actors.

Whose fault was it, in 1981, that savings were eroding, mortgages were out of reach for most families, able-bodied people could not find work, shabby industrial equipment was not being replaced, and we continued to import great quantities of oil from the Persian Gulf?[11] For political purposes the president blamed Congress and the regulators, while leaders in Congress blamed the president, OMB, the Federal Reserve Board, or one another. Meanwhile, the people did not know whom to blame, who was responsible. It was true that the president had a program; but Congress changed it, and the Federal Reserve Board counteracted it. Several leaders in Congress offered economic packages of their own that year (the chairman of the House Ways and Means Committee, on taxes, and the chairman of the House Budget Committee, for overall fiscal policy), but even when they seemed able to overcome the natural tendency of legislatures toward fragmentation, the president's veto loomed to dash their hopes.

The Fed's primary assignment—to control the supply of money— is fairly narrow and explicit, and it might be argued that, in this area at least, the rationale for its independence is somewhat analogous to the judiciary's. As Hamilton said in *The Federalist*, Number 78, courts have "neither force nor will." They depend on legislation and the Constitution for declarations of intent and on the executive for powers of enforcement. Their function is simply to ensure that the stated purpose of the law is carried out, unless it conflicts with the more fundamental intent of the people, as declared in the Constitution.

By this analogy, if we assume that the creation of the FRB is not intended to compromise the American commitment to popular government, the discretionary aspects of its mission ought to be discharged in the legislation that created it or by the administrative regulations promulgated by the executive. The work of the FRB should be purely ministerial: applying the intent of Congress to the evolving circumstances of the economy.

But is this so? In December 1985 a rash of corporate take-overs provoked the Fed to take an action that illustrates the kind of power it has and illustrates as well the conflicting authorities that are involved in regulating the American economy.

Throughout 1985 all debt—including that held by consumers, by corporations, and by the government at various levels—had been growing at twice the rate of the economy as a whole. This development worried the Fed, because one of its primary ways of regulating the economy is to raise or lower interest rates. If debt increased too much, even a slight upward adjustment of rates could reduce corporate profits, cause bankruptcies, raise unemployment, and trigger a harsh recession. Take-overs were adding to the problem because small companies were financing their bids to acquire larger companies by selling low-quality bonds, and corporate executives were fighting back by buying out stockholders, using the same device. Wall Street calls these junk bonds because the purchaser puts up very little of his own money to buy them. The Fed proposed to put a brake on take-over wars by raising the margin requirement to 50 percent, the same as that for common stocks. The change was to go into effect one month after its announcement on December 6, 1985.

The administration reacted sharply to the Fed's announcement. President Reagan's position was that restraints on borrowing were a mistake. It was better to trust the marketplace than to rely on the manipulation of a government agency. In a series of moves coordinated from the White House, the Justice Department submitted a request to delay the imposition of a margin requirement, and the Treasury, Commerce, and Labor departments, plus the Council of Economic Advisers and the Office of Management and Budget, all filed endorsements.

In an analysis of the administration's response the *New York Times* commented: "Such an exercise would have been impossible during the first Reagan term because the agencies were divided, and Mr. [Paul] Volcker [the chairman of the Fed] had important allies on the White House staff, in the OMB and in the CEA. The multi-agency initiative on this issue showed that this time around, Mr. Volcker has not a single body of support within the entire administration edifice of economic policy-making." The *Times* went on to observe that soon President Reagan would be filling two vacancies on the board, thus giving the president's appointees a majority. Presumably this would ensure that future decisions by the full board would be more sympathetic to the administration's general approach. But not interest-rate policy. That is made in a larger forum: the twelve-member Open Market Committee, which includes the seven board members plus the presidents of five of the twelve regional Federal Reserve Banks. Mr. Volcker, the *Times* noted, was expected "to continue to be the dominant force on the Open Market Committee."[12]

Two points are underscored by this episode. The first is that the Fed's mandate allows plenty of room for the exercise of judgment. It is not simply a board of experts, objectively applying agreed-upon principles to a shifting set of circumstances. The principles themselves are controversial, and political leaders work very hard to impose their opinions on the system. The chairman of the Fed is himself one of those political leaders.

That leads to the second point: Whatever public opinion and the law may hold, the president does not have the reins of the economy in his hands. It is hard enough for him to keep control over such political appointees as department secretaries and the heads of the OMB and the CEA, not to mention the members of his own staff. Over the FRB, once its members have been appointed, he has virtually no control at all. He and his aides can bristle at them. Gradually, by filling vacancies over the course of years, he can seek to reshape its makeup.* But a determined and astute man like Volcker can impose policies that are at odds with those of the administration.

There are constraints on the Fed, too, of course. If it were abusing its legislative intent, Congress could replace it or amend its mandate, narrowing its discretion.† Though members of Congress

---

* To insulate them from political pressure, the seven members of the board are appointed for staggered terms of fourteen years each. The president names the chairman to a four-year term. Volcker was named chairman by Carter in 1978; Reagan reappointed him in 1982.

† Milton Friedman, for example, argues that a "monetary rule" to control the supply of money should be imposed, either by legislation or, preferably, by constitutional amendment, and that the Federal Reserve Board should be absorbed into the Treasury Department.[13]

repeatedly threaten to do this, it has not happened.

But there is a deeper issue. Congress has apparently deemed it better for popular government to set monetary policy off limits for elected officials—in a way analogous to the Bill of Rights. If this is the rationale, however, we have acquiesced in a fundamental compromise of democracy. Monetary policy is different in principle from civil liberties, and the rationale for the independence of the judiciary to protect fundamental freedoms does not cover a central banking system. Not only is monetary policy highly controversial, but it works to distribute material benefits. All citizens have a stake in economic prosperity, but experts vehemently disagree about the proper monetary policy to follow in different cases. In these circumstances those who make these political judgments, for the effects of which elected officials are held responsible, ought themselves to be electorally accountable, at least indirectly (as the secretary of state is, for example).

In the existing constitutional framework the dilemma is acute. Congress cannot exercise the power of monetary control by itself. The president, whose special constitutional virtues are vigor, dispatch, and a capacity for secrecy, but not representativeness, ought not to have such policy-making power by himself without the guidance of clear and definite legislation, which in this case, as we have noted, is impossible. We are back where we started. There is nowhere in the constitutional framework to put this power. There is no power, capable of quick and decisive action, whose authority is based on broad and ongoing political accountability.

During the twentieth century the size and complexity of the public sector have steadily grown, increasing the government's impact on the economy and making management more difficult. Each of the government's new activities rests on legislation, which can be repealed whenever Congress concludes that it is no longer needed. Yet Congress has become the rallying place for those who deplore the growth of the public sector. In the deep postwar economic crisis of 1920 and 1921, for example, many voices cried out for curbs on the public sector. The congressional response was the Budget and Accounting Act of 1921, which created the Bureau of the Budget, put it in the Treasury Department, and required that all agency requests for public funds be channeled through this bureau and made part of an overall governmental budget. The idea was discipline. The executive branch must no longer send requests for appropriations to Congress piecemeal. But the effect was a further empowerment of the presidency.

By the late 1930s the scope and weight of the federal government had grown enormously. Then World War II produced another tremendous growth of activity for the government in the field of national security, much of which subsided after the war. But the long-term development of public responsibility for regulation and intervention in the domestic economy did not end. The Employment Act of 1946 made the federal government responsible for full employment, gave the task of proposing policies to meet this goal to the president, and created the Council of Economic Advisers, a team of economists assigned to supply information and analysis to Congress and the president, to enable them to meet the goals set for the new positive program of economic management.

Looking back on these developments, we are tempted to see a pattern and intention that were certainly not fully formed in the minds of those who promoted them. The New Deal, for example, was not planned and announced as Roosevelt's intention during the 1932 presidential campaign. It emerged as a collection of ad hoc responses to particular problems. Behind it was a pragmatism, a willingness to use the energy and authority of the federal government to deal with such problems as unemployment, the needs of the disabled and elderly, and distress in the agricultural sector.

The idea that the federal government should take positive steps to ensure the health of the economy as a whole dawned only gradually, and its implications for our system of government have never been more than dimly understood. We have never thought very carefully about the impact of these massive changes on our constitutional system. Some very thoughtful people addressed the question in one form or another—not only Brownlow's committee but two commissions under the chairmanship of former President Herbert Hoover, President Kennedy's task force on independent regulatory agencies under the direction of James Landis, and others. But these efforts, focusing on particular problems of governance, tended to skirt the fundamental constitutional issue.

The assumption of an active role in economic management has

caused great weight to swing to the executive, not only to administer the vast array of programs and to propose new ones but to assemble an annual budget and analyze the performance of the economy. It is worth noting that these last two functions, which were fundamental to the new responsibilities, were originally assigned by Congress to the executive in an effort to curtail executive aggrandizement. The Bureau of the Budget was set up to force the executive to fit proposed expenditures into an overall plan, and the Council of Economic Advisers was established by a conservative-dominated Congress to tell presidents, particularly Democratic ones, that the economy could not absorb their grandiose schemes.* In fact, both these new agencies readily became instruments of presidential policy-making. Budgeting is essentially an executive function. The president's power to appoint and remove its members made the CEA part of the president's political arsenal. The science of economics proceeds from theories which are fiercely controverted among the practitioners. Presidents from Truman to Reagan have differed sharply in their notions about the proper role of government in the economy and the proper limits of the public sector, but none has failed to find prominent economists who would give him the advice he wanted. Thus, ironically, a series of devices intended to discipline presidents in the name of natural truth have each turned into a tool of presidential leadership.[14]

By the 1970s Congress was ready to conclude that the new governmental activism ought not to be controlled exclusively by agencies within the president's own establishment. Yet Congress lacked the organs and procedures to analyze the economy and to develop, or even to criticize, an overall budget. To restore constitutional balance, Congress would first have to equip itself for a major role in fiscal policy-making. But was it possible? The natural forces of the system seemed to be opposed. The genius of Congress was to represent the nation's great internal diversity and to deliberate, slowly and carefully. Economic management required coherence, a comprehensive outlook, and decisiveness.

The Congressional Budget Act of 1974, passed in the midst of a

---

*It is somewhat ironic, in view of these partisan origins, that the CEA under Martin Feldstein's chairmanship was deeply resented by the Reagan administration for trying to perform the function envisioned by its Republican creators.

congressional "resurgence" against the "imperial presidency," imposed a new organization and discipline on legislative consideration of the budget. As the legislative equivalent of the CEA, Congress created the Congressional Budget Office (CBO) and equipped it with a strong staff to analyze the performance of the economy and project the cost and fiscal impact of public programs. The legislative analogue to the OMB was the budget committee in each house the function of which was to collect spending proposals from various authorizing committees and fit them into an overall budget resolution in time for Congress to adopt ceilings for each of its committees.

Many commentators predicted that the procedures adopted in 1974 would fail. They seemed to demand that institutions perform contrary to their design. Yet the record in these first years of trial suggests that congressmen know the stakes. There have been many temptations to compromise the integrity of the CBO, to miss deadlines, and to ignore the constraints of budget resolutions, and Congress has not always resisted them.[15] But the process has worked better than almost anyone expected, at least as far as giving Congress a serious role in budget making is concerned.

The question here is whether it has provided an effective, accountable process for managing a modern economy. Is the government able to develop an accurate and coherent picture of the performance of the economy? Is it able to react as fast and forcefully as it needs to when economic conditions change? Is the government able to impose sacrifices in order to achieve its economic goals? Above all, do current procedures facilitate popular government? Do they go as far as possible in encouraging the development of a popular will about the goals of the economy and in making that will determinative over the actions of public officials?

Even with the resurgence of legislative power, which (by the most hopeful interpretation) tends to restore the intended constitutional balance, two major problems remain. One is the persistence of independent centers of power over parts of the economy, such as the regulation of particular sectors by independent commissions and the control of the money supply by the FRB. The significance of these sectors for the performance of the economy as a whole is enormous, and while the commissions and boards that administer them are theoretically subject to political control through legislation, they are in fact and by inertia substantially autonomous. They remain so in part because of institutional jealousies between the two major political branches, and the result is a fundamental compromise of popular government.

The second major problem is that Congress, by itself, is an unfit instrument for popular control over economic management, which requires a comprehensive perspective. Congress has adopted internal procedures which strengthen its capacity to take such a perspective, but its electoral basis is still attuned to local considerations. Most representatives and senators do not rise and fall on the performance of the economy. They are elected and reelected on the basis of their ties to a particular constituency.[16]

While this remains true, a constitutional system that distributes power between the branches cannot give us effective and accountable governance over the economy.

CHAPTER 11

Making War

The provision of the Constitution giving the war-making power to Congress was dictated, as I understand it, by the following reasons. Kings had always been involving and impoverishing their people in wars, pretending generally, if not always, that the good of the people was the object. This our Convention understood to be the most oppressive of all kingly oppressions, and they resolved to so frame the Constitution that no one man *should hold the power of bringing this oppression upon us.*

> Congressman Abraham Lincoln,
> in a letter to his law partner, W. H. Herndon
> February 15, 1848*

Grenada is a small, lovely tropical island in the southeastern Caribbean Sea. It has a fine natural harbor at the capital city of St. George's. Until October 1983 it was known to Americans primarily as a yachting port. Its chief products are bananas, nutmeg, and cocoa beans, but it has lately had an adverse balance of trade, which makes it dependent on financial help from Great Britain, its principal trading partner.

Christopher Columbus discovered Grenada in 1498, but Carib

---

*Arthur Schlesinger contends that Lincoln's letter to Herndon "unquestionably expressed the original intent" of the framers.[1] I agree.

Indians controlled it until France claimed and settled it in the middle of the seventeenth century. It remained subject to the French crown until it was formally ceded to Britain by the Treaty of Paris in 1763. Apart from a brief interlude of French rule again in the late eighteenth century, it has remained in association with Great Britain ever since. In 1967 the island became a self-governing state within the Commonwealth of Nations. As such, the United Kingdom is legally responsible for its external affairs and defense, and its governor is appointed by the crown on advice of the British prime minister.

In the late 1970s Grenada became the scene of political unrest. Maurice Bishop seized power by a coup d'état in 1979 and installed himself as prime minister. At first Bishop espoused Marxism and allied himself with Cuba's Fidel Castro, but in May 1983 he visited Washington to seek better relations with the American government. He returned to Grenada with little to show for his efforts, and on October 13, 1983, a small group of military policemen seized him, along with three members of his cabinet and two labor leaders, and placed them under house arrest. The leader of this new coup was Bernard Coard, a former deputy prime minister and avowed Marxist. Coard resigned on October 14, citing "vicious rumors" that he planned to assassinate Bishop. The remaining leaders of the coup a week later staged a boisterous demonstration, during which Bishop was in fact murdered. The following day the new Revolutionary Military council claimed power, with former Army Commanding General Hudson Austin as its head.

Two factors drew American attention to this Caribbean turmoil. Grenada was the site of a medical school in which several hundred Americans were enrolled. Some feared that these students might be taken hostage in the event that the coup leaders wanted to embarrass the United States, as in Iran in 1979. The other factor was a report that Cubans were building a long, hard runway on the island, ostensibly to encourage the tourist industry.

Ever since Castro came to power in 1959, proclaimed himself a Marxist, and began to develop close ties to the Soviet Union, Americans have perceived in Cuba a threat to its hegemony in Central America. That sense of hegemony has deep roots. In 1903 President Theodore Roosevelt intervened against Colombia on behalf of pro-

American revolutionaries in Panama, securing their independence (despite treaty guarantees to Colombia) in return for rights to build a canal joining the oceans. Roosevelt justified American involvement in Central America by declaring that the United States would exercise "an international police power" over nations which, by their inability or unwillingness to ensure justice and order at home or in their relations with other countries, were violating the rights of the United States or inviting foreign aggression. Roosevelt's corollary to the Monroe Doctrine articulated the justification not only for his own intervention in Panama but for those of Presidents Pierce, Taft, and Coolidge in Nicaragua; Taft, Wilson, Kennedy, and Johnson in the Dominican Republic; and Wilson to occupy Haiti, invade Veracruz, and send General Pershing and a force of 15,000 soldiers into Mexico in pursuit of the outlaw general, Francisco ("Pancho") Villa.[2] The advent of Castro introduced a new and more dangerous aspect to the situation, one made grimly manifest in 1962, when President Kennedy took the world to the brink of nuclear war in order to block the placement of Soviet missiles there.*

In October 1983 American attention was concentrating on Lebanon, where a truck loaded with explosives crashed into a building and killed 241 Marines who had been sleeping there. While the nation was still reeling from this disaster, suddenly, early on a Tuesday morning, October 25, 1983, an invading force of about 1900 American marines and infantrymen swarmed onto Grenada. Native children and civilians awoke to the grinding gears of military vehicles. Medical students scrambled under their dormitory beds, terrified by the sound of artillery and rifle fire and the shouts of the invaders. Grenada had almost no police force, much less armed forces, and the invading American troops at first met little resistance. Soon, however, the clamor aroused some of the 700 Cubans who had been working on the runway, who took up small arms and began to fire

---

*Note, by the way, that there was no congressional consultation during the Cuban missile crisis. It was accomplished, said Theodore Sorensen, not apologetically, "by executive order, presidential proclamation and inherent powers, not under any resolution or act of Congress." When congressional leaders were informed at the last minute of the action President Kennedy was about to take, Sorensen found their reaction "captious and inconsistent," though he did note that they reacted to the plans outlined in the briefing "the same way most of us originally did."[3]

back. The fight was brief. Within a matter of hours the Americans were fully in control of the island and able safely to evacuate the American students and other citizens. It took just a few more days to root out pockets of resistance and round up Coard, Austin, three other coup leaders, and 7 soldiers of the defunct People's Revolutionary Army, all of whom were charged with complicity in the murder of Bishop and his associates.

In the context of other serious problems, notably the conflicts in Lebanon, El Salvador, and Nicaragua, the relative ease and tidiness of the operation in Grenada were a source of great satisfaction to the American people. We had, as the president pointed out, not only protected our own citizens but thwarted "a brutal gang of leftist thugs" and given "help in the restoration of democratic institutions in Grenada."[4] We had acted to remove a threat to our allies in Venezuela and sent a message to Marxists in Cuba, El Salvador, and Nicaragua that our toleration of their machinations could not be taken for granted. Our armed forces had also been given a proud outing, something they badly needed in the wake of the frustrations from Vietnam to Lebanon.

On the negative side, we had annoyed and embarrassed our allies, particularly Prime Minister Margaret Thatcher of England, who felt a special responsibility for Grenada as a partner in the Commonwealth and who was dealing at that moment with vociferous opposition to her decision to accept a new generation of American nuclear missiles on European soil. Despite her gratitude for firm American support during Britain's recent war against Argentina in the Falklands, Mrs. Thatcher spoke harsh words about the American invasion of Grenada. If we were so concerned about Cuba, she asked, why had we not taken the fight there, so much closer to our shores?

Criticism came from other quarters as well. Many feared that it had been foolish to assume responsibility for the "restoration" of democratic institutions in Grenada. Others argued that, in violating various provisions of the Charter of the Organization of American States and of the Charter of the United Nations, which forbids the "threat or use of force" in international affairs except for purposes of defense against "armed attack," we had undermined the rule of law and weakened the moral authority of our condemnations of Soviet actions in Poland and Afghanistan.

Almost lost in the controversy over policy were the constitutional issues. By what authority had the president ordered this invasion? Did he not need a congressional declaration of war in order to invoke his powers as commander in chief? Should he not have consulted with Congress before committing American troops to this operation? Is it possible and right for one man, on the advice entirely of men (yes, men) of his own choosing, to take this country to war? The episode in Grenada ended too quickly for these questions to receive much attention, but it was a haunting reminder of times when presidential war making involved great suffering and loss for the United States, and a grim warning that nothing in the Constitution or in nearly two centuries of legislation had been able to induce the president to share his war-making power with anyone not of his own choosing.

As we have seen in chapter 7, two factors underlie the modern constitutional position of the commander in chief: the availability of a massive standing army and a network of treaties, congressional resolutions, and executive agreements by which the United States has assumed responsibility for security around the world. Both factors are rooted in a consensus: that many nations are threatened by communism, that the might and ambition of the Soviet Union make communism menacing, and that the United States is primarily responsible for "containing" the Soviet Union and its allies.

Testifying before a Senate committee in 1963, political scientist Richard Neustadt remarked that "when it comes to action risking war, technology has modified the Constitution."[5] There have been no formal amendments relating to war powers. Presidents have always been able to use military forces to protect the nation's vital interests, and several have not hesitated to do so, in Latin America or the Far East, if they thought that a show of military force would serve American interests. But a massive standing army and modern weaponry have greatly increased the president's constitutional power because the president's judgment is finally decisive in assessing threats to American interests and in deploying and using military forces. The traumatic experience in Vietnam, a disastrous war perpetrated by a quarter century of presidential decisions, led to a search for remedies within the context of the Constitution as modified by modern technology, but events even after Vietnam have shown that one man is still capable of taking the United States to war.

To understand how the Constitution's war powers led us into the war in Vietnam, we must return to the last months of the Truman administration. In 1952, after nearly two years of bitter warfare in Korea, Truman's National Security Council produced a document outlining "United States Objectives and Courses of Action with Respect to Southeast Asia."[6] The statement declared that it was America's interest "to prevent the countries of Southeast Asia from passing into the communist orbit, and to assist them to develop will and ability to resist communism from within and without. . . ." If Southeast Asia fell to the Chinese Communists, the free world would lose access to important sources of rubber, tin, rice, and petroleum, but even more important, the way would be open for communism to spread through India and the Middle East toward Europe and through Indonesia, Formosa, and the Philippines toward Japan. It was therefore "imperative," said the National Security Council, to oppose vigorously any overt attack by Chinese Communists in Southeast Asia, even if it meant diverting military strength from other areas, and to counteract subversion—the more likely form of Communist assault—by propaganda activities, by economic and technical assistance to French forces (which in 1952 insisted on bearing primary responsibility for ground combat in Indochina), by diplomatic efforts, by covert actions to disrupt Communist communications and to encourage overseas Chinese communities to pursue anti-Communist activities, and by teaching the American people to regard Southeast Asia as vital to American interests. In all these efforts, the statement concluded, the United States should seek the cooperation of "at least France and the United Kingdom," but in the event that their concurrence was not forthcoming," the United States should consider taking unilateral action."[7]

This document, framed by the NSC in 1952, provided a complete blueprint for the war that helped to ruin the presidencies of Lyndon Johnson and Richard Nixon.

President Eisenhower came into office in 1953 pledged to end the war in Korea. It was apparent from the start that his administration, particularly his secretary of state, John Foster Dulles, shared vehemently the anti-Communist convictions of Truman's NSC. The president himself, however, took a cautious approach toward the commitment of military forces in support of these ideas. When French forces retreated to their fortress at Dien Bien Phu and it appeared certain that they would have to surrender, the American ambassador to France, C. Douglas Dillon, communicated an urgent French request for military assistance. There was specific evidence of Chinese intervention in Indochina, said Dillon. He reported the opinion of the French commander in Indochina that a "relatively minor U.S. effort could turn the tide," but that, without American help, by the end of that week the fate of Dien Bien Phu would probably be sealed. Admiral Arthur Radford, chairman of the Joint Chiefs of Staff, stood with Dulles in urging a positive response to the French request, but other service chiefs, including General Matthew Ridgway of the army, remembering the costly and protracted struggle in Korea, urged caution. President Eisenhower told Dulles to sound out opinion on Capitol Hill. Congressional leaders said they would not support intervention unless the allies, particularly Britain, joined in the effort. Dulles knew that Britain could not be brought along in time, if ever.

After a conference with the president, Dulles cabled Dillon that it was not possible for the United States "to commit belligerent acts in Indochina without full political understanding with France and with other countries." In addition, wrote the secretary of state, congressional action "would be required." These conditions were, of course, impossible to meet. As the French foreign minister said to Ambassador Dillon, the time for building coalitions had passed. The fate of Indochina would be decided within ten days at Dien Bien Phu. The French would have to fight alone.

Without help from the United States, Dien Bien Phu, as expected, fell to the communists. Again Dulles argued for American intervention in Indochina, and again the matter was canvassed. Perhaps the French would now be more willing to grant "genuine freedom" to their colonies in Laos, Cambodia, and Vietnam, as Congress insisted. President Eisenhower gave Dulles the go-ahead to draft a congressional resolution. This time the Joint Chiefs of Staff dragged their feet, warning that Indochina had no decisive military targets and that intervention would divert limited military forces. Meanwhile, the French position in Vietnam deteriorated so rapidly that the question of saving the French was moot. Another approach would have to be found.[8]

The approach that evolved included both overt and covert aspects. The United States delegation at the Geneva peace talks stood aloof from the accords on Indochina but promised to "refrain from the threat or the use of force to disturb them" and to support free elections as a step toward reunifying Vietnam. Meanwhile, the president authorized a covert mission, headed by Edward Lansdale, to seek to stabilize and strengthen the Saigon regime. Lansdale reported that he would undertake paramilitary operations in Communist areas and wage "psycho-political warfare."[9]

John F. Kennedy came to the presidency pledged to replace Eisenhower's reliance on massive retaliation with a more flexible approach, including a capacity for "counterinsurgency." In light of the Lansdale mission, this was a somewhat ironic emphasis, but it is in the nature of covert activities that a president cannot reply candidly to his critics. Our involvement in global security has plunged our political life into a whole range of such deceptions.

On January 6, 1961, as Kennedy was preparing for his inauguration, Soviet Premier Nikita Khrushchev gave a boastful, bellicose speech lasting eight hours, in which he set forth the notion that three kinds of conflict were possible against capitalist countries: nuclear wars, conventional wars, and wars of national liberation. Nuclear wars must be avoided, said Khrushchev, because there would be no victor. Conventional conflicts involving nuclear powers were also dangerous because they might escalate into nuclear warfare. Wars of national liberation, on the other hand, would have vigorous Soviet support because they were a "just" means of advancing the Communist cause. In his first State of the Union message, President Kennedy made his response. "We must never be lulled into believing that either power [Russia or China] has yielded its ambitions for world domination—ambitions which they forcefully restated only a short time ago. On the contrary, our task is to convince them that aggression and subversion will not be profitable routes to pursue these ends."[10] To give substance to these strong words, Kennedy embarked on a buildup of conventional and counterinsurgency forces.

It soon became apparent that Vietnam was one place where Communists were capable of mounting a major "war of national liberation."[11] In terms of the oratorical blasts exchanged in January 1961, it was imperative for Kennedy to meet the challenge. But how? Military advisers were divided. In 1961 the Joint Chiefs estimated that it would take 40,000 United States troops to "clean up the Vietcong threat." General Maxwell Taylor, the president's military adviser, following a meeting with South Vietnamese Premier Ngo Dinh Diem, recommended that a 6,000- to 8,000-man United States force be sent to support South Vietnamese units in the Mekong delta. Taylor discounted the risk of a "major Asian war," commenting that North Vietnam was "extremely vulnerable to conventional bombing." Secretary of Defense Robert McNamara was less sanguine. In reporting to the president that he and the Joint Chiefs were "inclined" to support Taylor's recommendation, McNamara warned that the "struggle may be prolonged." Even if it did come to involve direct confrontation with North Vietnam and China, however, he thought it would not require more than 205,000 troops.

President Kennedy was skeptical about the strategic significance of Vietnam and reluctant to commit combat forces. He was also troubled about "static" coming from Congress, where senators, especially, were beginning to raise hard questions about the reported corruption and incompetence of the Diem regime. In November 1961 Kennedy rejected recommendations that he send ground combat forces to South Vietnam and authorize the bombing of North Vietnam, which would have flagrantly violated the Geneva accords of 1954. But he did approve a set of somewhat less flagrant violations: the dispatch of advisers to work in the field with South Vietnamese forces, American-manned helicopters to improve their mobility, American fighters and bombers to provide close air support, and a continuation of covert activities in both halves of the divided country.

Premier Diem was reportedly disappointed by this American response.[12] To ease his feelings, Kennedy sent instructions to the U.S. embassy in Saigon to soften its demands for reforms and indicate that it sought "close partnership" and consultation rather than control over the government of South Vietnam. This squabble turned out to be a harbinger. Diem either would not or could not bring about the reforms demanded by Washington and gain the support of his people. The Communists, after all, were engaging in their own acts of terror and subversion. While the American military commitment grew and casualties mounted, opponents of the Diem regime offered dramatic evidence of the depth of their disaffection, including the suicide by fire of a Buddhist monk in the streets of Saigon in June 1963. Finally, in the fall of 1963, President Kennedy authorized a coup against Diem. It took place on November 1, 1963, and left Premier Diem shot to death in his own quarters. Although Kennedy had apparently not intended that Diem be assassinated, he could hardly avoid responsibility for it.

By the time of his own assassination three weeks later, there were more than 16,000 American troops in Vietnam. American casualties had grown from 14 in 1961 to 109 in 1962 and to 489 in 1963. It was time for a new decision about how much more to commit to the struggle against communism in Southeast Asia.

The decision to escalate the war in Vietnam, and to make it an American war, belonged primarily to one man: Lyndon B. Johnson. In Woodrow Wilson's prophetic book on the presidency—written, as Clinton Rossiter put it, "before [Wilson] came to the Presidency, but not before he had begun to think about it"—he declared that if a president once won the admiration and confidence of the country, no one could withstand him. "If he rightly interpret the national thought and boldly insist upon it," wrote Wilson, "he is irresistible. . . ."[13] President Johnson was nothing if not bold in his insistence that he rightly understood the nation's responsibility in Southeast Asia, and for at least four years (until the spring of 1968) he was indeed irresistible.

While serving as Kennedy's vice president, Johnson had been a staunch supporter of the American presence in Vietnam. Reporting on his mission to Saigon in 1961, he had said that we would either have to help the non-Communist regimes in Indochina or "throw in the towel" and "pull back our defenses to San Francisco."[14] Furthermore, he believed strongly in the president's responsibility to make such decisions. He had strongly supported President Truman's intervention in Korea, although he later judged that Truman had made a political mistake (not a legal or constitutional one) in failing to obtain explicit support from Congress.

During 1964 the focus was on the presidential election campaign. President Johnson was determined to appear statesmanlike and cool-headed. His opponent, Senator Barry Goldwater of Arizona, had a reputation for belligerent anticommunism. In the context of the campaign there was little danger that Johnson would seem like a warmonger. In August 1964 Johnson reported that the North Vietnamese had fired torpedoes at an American destroyer in the Tonkin Gulf and asked Congress to pass a resolution authorizing him "to take all necessary measures to repel any armed attack against the forces of the United States and to prevent further aggression." Congress responded quickly and nearly unanimously. In the brief debate some senators wondered whether the resolution would endorse a change in policy or authorize a land war in Asia. Senator William Fulbright, Democrat of Arkansas, managing the bill, said that it would not. It was consistent with "our existing mission and our understanding of what we have been doing in South Vietnam for the last ten years." Yet when Senator John Sherman Cooper, Republican of Kentucky, suggested that the resolution gave the president "advance authority to take whatever action he may deem necessary respecting South Vietnam and its defense," Senator Fulbright admitted that it was so.[15]

The legal significance of the Tonkin Gulf Resolution was later brought into question. Nicholas Katzenbach, undersecretary of state, called it the "functional equivalent" of a declaration of war, though he, like President Johnson, insisted that the president had inherent authority, based on the commander-in-chief clause, to wage war in Vietnam if he judged that the nation's vital interests were threatened by enemy action there. The legal adviser to the State Department in 1966 presented the official justification for the constitutionality of the war. Although it cited the Tonkin Gulf Resolution and the SEATO treaty, it relied ultimately on the "constitutional powers of the President." It was unquestionably the president's responsibility, the department noted, to respond to attacks on the United States. In the twentieth century we had come to realize that "an attack on a country far from our shores" might threaten American security. "The Constitution leaves [it] to the President . . . to determine whether the circumstances of a particular armed attack are so urgent and the potential consequences so threatening to the security of the United States that he should act without formally consulting the Congress."[16] Resting on this theory, President Johnson waged war from

August 1964 until he left office more than four years later without ever obtaining the explicit consent of Congress.

By the fall of 1965 there were 170,000 American fighting men in Vietnam, and American airplanes were bombing North Vietnam on a regular basis. Still, the enemy kept coming, and the Johnson administration kept escalating the American response. By the end of 1967 the commitment and the costs were staggering: 480,000 troops in Vietnam, at an annual cost of $25 billion (about one-third of the defense budget). There were more than 9,000 American casualties in 1967 alone. The air force lost 950 aircraft to enemy action over North Vietnam and about 450 in the South, and the army lost 420 aircraft, mostly helicopters, in the South. Accidents and operational failures resulted in the loss of an additional 1,200 aircraft, bringing the total losses to approximately 3,000 planes, at a cost of $2.9 billion, between February 1965 and the end of 1967.[17]

Inevitably, despite the president's efforts to mask the magnitude of the struggle, the war began to tear at the fabric of American life. Vietnam was the first war that television brought into American homes. Americans were appalled at the slaughter and incredulous that an enemy so ill equipped could fight so tenaciously. It was obvious, of course, that Russia, China, and other Communist countries were supplying the Vietcong and North Vietnamese and obvious, too, that a hit-and-run guerrilla war required fewer men and weapons than the defensive side needed. Still, the cost in American lives and wounds was frightful.

By the end of 1967 dissent had spread from college campuses to the floor of Congress, and in November 1967 Senator Eugene McCarthy announced his decision to challenge the president for the Democratic nomination, stating that "the administration seems to have set no limit on the price it is willing to pay for a military victory." Polls began to indicate, by a two-to-one majority (57 percent to 27), that the American people disapproved of the president's handling of the war. The *Saturday Evening Post* carried an editorial calling the war "Johnson's mistake" and adding that "through the power of his office, he has made it a national mistake."[18]

There were also signs of disarray within the Johnson administration. In August 1967 Secretary McNamara expressed doubts before the Senate Armed Services Committee about the efficacy of bombing North Vietnam. The committee report, issued on August 31, reflected great frustration among congressional supporters of the war. It called attention to the fact that the "top military leaders of this country" disagreed with McNamara. The committee urged that the president accept "professional military judgment" and permit air force and navy aviation to "apply the force that is required to see the job through." Secretary McNamara's influence within the administration was waning anyway, and in November a story that the president intended to nominate McNamara to be president of the World Bank leaked from the White House.

In January 1968 the enemy launched an astonishing assault, attacking thirty-five major cities and towns and occupying many of them for extended periods. The defending forces inflicted enormous casualties (estimated as high as 40,000); but large enemy forces remained in the suburbs of many cities, and they had the run of the countryside, from which most South Vietnamese units had been withdrawn to help in the defense of the cities. President Johnson insisted that it was time for courage and persistence, that the enemy had shot its bolt, but Walter Cronkite, the nation's most trusted television newsman, returned from an inspection tour and pronounced the war a "stalemate," adding that the only rational way out would be to negotiate "not as victors, but as an honorable people who lived up to their pledge to defend democracy, and did the best they could."*

In February President Johnson sent Earle Wheeler, chairman of the Joint Chiefs of Staff, to Vietnam to assess the situation. After conferring with military commanders, General Wheeler reported that it would require about 206,000 more troops to achieve American objectives in Vietnam. In view of the strains that were already evident in the economy, where military expenditures were causing deficits and fueling inflation, granting such a request seemed certain to require a surtax. It would also mean calling up reserves and increasing the level of inductions. None of these could be done without

---

*Austin Ranney concludes that Cronkite's report "may well have tipped the balance" in Johnson's decision to wind down the war.[19]

congressional approval, and the mood on Capitol Hill was growing ugly.

Clark Clifford succeeded McNamara as secretary of defense on March 1, 1968. His first assignment was to convene a task force to study Wheeler's recommendation. It included thirteen members of the administration (representatives of State, Defense, Treasury, White House staff, and military), but not a single legislator. After an intensive week of discussion the group recommended that the president accept a scaled-down version of Wheeler's recommendation. In communicating the result to the president, Secretary Clifford expressed his own developing "doubts" about what could be expected from a further large infusion of American troops.[20]

As March 1968 wore on, President Johnson's strategy of escalation came to a crisis. First, there was further evidence of erosion in the president's political standing when he won only a narrow victory over Senator McCarthy in the Democratic primary in New Hampshire. Two days later Senator Robert Kennedy of New York met with Secretary Clifford and asked him to tell President Johnson that he (Kennedy) would not feel obligated to run if the president would appoint a commission to conduct a complete evaluation of Vietnam policies. Kennedy proposed several names for the commission: four senators (including himself), two generals, and some private citizens with distinguished diplomatic and academic credentials: Edwin Reischauer, Kingman Brewster, Roswell Gilpatric, and Carl Kaysen.

Clifford agreed to communicate Kennedy's proposal to the president. The next day he reported back the answer. The president had rejected the plan, said Clifford, because it would raise grave doubts about present policy and encourage Hanoi to think that the United States was about to quit. In addition, the public appointment of an outside group would diminish the authority of the presidency. Besides, there was no necessity for a meeting of the people Senator Kennedy proposed; the president was well aware of their views.[21]

Three days later Senator Kennedy announced that he was entering the race for the Democratic nomination. Meanwhile, there were antiwar demonstrations on campuses and in the streets. The president hardly dared to appear in public, except at military bases and in other carefully controlled settings. George Kennan expressed the opinion of most intellectuals when he called Johnson's policy "grievously unsound," a "massive miscalculation and error of policy, an error for which it is hard to find any parallels in our history." He likened the president and his closest advisers to "men in a dream, seemingly insensitive to public opinion, seemingly unable to arrive at any realistic assessment of the effects of their own acts."[22] *Time* magazine reported that the president was consulting an ever-narrowing band of advisers.

As it turned out, reports of presidential isolation from criticism were inaccurate. In late February former Secretary of State Dean Acheson, whose advice Johnson had sought, complained that he was not satisfied with the briefings he was getting from the CIA and Pentagon staff and did not feel able to give the president useful counsel. Johnson offered to make other sources of information available to Acheson; this led to a series of meetings at Acheson's home with lower-level government specialists. Finally, at a private luncheon at the White House, Acheson told the president that his policy could not succeed without vastly greater resources and five years' time. He added that the country no longer supported his policy.

These were bitter words for Johnson to hear. Acheson was a member of the informal Senior Advisory Group on Vietnam, which had met with the president once or twice a year since 1965 to counsel about the war. At its most recent meeting, in November 1967, all members of the group except George Ball had supported the administration's policy and expressed satisfaction with the progress of the war. Secretary Clifford suggested that the president ought to have the benefit of the group's assessment of the American position in the wake of the Tet offensive before deciding on the recommendation to commit more troops and intensify the bombing of North Vietnam. The president agreed, and the group convened at the White House on March 25 and 26. Those present, besides Acheson and Ball, were McGeorge Bundy, Douglas Dillon, Cyrus Vance, Generals Omar Bradley, Matthew Ridgway, and Maxwell Taylor, Abe Fortas (an associate justice of the Supreme Court and a close personal adviser to President Johnson), Arthur Goldberg (a former justice, now ambassador to the United Nations), and four other men with distinguished records of diplomatic service (Arthur Dean, John J. McCloy,

Robert Murphy, Henry Cabot Lodge). Again, not a single member of Congress was present.

From the outset of the meeting it was apparent that the virtual unanimity of the preceding November had evaporated. A few (Taylor, Murphy, Fortas) still thought the policy of attrition was viable and proposed heavier bombing. Others (McCloy, Lodge, Dean, Bradley) were troubled but reluctant to call for a dramatic change in policy. Still, a clear majority wanted change—either some way to make the war politically and economically endurable for an extended period or outright disengagement. At the concluding luncheon Bundy offered a summary of the group's findings, to the effect that the present policy could not achieve its objective without the commitment of virtually unlimited resources, that the nation no longer supported the war, and that significant change was therefore imperative. Fortas objected that Bundy's summary did not reflect the views of the whole group, but Acheson supported Bundy, saying that his summary represented a clear majority of those present. He added that the insistence on military victory had dragged the president and the country into a morass which could only get worse until the policy was changed and that the thrust of our policy should now be toward deescalation, negotiation, and disengagement.

March 1968 ended dramatically. In a televised speech from the White House President Johnson announced that he had ordered a halt in the bombing, that South Vietnam was calling up more troops from its own reserves—and that he had decided to withdraw from the race for renomination, so that he could devote all his energies to the search for peace. The president had rejected the call for more American troops and reversed the tide toward escalation. He had certainly not decided to abandon the American effort in Vietnam, as he showed by his volcanic reaction whenever Vice President Humphrey, the eventual Democratic nominee, seemed to waver from total commitment to prevent a Communist take-over of Indochina. But by calling a halt to the bombing, he had decisively changed tactics. No longer would he rely exclusively on military means to resolve the conflict in Vietnam. There did not remain enough time in his term in office for him to clarify the alternatives he may have had in mind. By resigning the race, he left that task to his successor.

Reflecting later on the decisions President Johnson announced on

March 31, 1968, Clark Clifford remarked, "Presidents have difficult decisions to make and go about making them in mysterious ways."[23] In his memoirs Johnson himself insisted that the decisions were his. He could have reversed or modified them at any time prior to announcing them, he said, if the enemy had launched new attacks, for example, or if he had become convinced that his withdrawal from politics would have undermined morale in Vietnam, or if a serious incident had erupted elsewhere in the world. If any of these things had happened, he wrote, "I would have reconsidered my decisions and changed my course if necessary."[24] The affair was in the president's hands.

From Johnson's memoirs it is clear that he conducted exhaustive consultations during February and March 1968 before reaching his decision. He spoke almost daily with Dean Rusk, his secretary of state. He had frequent meetings with his "senior advisers," Vice President Humphrey, Secretaries Rusk, McNamara, Clifford, and Henry Fowler of Treasury, Generals Wheeler, Taylor, and other military officers, CIA Director Richard Helms, and members of his White House staff (Walt Rostow, George Christian, Tom Johnson, Harry McPherson and others). He received reports from the American ambassador in Saigon, Ellsworth Bunker, and several times during the month he asked for and obtained Bunker's soundings of reactions to various proposals by South Vietnamese officials. On a trip around the world in December 1967 he met with the Australian cabinet, visited troops in Vietnam, and saw Pope Paul VI at the Vatican.* He received a peace proposal from UN Secretary U Thant. He watched television reports and read newspapers, though he seems to have regarded them less as independent sources of information than as agents of public confusion about the true situation in Vietnam.

---

*He told the pope that he did not think that a bombing pause would produce useful results at that time, that he expected the Communists to use "kamikaze" tactics in the weeks ahead, and that he hoped that the South Vietnamese government's program of national reconciliation would succeed. Citing the pope's concern for men in all conditions, he asked his assistance in obtaining information about American soldiers held captive by the North Vietnamese or Vietcong. He left the Vatican, he said, convinced that His Holiness understood his policies. "As we walked out," his memoirs note, "one of the Pope's colleagues quoted His Holiness as saying: 'What a wonderful talk.' "[25]

Perhaps the best clue to the president's attitude toward dissenting advice came in his own account of the meetings on March 25 and 26 with the Senior Advisory Group or, as Johnson called them, the "Wise Men." In his memoirs he gives the impression that he had settled on his intended course before this group met, but he admits that he was dismayed by their pessimism. He attributed it to the possibility that his briefing officers may have used "outdated information" which failed to reflect the "sharp turnaround" which Wheeler and Westmoreland had reported both in the military situation and in the mood of our South Vietnamese allies. Still, these were "intelligent, experienced men," the president notes in his memoirs. "I had always regarded the majority of them as very steady and balanced." Did their counsel sway his thinking? Apparently only indirectly. Their defection stimulated a political reflection: "If they had been so deeply influenced by the reports of the Tet offensive what must the average citizen in the country be thinking?"[26]

One remarkable feature in Johnson's own account is his attitude toward Congress. Senatorial critics of the president's policy were getting a great deal of publicity during this period, but the president was also aware that members of the armed services committees actually wanted to intensify the bombing campaign. When the *New York Times* published a leaked report that General Westmoreland had asked for 206,000 more troops, the president worried that it would arouse congressional critics of his policies. As the discussions of March 1968 continued, it became clear that a call-up of reserves and reinforcements in Vietnam would increase the budget deficit by $8 billion to $10 billion over the next year or so. President Johnson called congressional leaders to the White House and told them that action on a tax bill was urgent. At the end of the month, when he had made up his mind how to proceed, he called in several senators to inform them of the military moves he was planning.

There is no indication, however, anywhere in the chapter describing his decision making on Vietnam in 1967 and 1968, that he solicited or received advice from any member of Congress. The Senate he perceived as a forum for amplifying doubts and criticisms that encouraged the enemy to think that the nation's resolve was weakening. He had to persuade Congress to make the necessary appropriations. He had to cope with criticism from senators. But members of Congress—like the "Wise Men" who were deserting him, like civilian critics in the Pentagon, like journalists who had overreacted to the suicidal Tet offensive—lacked the facts on which he and his chosen "senior advisers" were relying. Time alone would reveal whether his decisions on Vietnam were wise, wrote the president, "but good or bad I made them, and the full responsibility is mine."[27]

President Nixon assumed office in January 1969. He was deeply committed to the doctrine of containment on which the nation's policy toward Indochina had been based since the Truman administration, and he had no intention of abandoning South Vietnam. On the other hand, he recognized that the cost of the war, particularly in terms of lives and casualties, had to be reduced. He recognized that he would have to change tactics in order to achieve America's strategic purposes in Indochina. Instead of waging a ground war with drafted infantrymen, he would rely more on bombing and on mining harbors. Meanwhile, his publicists would emphasize the withdrawal of American forces and the declining casualty rates.

This strategy succeeded pretty well in deflecting public resistance until the traumatic events of the spring of 1970. On April 20 of that year President Nixon announced that he would reduce the number of American troops in Vietnam by 150,000 within the next year, to a level of 284,000. On April 23 he pledged to move away from the draft and toward a volunteer army. A week later he announced the "incursion" into Cambodia, which an astonished public immediately perceived as a widening of the war. College campuses exploded in outrage. Students and professors organized protest marches and lobbying campaigns to try to persuade Congress to cut off funds for the war. On the campus of Kent State University in Ohio national guardsmen, called out to maintain order during an antiwar demonstration, shot into an advancing phalanx of students and killed four of them, wounding eight others.

These tumultuous events rocked the foundations of government. Secretary of the Interior Walter Hickel wrote the president, complaining that the administration was failing the young people of the nation. (Hickel was dismissed from office the following November.) The stock market fell to its lowest level since November 1962. "Strikes" broke out at more than 200 colleges and universities, and students descended on Washington to demand an end to the war. At dawn on May 9 the president paid an unscheduled visit to students camping at the Lincoln Memorial and stayed with them for an hour to discuss the war and racial problems.

In retrospect, what is most remarkable about this turmoil is how little impact it seems to have had on American policy toward Vietnam. President Nixon continued to reduce troop levels and to substitute air and naval power for ground combat forces. He continued to conduct secret warfare in the neighboring countries of Indochina. He continued to claim to be seeking an end to the war (as President Johnson had), while insisting that South Vietnam must remain independent and non-Communist.

One great object of the protests of May and June 1970 was the enactment of the so-called Cooper-Church Amendment, sponsored by the Senate Foreign Relations Committee, calling for an end to American military activity on the ground or in the air over Cambodia. Despite the hue and cry, the Senate did not pass the amendment until after all United States forces had departed from Cambodia, and the measure never did come to a formal vote in the House of Representatives. Six months later Congress and the president agreed on legislation which provided that "in line with the expressed intention of the president," no funds could be used "to finance the introduction of United States ground combat troops into Cambodia" or to provide American advisers to Cambodian military forces in Cambodia.[28] Significantly, the provision failed to mention combat activity in the air above Cambodia.

Opponents of the war did achieve one goal during this period: On July 10, 1970, the Senate repealed the Tonkin Gulf Resolution. The Nixon administration offered no overt resistance to the repeal, arguing almost contemptuously that the president's authority to conduct the war in Vietnam rested on his constitutional role as commander in chief, supported by congressionally enacted appropriations and by the draft laws.

A more serious challenge to President Nixon's leadership came in the so-called Mansfield Amendment, offered by the majority leader, Mike Mansfield of Montana. The amendment, part of the Defense Procurement Authorization Act of 1972, said that "the policy of the United States [was] to terminate at the earliest practicable date all military operations of the United States in Indochina, and to provide for the prompt and orderly withdrawal of all United States military forces at a date certain, subject to the release of all American prisoners of war . . . and an accounting for all Americans missing in action. . . ."[29] In signing the act, other parts of which were essential to the American military effort, President Nixon stated that Mansfield's provision did not represent the policies of the administration and that he intended to ignore it. At the same time he insisted that his own policy was to end the conflict in Vietnam as soon as possible—as soon, that is, as South Vietnam was able to defend its own independence.

Opponents of the war, unable to devise a legislative strategy for forcing an American withdrawal, took the issue to court. In a series of suits directed at Secretary of Defense Melvin Laird, draftees sought to escape induction by arguing that in the absence of a congressional declaration, the government was waging war unconstitutionally. In 1971 the courts rejected this argument, noting that the Constitution granted war-making powers jointly to the president and Congress, that there were abundant precedents for American involvement in hostilities abroad without a formal declaration of war, and that in this case Congress had indicated its willingness to fight by repeatedly providing financial support, renewing the draft, and foiling efforts to set limits on the scope and duration of the war. Thus, the court concluded, the branches were not in opposition, and there was no constitutional relief for individuals who disapproved of the president's policy.

By 1973 the atmosphere surrounding the war in Vietnam was again changing. Late in the presidential election campaign of 1972 Henry Kissinger, serving then as the president's national security adviser and having been dispatched to spur the "peace talks" with the North Vietnamese in Paris, told reporters that peace was "at hand." Nixon won a landslide victory in the election; but the momentum toward peace seemed to stall,* and in late December the

---

*Kissinger's memoirs give his account of how events proceeded from his widely publicized statement that "peace is at hand" to a massive resumption of the bombing. He likens the attempt to pin the diplomatic fiasco on him to "life at royal courts," where

president ordered a withering campaign of bombing over North Vietnam.

The apparent renewal of the war brought a new spate of suits seeking to stop the administration's effort, but the courts were still unwilling to intervene. The rationale, however, had shifted significantly. Plaintiffs contended that the president's unilateral decision to bomb North Vietnam and mine its harbors constituted an escalation of the war which was illegal in the absence of congressional authorization. Judge Irving R. Kaufman, on the circuit court of appeals in New York, ruled that the court was incapable of assessing the facts. "It was the President's view," he wrote, "that the mining of North Vietnam's harbors was necessary . . . to bring the war to a close." Judges, sitting thousands of miles from the field of battle and lacking military training and fresh information, could not determine whether a specific military operation constituted an "escalation" of the war or was merely "a new tactical approach within a continuing strategic plan." It was, he concluded, a political question, and it would have to be fought out in other arenas.[31]

By mid-1973 American ground forces had been removed from Vietnam, but the bombing of Cambodia continued. It was at that time that judicial consideration of the constitutionality of the war in Vietnam finally came to a head. Thirteen members of the House of Representatives, led by Parren Mitchell, Democrat of Maryland, had brought suit in 1971, alleging that for seven years, by the actions of two presidents and their appointees, the United States had been engaged in war in Indochina without obtaining "either a declaration of war or an explicit, intentional and discrete authorization of war" and that they, as members of Congress, had been deprived thereby of their constitutional right to "decide whether the United States should fight a war." They asked the court to enjoin the administration from prosecuting the war unless Congress, within sixty days of the court's order, had explicitly authorized its continuation.

The case slowly wended its way through the judicial system, and

an aide who incurs the monarch's displeasure becomes fair game for other aides, and foreign governments "draw their own conclusions from an appearance of division in high councils."[30]

it was two years before the circuit court of appeals in Washington issued its decision. The opinion, written by Judge Charles Wyzanski, acknowledged that courts had heretofore found authorization for the war, first, in the Tonkin Gulf Resolution and then, after its repeal, in appropriation acts, draft extensions, and various related measures. The court renewed its affirmation that "it is constitutionally permissible for Congress to use another means than a formal declaration of war to give its approval to a war such as is involved in the protracted and substantial hostilities in Indochina," and it conceded that the "overwhelming weight of authority" justified the constitutionality of the war in Vietnam on that ground. But now, he wrote, the court had come to regard that body of authority as "unsound." There is a "special problem," he wrote, when one seeks to draw an implication of approval from legislation relating to a "war already being waged at the direction of the president alone." Judge Wyzanski used strong language to repudiate the government's argument:

> This court cannot be unmindful of what every schoolboy knows: that in voting to appropriate money or to draft men a congressman is not necessarily approving of the continuation of a war no matter how specifically the appropriation or draft act refers to that war. A congressman wholly opposed to the war's commencement and continuation might vote for the military appropriations and for the draft measures because he was unwilling to abandon without support men already fighting. An honorable, decent, compassionate act of aiding those already in peril is no proof of consent to the actions that placed and continued them in that dangerous posture. We should not construe votes cast in pity and piety as though they were votes freely given to express consent.[32]

Judge Wyzanski concluded that "none of the legislation drawn to the court's attention may serve as a valid assent to the Vietnam war."

Yet the court drew back from issuing the injunction sought by Congressman Mitchell and his colleagues. It had to be recognized, wrote Wyzanski, that when President Nixon took office, he was confronted with a situation not of his own creation. "Obviously" the president could not properly execute his duties by ordering a cessation of hostilities on the very day that he took office. "Even if his predecessors had exceeded their constitutional authority, President Nixon's duty did not go beyond trying, in good faith and to the best of his ability, to bring the war to an end as promptly as was consistent with the safety of those fighting and with a profound concern for the durable interests of the nation—its defense, its honor, its morality."[33] Whether President Nixon was discharging his duty properly or not, no court was competent to say. Courts could not procure the necessary evidence to make a judgment, and even if they could, the Constitution gives the president "an unusually wide measure of discretion in this area," with which courts must not interfere "if this country is to play a responsible role in the council of the nations." In short, the case presented "a 'political question,' which is beyond the judicial power conferred by Article III of the United States Constitution." On that ground the complaint had to be dismissed.

Judge Wyzanski's opinion was persuasive on two key points: that Congress never gave free and knowing consent to the war in Vietnam and that the courts are not fit to determine whether a president, in making war, is abusing his powers or not. But if presidents acting without congressional affirmation can wage war without violating the Constitution or incurring judicial interference, is it possible to prevent a president from abusing his power to make war?

The war in Vietnam was instrumental in bringing Presidents Johnson and Nixon to political disaster. Their power to wage war was never successfully thwarted, but opponents of their conduct eventually found other ways to hound them from office. There is no doubt in either case that opposition to their war making was a prime contributor to their political collapse.

In this sense American presidents are not free from constraint in war making. The complexity of their responsibilities means that they are never wise, in pursuing one goal, to neglect the impact of their success or failure on other aspirations. They pay a high price for embarking on any campaign they cannot win. A president's ability to wage war is limited by the ability of the adversary to prolong the conflict and raise the price of victory, by his ability to persuade the public that the necessary sacrifices are justified, by the willingness of Congress to raise revenues and appropriate support and to provide an acceptable level of support for the rest of his program.

But the lesson of Vietnam is that despite these constraints, it is finally the president who takes the nation to war, who conducts the war, defines its purpose, and sets the terms for ending it. Even though majorities in Congress may come to doubt the wisdom of the war or wish that it were being fought for other ends, they cannot stop it or alter its course once it has begun. They can raise the political cost, and eventually the president may be persuaded to modify his strategy. But it is he who assesses the evidence of political defection and he who determines what route to take toward extrication.

The frightful costs of the war in Vietnam and the agony of the nation during the process of extrication made many people eager to devise ways to involve Congress in the decision to go to war in the first place. The provisions in the Constitution seemed inadequate. Everyone recognized that there had been, and would doubtless continue to be, occasions when a formal declaration of war was inappropriate. The availability of a massive standing army meant that the means of making war were constantly available, rendering the congressional authority to raise armed forces and appropriate supplies an inadequate control.

Was it possible in these circumstances to compel presidents to share their power to apply military force in support of the nation's strategic objectives?

Congress gave its answer in the form of the War Powers Resolution, enacted on November 7, 1973, by an override of President Nixon's veto. The resolution posed as a clarification of the Constitution's provisions. It was meant, said the preamble, "to fulfill the intent of the framers of the Constitution . . . [to] insure that the collective judgment of both the Congress and the president will apply to the introduction of United States armed forces into hostilities. . . ."[34] It required the president, "in every possible instance," to "consult with Congress" before introducing armed forces into hostilities or into situations where hostilities seemed imminent. If the president decided to send troops without a declaration of war, or if he substantially enlarged an existing commitment of troops, the resolution required him to submit a report to Congress within forty-eight hours. It also required him to withdraw the troops within sixty days unless Congress declared war, extended the deadline by law, or was physically unable to meet. In the absence of affirmative action by Congress, the president could have another thirty days to withdraw the troops.

No part of this resolution escaped censure. Critics rejected its pose as a clarification of the Constitution, arguing instead that Congress was seeking to enlarge its role. Its requirement of consultation with Congress "in every possible instance" was questioned primarily because of its vagueness. What exactly did "consult" mean? Who would act for Congress? The provision seemed to express a pious hope, in terms not legally enforceable. As far as the requirement to report was concerned, Presidents Ford, Carter, and Reagan challenged its constitutionality on grounds that Congress could not by law require that the president take specific acts on duties assigned to him by the Constitution. Furthermore, these reports had the effect of triggering the sixty-day limit, and presidents were not willing to do that. Why should the president's hand be stayed just because Congress was unable to agree on a course of action?

The basic issue was whether the president could, or should, be forced to share his power as commander in chief. In the resolution Congress declared that the president's power (as commander in chief) to send troops into combat required a declaration of war, a specific statutory authorization, or an attack on the United States, its possessions, or its armed forces.* But events in the decade following the enactment of the resolution suggested that this language was unduly restrictive.

First, there was the ghastly retreat from Indochina in April 1975.

---

* The original Senate bill would have allowed the president to introduce armed forces into combat on his own authority only to repel an armed attack on the United States, its territories, possessions, and armed forces; to take appropriate retaliatory action for such an attack; to forestall the direct and imminent threat of such an attack; or to protect evacuating citizens.[35] In testimony before a House subcommittee a State Department official listed other circumstances in which a president might feel compelled to use military force: to rescue American citizens abroad, to protect U.S. embassies, to implement the terms of an armistice, and to carry out the terms of security commitments made in treaties. He added that no definitional statement could encompass "every conceivable situation in which the president's commander-in-chief authority could be exercised."[36]

As South Vietnam and Cambodia fell to Communist forces, President Ford reported to Congress that he was ordering 350 marines equipped for combat to assist in the evacuation of refugees and American citizens. Besides the War Powers Resolution, the president's orders seemed to conflict with legislation which prohibited the expenditure of funds for combat activities by American forces anywhere in Indochina after August 15, 1973.[37] On April 10, 1975, he went before a joint session of Congress to ask for immediate clarification of this restriction: Did it apply to the use of American forces for evacuating Americans and South Vietnamese from Indochina? Two days later, as Phnom Penh was falling to the Khmer Rouge, President Ford ordered American soldiers to proceed with the planned evacuation. No casualties were suffered in the operation, although the last helicopters leaving Phnom Penh were fired upon. On April 14 Senate leaders offered legislation to authorize the evacuation of American citizens from Vietnam. The Ford administration countered with a bill that would have construed the earlier restrictions as not intended to prohibit a "humanitarian evacuation." On April 29, as it appeared that the Senate was about to enact its own version, President Ford ordered the evacuation of Saigon and Da Nang. South Vietnam surrendered later that day. During the evacuation American forces suppressed antiaircraft fire and returned enemy rifle fire, and four American soldiers were killed. No one seemed to doubt the necessity of doing what President Ford had done, and no one challenged its legality, though it appeared to violate both the War Powers Resolution and the funding restriction.

Both pieces of legislation were still in effect a month later (May 12, 1975), when a Cambodian naval patrol seized the S.S. *Mayaguez*. President Ford immediately declared that the ship had been seized in international waters and ordered American forces to rescue both ship and crew. There ensued the sinking of Cambodian gunboats, the bombing of a Cambodian military airfield and oil depot, and an amphibious assault on an island where the crew was mistakenly believed to be held. The operation resulted in the recapture of the ship and the rescue of forty crew members, but forty-one Americans were killed and seventy-one injured. Again, as in the evacuation, there seemed to be little concern that the funding restrictions had been ignored, as had the requirements of the War Powers Resolution for prior consultation with "Congress."* Most observers in and out of Congress seemed tacitly to agree that the operation, while surprisingly costly, had been justified by the need to respond quickly and to demonstrate that American dignity and self-respect had survived the miserable collapse of the American effort in Indochina.

President Carter's relations with Iran provided another test of the War Powers Resolution. President Carter strongly affirmed an American policy that regarded Iran as a firm ally, a western-oriented country on the southern flank of the Soviet Union. During Carter's first year in office the shah visited the White House, and shortly thereafter the president himself visited Iran. In a toast he referred to Iran as "an island of stability in one of the more troubled areas of the world."[39]

By the end of 1978, however, Iran was a scene of turmoil. Reluctantly the administration concluded that the shah's continued presence was fueling unrest and acquiesced in his decision to go into exile abroad. As the shah moved first to Egypt, then to Morocco, and finally to Mexico, pressure mounted on President Carter to invite him to come to Walter Annenberg's estate in California, but the president, fearful for the safety of Americans still in Iran, resisted.[40] In October 1979 the president learned that the shah was seriously ill and agreed that he could go to New York for tests and treatment, provided that he returned to Mexico as soon as medically possible.

As soon as it was announced that the shah was in the United States, demonstrators in Iran demanded that the shah and his estate be delivered up to Iranian "justice." On November 4 the American Embassy in Teheran was overrun, and when the dust cleared, a group of militant students held sixty-six Americans hostage.

In the early hours and days after the seizure President Carter was "reasonably confident" that the Iranians would soon remove the attackers from the embassy compound.[41] At the same time he began

---

* In remarks made in December 1983 President Ford noted that "we never conceded that the War Powers Resolution was applicable" in the *Mayaguez* case. The challenge to his administration, he said, was to "get the crew back without any loss of life and . . . recover the ship itself." The result of his action, he added, was the "the crew and ship were recovered from the enemy." He made no mention of the heavy American casualties.[38]

to consider other options. Two days after the hostages were taken, the president and his advisers broached the possibility of a rescue mission. Incidentally, only Vice President Walter Mondale, Secretary of State Cyrus Vance, National Security Adviser Zbigniew Brzezinski, Defense Secretary Harold Brown, and General David Jones, chairman of the Joint Chiefs of Staff—but no members of Congress—were privy to these discussions.

Throughout the winter a variety of economic sanctions and diplomatic pressures were applied, to no avail. Finally, on April 4, Carter broke off diplomatic relations with Iran, expelled all Iranian diplomats, and declared an embargo on all shipments to Iran except food and medicines.

Meanwhile, plans for the rescue mission were moving forward. The final decision to proceed was made at a meeting on April 11, attended by Mondale, Brzezinski, Brown, Jones, Deputy Secretary of State Warren Christopher, CIA Director Stansfield Turner, and two White house aides (Hamilton Jordan and Jody Powell).* Again, no member of Congress was involved.

Every effort was made to maintain secrecy about the mission. On April 9 the president called President Valéry Giscard d'Estaing of France and told him that he was about to take military action, but he did not specify what it was. Later, when stories began to circulate that American planes were in Oman and loaded with ammunition and supplies for Afghanistan, intelligence sources traced them to a former British officer. President Carter dispatched an aide to London to brief Prime Minister Margaret Thatcher about the true purpose of the planes. Otherwise, no allied leader learned in advance of the attempted rescue.

On April 18 President Carter met with senior advisers to discuss "how to deal with the congressional leadership" about the rescue mission. Vice President Mondale argued for minimum advance notice. Secretary of State Vance urged that Democratic and Republican

---

*Secretary Vance was on vacation. When he returned, he presented a dissenting opinion on the mission, urging that nothing be done to endanger the safety of the hostages. The president rejected this advice, and on April 21 Vance submitted his resignation.

leaders in the House and Senate be informed. The president sided with Mondale.[42]

The mission was scheduled to be launched on April 24. The evening before, Carter met with Robert Byrd, the Senate majority leader. Later that night he made the following entry in his diary: "I told him that before we took any of the military acts that had been prominently mentioned in the press—mining, blockade, and so forth—I would indeed consult with Congress. And that at this time I had no plans to initiate this kind of action. He [Byrd] drew a sharp distinction between the need to consult on a military plan and the need to inform Congress at the last minute on any kind of covert operation."[43] Carter decided not to tell Byrd, though the mission was just a few hours from initiation, that it was imminent. In his memoirs Carter added, poignantly, "After [Byrd] left the White House I wondered if it would have been better to involve him more directly in our exact plans for the mission. His advice would have been valuable to me then—and also twenty-four hours later.[44]

It is not clear what contribution Senator Byrd could have made at that point. The mission began that very night. Almost immediately two of the eight helicopters crashed. Then another developed a hydraulic problem, leaving fewer than the minimum of six which the plans required. Within minutes the president had to decide whether to terminate the mission. On the advice of the commander at the site he gave the order to abort and return. Then tragedy struck. In taking off near the transport plane in the desert, one helicopter crashed into the larger plane, leaving eight men dead and three burned. When the remaining men and movable equipment had cleared Iranian airspace, President Carter went on television at 1:00 A.M. to announce the debacle, then began his calls to congressional leaders.

In a way, it is almost absurd to ask whether Carter complied with the War Powers Resolution. The episode was over almost before it began. What it showed was not the continuing willfulness of presidents but the foolishness of demanding that the president "consult with Congress" before sending military forces into potentially hostile situations. The resolution requires consultation "in every possible instance," but if this episode is exempted on grounds of the need for secrecy, and if it is admitted that only the president can determine the need for secrecy, has he not effectively been given the authority to decide whether or not to engage in a particular invasion or raid? What is the alternative?

The attempted rescue of the hostages raises hard questions in this area. From the standpoint of military planning and execution it was apparently bungled. It cannot be denied, however, that a sovereign nation must be able to undertake expeditions of this kind or that they require secrecy and unified command. As Clinton Rossiter has written, where else could such power be placed? The genius of Congress is deliberation, the gathering of opinions from a wide variety of perspectives. Those qualities may have a place in administration, but not at the point where a commander must decide whether or not to undertake a surprise raid on foreign soil.

Yet we cannot rest here. If a president, pleading the need for secrecy and dispatch, can decide on his own to rescue hostages, can he not also respond to attacks on American ships like the *Mayaguez?* And if so, is he not the one who must decide whether the circumstances in another case—such as the Gulf of Tonkin—justify a response?

There is another ambiguity in the War Powers Resolution. It turns on the word *hostilities*, in the following phrase: The president shall report to Congress whenever he sends armed forces "into hostilities or into situations where imminent involvement in hostilities is clearly indicated by the circumstances. . . ." Several times President Reagan has sent troops into situations which resulted in casualties to American forces without submitting the report required by the War Powers Resolution. In El Salvador he consistently took the position that United States military advisers there were not involved in hostilities, even after (on February 4, 1983) an unarmed adviser was wounded by sniper fire when his helicopter flew low over a rebel position.[45] Eleven members of Congress brought suit, asking the court to declare that President Reagan had violated the resolution, but the court dismissed the suit. The court suggested that the issue would be better framed if Congress had passed a resolution to the effect that circumstances in El Salvador required a presidential report. If the court acted in the absence of such a resolution, congressional inaction might have the effect of requiring the withdrawal of American forces after sixty days, even if a majority in Congress concurred in the president's appraisal that no report was required. Besides, there were no "judicially discoverable and manageable standards" for determining when hostilities had begun.[46]

Similarly, in 1983 President Reagan sent marines to keep the peace in Lebanon in the wake of the Israeli withdrawal. Even after two marines had been killed by hostile mortar fire and United States warships in retaliation had shelled artillery positions, he refused to file the report required by the War Powers Resolution. "Isolated or infrequent acts of violence," said the president, do not necessarily constitute "imminent involvement in hostilities."[47]

By September 1983 members of Congress became convinced that our involvement in Lebanon had changed from peacekeeping to support for one side in a bitter civil war. After intensive negotiations with the administration Congress enacted a resolution, signed by the president on October 12, extending the limit on military involvement in Lebanon to eighteen months. Three weeks later a young driver drove a truckful of explosives through a barricade and into a building in which United States marines were sleeping. When the building collapsed into a heap of rubble, 241 of them died. A rancorous public debate ensued about the purposes and prospects of American involvement, and on February 7, 1984, President Reagan ordered the evacuation of the 1,400-man marine contingent, more than a year short of the eighteen-month deadline.

The Constitution distributes war powers between Congress and the president. Not only does Congress declare war, raise armed forces, and (in the Senate) confirm diplomatic appointments and ratify treaties, but its powers to appropriate funds and to make appropriations conditional also have impact in the field of foreign relations. It cannot prevent a president from recognizing a foreign regime or breaking off diplomatic relations, but if the president decides to send an ambassador, the Senate must approve the appointment.* If he wants to send military aid, Congress must appropriate the funds. If he wants to send military advisers or covert aid, Congress must have provided them, and Congress by law can restrict their use.

*President Truman's plan to open full diplomatic relations with the Vatican was foiled in 1951, when the Senate balked at confirming his appointment of General Mark Clark as ambassador.

As a practical matter, however, presidents have enormous leeway in the use of war powers. Where there are laws, they normally control a president's actions; but there are vast areas where no law applies, and here a president and his advisers have wide discretion. The executive branch gathers information about foreign developments,* prepares and analyzes options, and sends military force into action. No one else has the nation's armed forces ultimately at his command.

Does this give the president unlimited authority over war powers? No, it does not. The president is a political leader with broad responsibilities, and he operates in a complex field of influences. A president must contend with the press; with members of the military bureaucracy (technically under his command but having opinions of their own); with allies, adversaries and nonaligned leaders abroad; with ethnic groups and churches, industrialists and investors, trade unionists, political rivals, and public opinion. Even in wartime, when people in other positions are most inclined to defer and the nation is most likely to rally (at least initially) to the commander in chief, a president must be sensitive to all these political signals.

After all this has been said, however, the commander in chief of American armed forces has vast military might at his disposal and virtually unlimited precedents for using them. The War Powers Resolution must be judged a failure in seeking to compel the president to share these powers with Congress. If senators and representatives were "trustworthy" and if they were available in times of crisis, most presidents (but not all) would want to consult with them. But members of Congress, like presidents, are talkers, and like presidents, they resist being gagged when they feel they have something important to say. Thus, even well-meaning presidents, even those, like Lyndon Johnson and Gerald Ford, themselves with long congressional backgrounds, often proceed without full consultation with Congress.

*Congress gathers information, too; so do newspapers, television reporters, and academic researchers. But the information that affects presidential decision making is filtered through executive branch machinery. Ultimately it is the president himself who decides what weight to give to the various pieces of information that come to his attention.

There is much to be said for existing arrangements. As long as we have presidents of solid intelligence, wise in the uses and limits of military force, capable of choosing experienced advisers and determined to draw advice from many and varied sources, it is advantageous to have unified command and clear accountability in this area.

There are also great dangers and important drawbacks. Presidential politics is volatile. There are often distinct changes in policy from one administration to the next and far-reaching changes in personnel. When a new administration comes to office, allies must wait many months for new people to learn the ropes, and adversaries may have opportunities during these months to gain advantages over their inexperienced counterparts. (The permanent bureaucracies in the foreign service, intelligence, and military sectors are probably better at preventing damage during these periods of transition than at seizing new opportunities for cooperation.) Another danger is the weight attached to the perceptions of one man and his advisers. During the Reagan administration arms control negotiations broke down completely. When the Soviets made an overture to resume them, a White House official said that the administration was trying to find out whether the proposal marked a real shift in Moscow's attitude or was aimed at embarrassing the president. It was up to one man, finally, to play this fateful hand of poker for the United States.

There are also dangers of insulation, when an administration becomes embattled and loses contact with the nation. No case of this was more poignant than that of Lyndon Johnson, the quintessential senator, the most sensitive of men, who drew himself into an ever-tightening circle of advisers when his policy in Vietnam began to fail. This tendency toward insulation seems almost irresistible. In their memoirs both Presidents Johnson and Carter express great anger in telling of aides who apparently took their disagreements over policy to newspaper reporters.[48] President Nixon's efforts to plug these leaks were instrumental in bringing his administration to a premature end.

It is not hard to understand why presidents feel so strongly about disloyalty among their aides. But the situation also reflects a determination among the American people to open the war-making power to wider participation. In view of the centralization of war powers in one man, Congress will not pass an "official secrets" act, like the one in Britain that prevents the press from publishing material which the government wants to protect. If presidents had the control they want, we would indeed come close to autocracy in foreign relations.

PART V

Renewal

CHAPTER 12

Rounding Out the "Constitutional Revolution"

> . . . *Unless we are prepared to forgo altogether the values of constitutionalism,*
> *we need to give some deliberate attention to that element of the Constitution*
> *which has remained comparatively unresponsive to crisis; I mean the structural*
> *element.*
>
>
>
> Edward S. Corwin,
> "Our Constitutional Revolution and
> How to Round It Out" (1948)[1]
>
>

An organism must be judged according to its fitness to perform the tasks we assign to it. A horse is fit to pull a carriage, but it cannot take a person to the moon.

When the Constitution was framed two centuries ago, there were a few crucial tasks that required national government. National security was one; Americans needed to define a common policy toward foreign powers and to cooperate in implementing it. The second major requirement was to establish a common market among the states. The list of powers and prohibitions contained in Article I, Sections 8, 9, and 10 and Article II, Section 2 gives a good clue to the framers' notion of the role of the national government.* It focuses

---

*An exchange between Roger Sherman and James Madison early in the convention (June 6, 1787) sheds light on these intentions. Sherman would have restricted the

essentially on foreign relations, national defense, and the regulation of commerce, both foreign and domestic.

In support of these two broad areas of governance, the Constitution assigned certain functions to Congress and others to the president. The effective discharge of these responsibilities required energetic administration, and the framers did not hesitate to provide it. They knew that the nation, its economy, and its social structure would not always be primitive. Believing that they were building a constitution for a great empire and for the ages, and having read Blackstone and Hume on the growth of ministries in Britain, they were aware that the executive would grow as the nation grew, particularly as the nation came into contact with other nations that posed a threat to its security.* Even the boldest spirits, however, did not foresee—could not have foreseen, any more than Blackstone and Hume did—the full contours of the modern welfare / garrison state. They did not foresee a world in which even the proponents of limited government, the self-proclaimed disciples of Adam Smith, would campaign for the presidency, as the Republicans did in 1980, on a platform that pledged federal subsidies and incentives in the fields of health care, education, housing, transportation, and environmental protection, not to mention assistance for workers left unemployed by "technological obsolescence or imports."[2]

A government that decides in a few days to allocate billions of dollars to a road-building program partly in order to alleviate unemployment must be set up differently from one that frets for decades

federal government to national defense and foreign relations; Madison thought it must also protect private rights and establish justice. It is not clear exactly what Madison meant, but in *The Federalist*, Number 10, he argues that the principal task of modern legislation is the adjustment of relations between groups involved in commerce. The list of powers in Article I, Section 8 probably represents Madison's concept pretty closely. But see also his motion on August 18, 1787, to give Congress power to "establish an university." The motion was defeated on September 14, partly on Gouverneur Morris's argument that it was not necessary, being encompassed in the power of Congress to make laws for the national capital.

*Indeed, many of the leading framers (Hamilton, Gouverneur Morris, Rutledge) were impatient to spur the nation into greater involvement with the cosmopolitan world. Others (Gerry, Randolph, and Mason, as well as Jefferson, watching from Paris) were more apprehensive about this imperial impulse, but they were dissenters, not prime movers, in the constitutional revolution of 1787.

about whether it has constitutional authority to build a road from the coastal area to the interior. A government that monitors and adjusts the amount of money in the system on virtually a daily basis requires a different structure from one that debates for decades whether or not it needs a national bank and, if so, whether it has the constitutional authority to set one up. A government that might have to decide in minutes whether or not to return nuclear fire must be structured differently from one that does not learn for several weeks whether its envoys have been able to buy the Louisiana Territory.

From the beginning the theory of the Constitution was that Congress, by writing laws, would define crimes, raise military forces, create public enterprises, and secure revenues to support them, while the president, as chief executive, would preserve public order, conduct foreign relations, command the armed forces, and administer public services in accordance with the laws. This clear division of responsibility reflected the composition of the bodies. Congress, by its size and close ties to the communities of the nation, ensured that the popular will would direct what the government undertook, while the presidency, centering on a single individual, caused the government to use its resources vigorously and efficiently in service of this will.

The Constitution's design is not neat. From the beginning in 1789, Congress by law has shaped administrative agencies and monitored the performance of the executive branch. The Senate has shared in the leading appointments in the executive branch, and Congress, by manipulation of the purse strings, has gained a share of patronage. On the other side, the executive has had a share of legislative power in the right to recommend measures and veto acts of Congress, and some presidents have been able to exert considerable influence over the course of legislation by informal persuasion. Nevertheless, for most of the nineteenth century the Constitution worked more or less according to the doctrine of separation. Congress by its lawmaking powers took the initiative in policy-making, while the executive concentrated on enforcement and administration. If the record gave cause for dismay from the framers' standpoint, it would have been in the weakness and dependence of the executive during the heyday of the congressional caucus (1796-1824) and in the corruption that resulted from congressional hegemony for much of the period from the end of the Civil War to the end of the century, especially 1869 to 1892.

During the twentieth century, however, this pattern has changed decisively. Congress continues to play a major role. It is probably the strongest, most independent legislature in the world. It can still force the president to take its judgment and desires into account. Nevertheless, Congress rarely takes the initiative anymore in defining the nation's policies. Most of the time it lets the president define the agenda, then reacts to his proposals. Moreover, it has equipped him for leadership by placing a host of policy-planning councils at his disposal. Meanwhile, the Supreme Court has ruled that congressional attempts to keep a hand in rule making by reserving a legislative veto violates the Constitution. The result is that the presidency, resting on the popular choice of a single individual once every four years, exercises power over the priorities of government, its rule-making powers, and especially the use of force in foreign relations that is incompatible with the traditional American commitment to representative government.

To understand this point, it is essential to recall why the framers separated the powers of the federal government. There were two reasons: to promote vigorous administration and to prevent "tyranny." As Hamilton makes clear in *The Federalist*, the framers created a separate executive so that compromises, which were unavoidable in the legislative process, would not carry over into the administrative process and hobble it. Other numbers of *The Federalist*, particularly those written by Madison, emphasize the dangers of oppression when all the powers of government are united in one place. Americans of the founding generation feared that a "party" might use its powers of appointment to corrupt the legislature. This concern is basic to the rationale behind separation of powers. Madison's constitutionalism was intended to frustrate the control of government by a unified national party. It cannot be stressed too much that it was *not* Madison's intention to cripple the federal government, to make it incapable of formulating a policy and implementing it. His own performance as leader of the House of Representatives during Washington's first term shows that he had no aversion to legislative leadership. What he wanted to prevent was the president, by adroit use of patronage, dominating the legislative process to serve the purposes of a national "faction."

To ask whether Madison and Hamilton and the other framers would have been pleased with the way the system has worked—whether it works as they "intended"—is a question of infinite complexity, as difficult and probably unanswerable as it is, fortunately, irrelevant for our purposes. What we do need to decide is whether the system now serves the fundamental constitutional values which we share with the founding generation.

These constitutional values are complex and subtle, but two are fundamental: Power must be checked and balanced, and authority must be kept accountable to popular will. The framers were aware that these values were sometimes in tension, but they were convinced that they were not contradictory. Furthermore, they believed that the viability of the republic—indeed, the future of republican government generally—required that they both be achieved. Ultimately the people must rule,* but no one—no person, no group, no class—is virtuous enough to rule alone. Reinhold Niebuhr captured the faith that holds these propositions together in a famous aphorism: "Man's capacity for justice makes democracy possible; but man's inclination to injustice makes democracy necessary."[3] Thus, the trick in incorporating these values into a constitutional scheme is to see that the will of the people, which must ultimately prevail, does not become tyrannical.[4] Madison, in *The Federalist*, offers two solutions to this problem. One (in Number 10) is to "extend the sphere" to include a large, varied population so that there will be many interests but no simple majorities. The other (in Number 51) is to complicate the structure and processes of government (by the separation of powers, bicameralism, judicial review, federalism) so that the enactment of new policies will take time, and foolish and wicked schemes can be exposed and popular majorities rallied to oppose them. Madison remarks that a reliance on the people, through elections, is the first line of defense for popular government, but experience has

---

*Note Madison's speeches on August 7 and August 31 at the convention of 1787 and his arguments in *The Federalist*, Number 51, that a dependence on the people is the primary control on government and, in Number 63, that the "cool and deliberate sense of the community" must ultimately prevail over the views of its rulers. Also, see Hamilton's speech on September 8 at the convention and *The Federalist*, Number 71, in which he argues that the deliberate sense of the community must govern the conduct of officials.

taught the need for "auxiliary precautions." The conflicting ambitions of public officials occupying juxtaposed positions in the constitutional structure provide that additional safeguard in the Madisonian
framework.

How have these safeguards worked, and what is their status today?
Certainly the first, what we might call cultural pluralism, still operates to protect liberty and foil tyranny. The country is far larger and
more complex than it was in 1787, and it is even more difficult now
to piece together a majority coalition in support of legislation or policy. Note, for example, how difficult it has been to achieve legislative majorities for welfare, immigration, or tax reform.

Certainly, too, Madison's second protection, outlined in Number
51, stands. The American governmental process is nothing if not
complex. A proposal must pass through a bewildering maze of subcommittees and procedural hurdles before becoming law. Nor do
the obstacles melt away at that point. At the implementing stage
there are many additional opportunities to block or rebend the compromises that emerge from the legislative process. In short, the system operates to make it extremely difficult for the federal government
to take coherent action.

So the main cultural and institutional features on which Madison
relied are still in place. Does the system then serve the constitutional
values to which he and the other leading framers were committed?
In two important respects, I think not. In the first place, the framers
would have been appalled at the extent to which the spirit of the
legislature now infects the administrative process. In their view,
responsiveness to interest groups was a virtue in the legislative process but not in the executive. "Factions" were the bane of administration. Administration needed to be vigorous, decisive, and objective.
That was the primary purpose of the separation of powers, as that
doctrine was understood in 1787.[5] Let the representative assembly
reflect various interests; but let the executive be unified, and let him
or her be chosen through a process that encourages the winner to
transcend the factions that compose the nation so that he or she can
administer the law energetically and fairly.

What has happened instead is that the spirit of the legislature,
operating primarily through legislative committees, permeates the
administrative branch. Through the appropriations process and

through oversight hearings, links are forged between congressional committees, administrative bureaus, and groups in the private sector (suppliers of goods and services, professional associations) that have a particular concern about a given area of policy. In the typical situation the general public has little knowledge of or interest in the policy in question, so the policy subgroup is left pretty much free to its own devices. Sometimes a scandal or a disaster will bring one of these hidden corners of policy to light; sometimes they are hit by a tidal wave, such as a decision to cut domestic spending across the board. Normally, however, they are immune from such external shocks.

From a constitutional standpoint the important thing about these policy subgroups is that they operate virtually without reference to the separation of powers. The authorization, appropriation, and administrative processes are of a piece, dominated by the same considerations and often by many of the same people. The administrative bureau is responsive to the same forces that operate in the legislative arena. When the party that controls the White House is different from the one that dominates on Capitol Hill, the coalition that administers a program may be organized differently from the one that passed the legislation and appropriated the funds, resulting in a frustration of the legislative intent. This, however, is no less a perversion from the standpoint of the framers' doctrine. What the framers sought was vigorous administration of the law, once enacted. What we have instead is a continuing political process.

Considering the shift of initiation and discretion in modern times from the legislative to the executive branches, there is something to be said for the fact that the executive is not free to exercise discretion without ongoing political constraint. The point here, however, is that the separation of powers is not operating as the framers intended.

This brings us to the second respect in which the current operation of separation of powers violates constitutional values. According to Madison's exposition in *The Federalist*, Number 51, the system was designed to make innovation difficult and thus to prevent the quick adoption of unwise schemes. The strategy was basically conservative, to block new departures until there was a broad consensus that they were needed and well conceived. The framers were leery of the tendency of governments to attempt too much, in terms of both domestic engineering and imperial adventures. They thought government should be modest in its ambitions and lean in its structure, so they created a government that would scrutinize ambitious schemes closely and give skeptics a good opportunity to show that proposals were flawed or ill advised or contrary to the public interest. In other words, the structure they created was biased in favor of opposition.

Ironically, this structure now operates to protect a bloated government. Just as it was terribly difficult to pass federal aid for health care, so now it is virtually impossible to enact reforms to "contain" the cost of hospitalization. Just as it was perilously difficult to prepare for World War II and to agree in 1950 to back up our international commitments with strong military forces, so now it is almost impossible to impose rationality and efficiency on defense procurement.

The history of policy-making in the twentieth century shows a pattern. A need emerges. Groups organize to promote a federal response to that need, but constitutional processes foil those groups for many years. A crisis develops. The electorate finally chooses a president and clear majorities in both houses of Congress with a mandate to meet the need. The stalemate is broken. The president proposes and Congress enacts a sweeping program to meet the demand. Then the system settles back into a deadlock that lays an icy grip not only on groups that see other needs but on those that seek to reshape or terminate existing programs.

Thus, in crucial respects the constitutional system no longer operates as the framers intended. It impedes the effort to frame coherent policy, and it hinders executives from giving vigorous, steady enforcement and implementation to the law. It deflects the electorate from rendering a coherent and meaningful judgment on the performance of the government and the promises of the opposition. It encourages administrative and judicial confusion by dividing the will that appoints people to these positions. It induces candidates, the press, and the public to give excessive attention to electoral politics and to slight the process of governing per se.

How have we survived for 200 years with such a system? For three reasons: first, because we are a rich and patient nation, able so far to prosper despite gross inefficiency and the neglect of many problems; secondly, because of innovations of dubious constitutionality, such as the regulatory commission and the legislative veto; and thirdly, through the practice of presidential "dictatorship," particularly in foreign relations.[6] Can we, by these means, survive much longer as a constitutional democracy? I doubt it. If we are to continue faithful to the principles to which the framers committed us, we must disenthrall ourselves from the external forms of an eighteenth-century system of government.

We pass at this point from diagnosis to prescription. Having traced some fundamental problems of modern governance to their roots in the Constitution, we can now inquire whether there are remedies which accord with American values and which offer promise of correcting the defects without creating new dangers.

At the threshold we confront the question of how radically we should seek to modify the existing structure and processes. Because the commitment to the existing system is so strong and the process of amendment so difficult, some people have concluded that it is better to work for small changes that would bring about at least some improvement than to seek a fundamental revision that would address several problems at once. Former Representative Henry Reuss, a thoughtful legislator who has himself proposed a number of constitutional revisions, recommends an incremental approach,[7] but I disagree. It is true, as Reuss notes, that the amendment process is daunting, but it is not much more inviting for small changes than for large ones. The Constitution has been amended sixteen times since the Bill of Rights. Eight of these changes deal with the rights of citizens (blacks, women, eighteen-year-olds, and those who make or sell alcoholic beverages). Two of them clarify ambiguities in the power of Congress (to enact an income tax) and of the judiciary (to entertain suits against states). The other six bear on the structure of the government, but four are of marginal significance. One provides that candidates for vice president be separately designated; one specifies a time for presidential and congressional terms to begin and provides for the death of a president- or vice president-elect before his term begins; one authorizes a nonvoting representative in Congress for the District of Columbia; and one establishes procedures to fill a vacancy in the vice presidency and to replace a disabled president. Only two of the existing twenty-six amendments affect the basic structure of the Constitution even a little bit: the Seventeenth, which provides for the direct election of senators; and the Twenty-second, which limits a president to two full terms. The fact that there have been only two structural changes in almost 200 years does not encourage the thought that changes of this kind are easy to make, however mild they may seem to their proponents.

Against this modest record of success one must weigh the history of massive frustration for incremental reformers. Take the electoral college, for example. The need for reform is obvious. Three times the constitutional process has resulted in the election of presidents who failed to win even a popular-vote plurality. Twelve times electors have voted for candidates other than those to whom they were pledged when voters chose them as electors. It is not hard to imagine circumstances in which "faithless electors" might throw the nation into crisis. Yet the electoral process remains unreformed despite decades of effort and hundreds of proposals offered by such distinguished and disinterested groups as the American Bar Association and a panel of experts gathered by the Twentieth Century Fund.

Even if a specific, limited proposal such as the single six-year term for presidents had a chance of enactment, which I doubt, it could not correct the derangement of our national governance. Is it realistic to expect that a single, isolated politician, however long his term and whether he is looking forward to reelection or not, could command support in Congress for his program? It is possible that a political genius could do that, but if we ever found such a person, would we be happy or wise to limit him or her to a single term? And what if the president were not a genius, were, in fact, incompetent, though not guilty of "treason, bribery, or other high crimes and misdemeanors"? For six years that person would be our president. What tensions would build up? What suffering would occur? What dangers would mount? Or—the likeliest case of all—what if the president were competent but at odds politically with Congress? What if a stalemate developed between a president who saw the public interest one way and a Congress dominated by people who saw it another way? How would the length of the president's term or the certainty of his retirement affect that? We cannot be sure, but it seems as likely to exacerbate it as to relieve it.

The system's faults are unlikely to be corrected by narrowly focused changes. A constitution is an organic whole. Its parts interact. We cannot change one part without causing other parts to act differently. When the Seventeenth Amendment brought about the direct election of senators, the whole party system underwent fundamental change. If a proposed change is profound enough to correct a major problem, it is almost certain to produce effects in far-flung parts of the system. No one will be wise enough to anticipate all these effects, any more than even the wisest framers accurately predicted how their system would operate. Still, it behooves us to recognize that we cannot correct fundamental problems by making minor adjustments. If the problems are minor, we probably ought not to tinker with the system at all. If they are major, we need to take the whole system into consideration.

If the current derangement is fundamental, then we need to consider some basic revisions in the constitutional structure. What are the general principles that should guide the search for these modifications?

First, we need to remove features which serve primarily as deterrents to coherent political action and accountability. In other constitutional democracies the intermediary between the nation and the government is a strong system of political parties. America's parties have not performed very well in helping shape a coherent national will and holding government accountable to it. As a result, they have a poor reputation, and no one wants to rig a constitution in their favor. However, since the character of American parties derives in large part from the system in which they operate, changes in that system would no doubt affect the character of the parties. They would not become programmatic parties on the European model— distinctive features of the American culture would prevent that— but they might move a little in that direction, and the result would be heightened popular accountability.

We need not deal directly with the parties in our reforms, any more than the framers did. If we modify some of the features of the system that were designed to frustrate parties and thereby encourage a broader and more coherent pattern of accountability, political leaders and voters will adapt their behavior to the new framework. The result will be an enhanced environment for the development of responsible political parties.

Secondly, we need to provide a way to resolve deadlocks between the branches. With the separation of powers, stalemates readily develop. Sometimes they reflect the absence of a national will. When there is no regular method for referring basic issues to the nation, however, leaders are sometimes tempted to blame the other side for deadlocks and to play on them for political purposes. If it were possible to go to the electorate when fundamental differences paralyze the government, it would be less tempting to play this costly and disheartening game.

With these considerations in mind, the following proposals may be set forth as one way to accommodate the deepest traditions of American constitutionalism to the demands of modern governance.

1. Repeal the second paragraph of Article I, Section 6 of the Constitution (which prevents any person who holds an appointment in the executive branch from being a member of Congress). Allow the president with the advice and consent of the Senate to appoint members of Congress to administrative offices and to dismiss them from these offices.

2. Provide four-year terms for the president and members of the House and eight-year terms for senators, and leave them all eligible for reelection.* Provide for the election of the presi-

---

*This would involve repealing the Twenty-second Amendment, which limits presidents to two full terms. Republicans resentful of Franklin Roosevelt's four victorious campaigns led the drive for this amendment. Ironically, since its ratification in 1951 only three presidents—Dwight Eisenhower, Richard Nixon, and Ronald Reagan, all of them Republicans—have been reelected for second terms and been ineligible for reelection. The political effect of the amendment has been to make presidents lame ducks during their whole second term. Many Republicans now wish that President Reagan were free of these fetters. The repeal of this amendment is a cause in which Americans irrespective of party affiliation ought now to join.

dent, all members of the House of Representatives, and half the senators (one from each state) at each federal election.

3. Provide for the calling of new federal elections at any time within the four-year period for full terms, either by presidential proclamation with the consent of one-third of either the House or the Senate or by joint resolution—that is, by a majority of both houses of Congress with the president's concurrence. If the president refuses within two weeks to sign the resolution calling for federal elections, provide that the resolution be resubmitted to Congress; if it be passed again by majority votes in both houses, provide that the nation proceed to federal elections. Provide that elections be held within sixty days of the call, whether by proclamation or resolution. Provide that the newly elected president and members of the House begin four-year terms, and the newly elected senators eight-year terms, within two weeks after the elections, unless those terms be shortened by the aforementioned procedures of presidential proclamation or joint resolution.

4. Establish a national (or federal) council, consisting of 100 notable persons chosen for life by the president with the advice and consent of both houses of Congress. Let the council elect one of its members to serve as chief of state for a term of two years, and let the chief of state issue the call for elections and superintend their conduct. Give the council power to review certain types of legislation, and give it power to suspend such statutes for a limited period, pending further consideration by Congress.

The primary purpose of these revisions would be to modify, though not to eliminate, the separation of powers. As we have noted, the essential purpose of the separation of powers is not to clog the machinery of government but to avoid the concentration of power in one place. It serves liberty, not by blocking action but by requiring cooperation. Separation now operates as an almost insurmountable obstacle to sustained cooperation between the branches.* It interferes with the viability of government and thereby creates a temptation to autocracy.

The revisions outlined here preserve an independent executive and legislature. Building on the American tradition of local roots in legislative elections, they retain an independent legislative assembly, with the means and incentive to oppose a president who departs from the popular will or abuses his trust.

At the same time the first proposed revision would encourage cooperation by both the carrot of permitting the executive to appoint members of Congress to his cabinet and the stick of allowing either branch to take the government to the nation in the event of an inability to agree on fundamental policies. The framers in 1787 forbade the appointment of legislators to the cabinet for fear that the president would corrupt Congress by dangling lucrative offices before its members. As several framers anticipated, however, presidents have nevertheless been able to influence legislators by offering administrative appointments to their cronies. By eliminating the constitutional provision which prevents legislators from serving in the executive branch, we would open the way for able leaders in Congress to display and develop executive talents, thereby encouraging the integration of legislative and administrative approaches to policy.

*In November 1980 a panel of the National Academy of Public Administration, cochaired by Don K. Price and Rocco C. Siciliano, issued "a report on presidential management," entitled "A Presidency for the 1980s." The report contained these observations: "In dividing powers among the branches and levels of government, our Constitution deliberately was designed to require cooperative unified action. . . . We now have to face the reality that political power has become fragmented beyond what the founding fathers could have imagined. The cooperation so essential for coping with our national problems is not merely difficult, it has become nearly impossible." The panel went on to argue that constitutional revision is not the proper remedy for this situation; it would be extraordinarily difficult to achieve and might entail "unintended adverse consequences." It preferred instead "a strategy for change within present constitutional boundaries," including various measures "to strengthen the forces of cohesion and integration in our political system by strengthening the capacity of the presidency for leadership."[8] Though the panel's analysis and many of its recommendations seem to me meritorious, I do not see how institutions which have fallen so deeply into fragmentation can be expected to adopt measures to end it without some change in the framework and its incentives.

The second proposal calls for the concurrent election of the president and members of Congress. The framers in 1787 provided that the president, senators, and representatives in Congress serve non-concurrent terms, so that passionate public opinion raging at a given moment could not sweep the nation toward disaster. Such a gust might produce the election of a president and a majority in the House, but two-thirds of the Senate would presumably be immune, having been elected earlier.*

Staggered elections have indeed been a centrifugal force in national politics. After midterm elections Congress usually displays fresh independence of the president, even when he has been able to dominate during his first two years in office. Sometimes the patterns are surprising. Ronald Reagan's strong victory in 1980 was accompanied by a Republican victory in the Senate, the chamber that is supposed to resist sudden shifts, but not in the House. Typically, however, nonconcurrent elections and the differing length of terms have contributed to a situation in which the president and Congress are at loggerheads, especially after the midterm congressional elections. Thus, staggered terms inhibit the concerting of policy. That may sometimes prevent errors, but it always frustrates a clear electoral verdict on the government and its policies.

If we adopted concurrent elections, would there be sufficient resistance to the momentary delusions of popular opinion? I think there would be. It would come from the deep-rooted traditions of localism in legislative elections. As the late Willmoore Kendall, a conservative political theorist, once pointed out, the framers' system set up "two majorities." One, the presidential, focuses on the nation's ideals and its global context, which are relatively abstract considerations in the minds of most voters. The other, the congressional, counts the costs of policy very carefully. Kendall argued that electoral campaigns in the presidential arena tend to be plebiscitary; would-be leaders and their campaign organizations manipulate gross images in an effort to attract huge groups of voters. Congressional politics is less grand, more intimate. During campaigns and in between, mem-

---

*The judiciary is, of course, also insulated from such momentary passions, but we do not propose to change that. The ability of courts to protect the rights of individuals and such organizations as churches and publishing companies in the face of strong political currents is an essential ingredient of constitutional liberty.

bers of Congress tend to deal with their districts through the leaders of particular groups. Kendall argued that the framers established these two majorities in national politics deliberately, believing that policy which resulted from an accommodation of these two outlooks would be stronger and sounder than that which would issue from either alone.[9]

Kendall saw staggered elections as a crucial device for keeping the president and Congress separate and independent. Writing in the 1950s, he was less concerned than I am about the dangers of stalemate and incoherence. If we sought to induce greater effectiveness by eliminating staggered elections, would the distinctive contributions of the presidential and congressional "majorities" survive? I believe they would, perhaps in a somewhat weakened form but sufficiently for the purposes of liberty and sound policy. This nation is not dominated by a single capital, as Great Britain, France, and Japan are. Its regions are strongly marked by varying conditions and traditions. The same district can repeatedly give a clear majority to Democratic candidates for president and Senate, for example, but retain a liberal Republican representative in the House. A state can vote for a Republican candidate for president but keep its conservative Democratic senator. In a country as diverse as the Untied States there is no reason to suppose that the electorate will be so seized by an ideological passion that it will sweep away its traditions of localism in a single swing. Nor will members of Congress once elected, or candidates for Congress, lack incentive to establish their independence from national trends when those trends are at variance with local opinion.

The third proposal is perhaps the most radical and the most important. It calls for introducing a power of dissolution into the American system.

As it stands, the Constitution contains no provision for removing a failed government before the end of its term, except for impeachment and the clauses of the Twenty-fifth Amendment relating to presidential "inability." It is owing to our relatively primitive and isolated situation for most of our history, and to good luck since the 1930s, that we have survived without such a provision.

The demise of Richard Nixon's presidency provided a test for the Constitution in this regard, and some people think that it "worked." In fact, our escape from that predicament was made possible by two fortuitous circumstances: the existence of a tape that proved President Nixon's complicity in criminal acts beyond a reasonable doubt and the resignation of Vice President Spiro Agnew. The latter aspect is not always accorded its proper weight. If Agnew had been merely a nonentity, as Nixon thought, rather than guilty of indictable acts of corruption, then the Watergate process would have ended in our having a manifestly incompetent president who had attained the position solely as Nixon's personal choice. Would that not have been a disaster? As it was, Agnew was forced to resign, and Nixon, by then politically impotent, was forced to negotiate his choice of a successor with Congress. In that episode we came closer to the reality of parliamentary government than at any time in our history since the early nineteenth century, when presidential candidates were nominated by congressional caucuses.

The end of Nixon's presidency shows not that the Constitution "works" to provide a smooth transition out of a failed presidency but that in all but the most extraordinary circumstances it is likely to deliver us into an impasse. An impeachment and trial may be a proper way to deal with "treason, bribery, or other high crimes and misdemeanors," but they do not solve the problem of succession, and they are altogether inappropriate for other likely causes of governmental breakdown and failure.

Without a dissolution mechanism, the constituent elements of our government can virtually ignore public sentiment during their terms in office without having to leave public office. No matter how embattled his policy became, Lyndon Johnson knew that he would serve at least until January 1969, God willing. Same thing (mutatis mutandis) for the senators who thwarted Woodrow Wilson's treaty. Outraged public opinion can cripple the government, shame it, virtually immobilize it, but it cannot dislodge it.

Another consequence is that, without a dissolution mechanism, elected officials shift the blame for policy failures, and the electorate has no way to render a judgment on fundamental disputes. The president wants to reduce the deficit one way; the House and Senate each have different plans. John Locke said that when elements of the government are in fundamental dispute, "the people shall judge." It may be that the public mind itself is unresolved and that a new election would result in a return of the same divided elements; but at least we would know that the electorate had had a chance to change things, and politicians would have to compromise as best they could, without pretending that the issue pitted one side, supported by the public will, against a selfish minority.

It is difficult to devise a dissolution mechanism for the existing American constitutional system because several of its features are ill adapted to it.[10] First of all, we have no head of state, separate from the active political leadership, who might issue the call for new elections and guarantee routine administration during the hiatus between the call and the elections. In addition, our bicameral legislature gives us three separate arenas of power.* When one party has a majority in all three arenas, we can theoretically have something approximating a government and opposition, though the Carter presidency reminds us that it is not neat even in these relatively simple, though increasingly rare, circumstances. When one or both legislative chambers are controlled by the party that loses the White House, the situation can no longer be described, even loosely, as government and opposition. Thus, it is difficult to frame political choices in terms that can be resolved by a national election.

Besides these structural problems, there are cultural factors that complicate the search for a dissolution mechanism. We are deeply committed to the habit and expectation of fixed elections—certain dates for national elections and certain lengths for terms in office.

---

*The easiest way to overcome this difficulty would be to replace our bicameral legislature with a single chamber, providing representation in it by the formula used for the electoral college. Such a change would depart from the "great compromise" of 1787, and it might weaken the role of states in the federal system. Its advantage, in addition to facilitating a dissolution mechanism, would be to strengthen the legislature in its dealing with the executive. *The Federalist*, Number 51, makes clear that the division of the legislature into two chambers was intended partly to weaken it in relation to the executive. As we have seen, the requirements of modern governance have greatly strengthened the executive's hand. If we value the contribution of a representative assembly to constitutional government, it may be necessary now to redress the balance. A unicameral legislature would be in a much stronger position to "consult" with the president, as the War Powers Resolution, for example, requires.

Also, we tend to reelect incumbents,* making one wonder whether new elections would very often produce a change in the pattern of government. Finally, there is the length of time we now devote to all the stages of a national election (primaries, caucuses, conventions, general electioneering) and to the period between the election and the inauguration of a new administration. It takes a full year from the opening of the presidential campaign in Iowa and New Hampshire until the inauguration the following January. Presumably this could be shortened, but how much? Certainly a year, or any substantial fraction thereof, would be an intolerably long time for a legally dissolved government to flounder along.

These are daunting problems for those who seek a better way to remove a disgraced or deadlocked government. The inescapable conclusion is that unless we are willing to make other revisions in the existing constitutional structure and unless the culture is willing to modify certain long-standing habits, dissolution will not improve our system.

A minimum essential change is the one we have outlined in the second proposal, providing for the concurrent election of the president, all members of the House, and one senator from each state, with the president and House members being elected to terms lasting up to four years and the senators for terms lasting as long as eight years. Some people have argued for this change to coordinated terms on its own merits, to reduce the tendency of our system toward incoherence.[12] If such a revision were adopted, however, we would be compelled, it seems to me, to consider a dissolution mechanism. Would it not be intolerable to be stuck with a floundering government for two or three years? We ought not in any case to go four years with no way for the people to register an electoral judgment on the government's performance. No constitutional regime in the world is impervious to popular disaffection to this extent.

There are, it seems to me, three criteria which a dissolution mechanism must meet. First, it must not destabilize the system. It must not make the government overly sensitive, vulnerable to every

---

* In House elections between 1950 and 1982, 91.8 percent of those who sought it won reelection. The figures for Senate elections are somewhat lower: 76 percent for the same period.[11]

opportunistic effort, every impulse of criticism which political opponents are bound to mount.

Secondly, it must not weaken the presidency, which is the primary force for coherence in the government. The president is the regime's integrator, its mobilizer in times of crisis, its principal agent in foreign relations. Michel Debré, former prime minister of France and a leading framer of its current Fifth Republic constitution, notes that France during the Fourth Republic (1946–1958) found itself unsuited for modern governance by the absence of an executive capable of conducting the nation's foreign relations, commanding its strategic forces, and coordinating its energies in times of domestic crisis.[13] The constitution of the Fifth Republic finally provided France with a strong president. We ought not to weaken the one we already have.

Thirdly, our mechanism for dissolution must not weaken Congress, which is the primary arena for representation in the regime, the locus of open deliberation, and the voice of regions and localities. Our representative assembly must be separate and independent, an opening for dissent and the representation of interests that have lost out in the contest for control of the executive. It must be capable of calling the executive to account when the nation deems that the executive is abusing its power.

With these considerations in mind, is it possible to design a dissolution mechanism for the American system? To do so, we must face and decide the following questions.

Who should be able to invoke special elections?

The president, if he or she is blocked by Congress, ought to be able to take the deadlock to the nation. However, since our purpose is to build incentives for cooperation and cohesion, we should require that he or she gain support from at least part of Congress before issuing the call for elections. I have suggested one-third of either house of Congress. If the standard were much higher, it might not be possible to break deadlocks.

There may also be occasions when Congress needs to take the executive to the nation. We need to provide for that, with suitable restraint to prevent abuse. I have suggested the requirement of a simple majority of both houses of Congress, with an opportunity for the president to require a reconsideration by Congress, presumably in light of his objections.*

Ultimately, when elected officials are at loggerheads, the people must judge. A case can be made that the people should also decide when new elections are needed, but most of us recoil from the notion of using a referendum for this purpose. It smacks of plebiscitary democracy and seems to invite demagoguery, and there is no precedent for it in the United States or in any other modern democracy. Besides, popular disaffection can register itself in other ways. If the public demand for elections is powerful enough, politicians will feel and act on it.

Should we try to define the circumstances that justify new elections?

My answer is no. In 1974 several members of Congress tried to write such a prescription, without success.[15] The best solution is to provide a carefully regulated process and trust to the interplay of public opinion and the incentives that guide elected officials to develop a tradition.

Which offices should be at stake in the new elections?

Dissolution ought not to be seen primarily as a punishment meted out by one branch on the other, but rather as reflecting the breakdown of normal political processes. Furthermore, its purpose is to produce a new popular mandate. The whole government should be put before the nation. Under the present constitutional framework, it would probably be best to leave two-thirds of the Senate in place, for purposes of continuity; under the revisions proposed here, half the Senate (one senator from each state) would remain in place. If the senators who had not faced elections adamantly refused to respond to the spirit of the mandate and blocked the new government's program, another round of elections might be necessary to resolve the logjam. This would be an unlikely outcome, however, in view of the sensitivity of elected officials. It is not only the Supreme Court that reads election returns.

---

*Sundquist asks whether a minority party in Congress (for example, the Democrats in 1931 or the Republicans in 1979) could ever muster a majority to call new elections, no matter how ineffective the president was.[14] My answer is, it could, if public demand were strong enough. Otherwise it ought not to be able to.

Should there be full new terms for the winners, or should they fill the unexpired terms?

If the opposition wins the election, it makes no sense to give them abbreviated terms. Even if the incumbents win, they ought to have a full chance to carry out their program, subject, of course, to the possibility of failure and the demand for new elections before the end of their terms. In the event of deadlock, we seek renewal and clarification of the people's mandate. We should emerge from the elections with a fresh government, ready and capable to govern. Dissolution with unexpired terms undermines that goal; dissolution with new terms contributes to it.

How soon should elections come after the decision to have them has been made?

If parties and candidates continued to organize their affairs as they do now, we would need to allow many months. But if we shortened the time available, campaign organizations would have to make some of their preparations before the decision to proceed to new elections was made. They would have to stand ready for elections more or less perpetually, as they do now in other democracies. Thus, the effect of dissolution and irregular elections would be to strengthen the parties, to shorten campaigns, and to reduce the cost of campaigning. These important goals of reform have proved elusive under the existing Constitution, but with these revisions they would be attained indirectly.

How much time would be needed between elections and the inauguration?

Here again we ought not to be constrained by present practices. There ought to be some reasonable compromise between our present practice of waiting two and a half months for the inauguration of a newly elected president and the parliamentary habit of turning over the reins almost immediately. I would suggest a brief period, two to four weeks at the most, to encourage a more continuous state of readiness on the part of the opposition and to cut short the death rattle on a repudiated government. It would also be healthy, I think, if we cut back on the pomp and circumstance that accompany our present inaugural circuses.

In sorting through these questions, I am reminded of the maxim that in a democracy the longer you examine an issue, the more complicated it becomes. Despite the difficulties, however, one keeps coming back to dissolution. It is absolutely essential for the renewal of American constitutionalism. The basic problems with our regime are twofold: its rigidity and its lack of accountability, both internally and to the nation at large. A mechanism that induces the government to cooperate internally, that enables us to replace a failed government, and that provides a way for the nation to resolve fundamental disputes can help correct these problems.

Finally, let me add a word of explanation about my last proposal, which calls for a new national (or federal) council. The American tradition lacks two elements found in most constitutional regimes: a chief of state separate from active political leaders and a council to which public notables might retire at the end of their active service and from which they might, on occasion, make useful contributions to the national well-being. These deficiencies might be solved by the creation of a national council, composed of former elected officials (presidents, members of Congress, perhaps governors) and possibly other persons appointed by the government for distinguished national service. Or it might be a federal council, with one member chosen from each of the fifty states, either ex officio (such as the governor or lieutenant governor) or someone specifically elected for a term of office. If its membership made it appropriate, certain types of legislation might be referred to this body for review and the consideration of amendments, with the proviso that it not delay the enactment of legislation by more than, say, sixty days. The council, however constituted, could choose from its own membership one person to act as chief of state for a fixed term, who could issue the formal call and superintend federal elections when the government directed and provide continuity during the period between governments.

Would these revisions give the United States a parliamentary system? No, they would not. The essence of a parliamentary system is that the legislature chooses the chief executive and cabinet—or rather, the electorate chooses between partisan candidates for seats in an assembly, and the prevailing party or coalition in the legislature in turn chooses the executive. In the American system the executive and the legislature are separately and popularly elected. That is the crucial difference between the American system and parliamentary democracy, and these revisions would retain it.

It is possible, of course, that parties may attempt to bridge the separation. It happened between 1796 and 1824 under the current Constitution, when congressional caucuses nominated presidential candidates. The Democrats made another feeble attempt during the late 1950s, when Paul Butler, their national chairman, tried to organize a council consisting of legislative leaders in association with other leaders of the party for the purpose of periodically renewing the party's position on evolving issues. Ever since the Jacksonian Democrats adopted the national convention, however, such attempts at "party government" have had little effect. The revisions proposed here would be more hospitable to party government than the design of 1787, but the persistence of the separation of powers in modified form would still constitute an obstacle. Everything would depend, as it does now, on the skill of political leaders in putting together a group of candidates for executive and legislative office that could win a national majority.

Epilogue

The attempt here has been to renew the American system of government using American materials. There is no social engineering in these proposals and no attempt to graft a foreign system onto this nation. I begin with American political ideals and principles and with American forms of government. Having concluded that the design of 1787 no longer serves those ideals and principles and having determined that the Constitution as framed in 1787 is no longer "adequate to the exigencies of government and the preservation of the Union" (quoting the resolve of Congress that called the convention of 1787 into being), I have proposed a rearrangement of some of its elements. It would retain essential features of the original design:

A bill of rights
An independent judiciary with powers of judicial review
A separation of executive and legislative branches, rooted in separate constituencies, and
A federal system.

It would remove a key barrier to cooperation between the political branches by allowing members of Congress to serve in the cabinet, but it would permit the retention of the traditional legislative committees. Indeed, there is no reason to assume that the committees of Congress would not flourish in this system. It would retain the traditional way of allocating weight in the electoral process for the presidency.

The most radical departure here from the design of 1787 is the provision for calling federal elections by presidential proclamation or joint resolution. I make this suggestion to deal with the tendency of the government to fall into stalemate, particularly during the last two years of a president's term, and to encourage more harmonious, cooperative relations between the president and Congress. Under present arrangements, when the president and Congress are politically estranged, the president is sorely tempted to govern autocratically. Until the four-year term has run its course, decisions must be made, the bureaucracy must be guided, and foreign relations must proceed whether the president and Congress are working harmoniously or not. There is no way to resolve stalemates, no matter how deeply antagonistic the political branches may be, and no way to remove a discredited administration. Even impeachment removes only one person, and he or she must be proved guilty of a gross crime. Otherwise, an incumbent president is secure in office, no matter how incompetent he or she may be, or how alienated from Congress or the prevailing temper of the nation.

The other advantage of elections that are freed from the calendar is that the time devoted to electioneering could be greatly shortened. In fact, this is the only way to control the length of campaigns, short of repealing the First Amendment. In regimes where it is possible for the government to call elections at any time within a prescribed limit, parties must aim to be in a state of readiness at all times. They cannot gear their operations toward specific dates. In consequence, they tend to have regular conferences for renewing their platforms and to have strong central coordinating committees and strong district committees, ready to mobilize quickly for an election. They also have shadow leadership, including potential cabinet ministers, ready to assume responsibility in the event of a favorable election outcome.

Parties in such regimes are not always "strong." They can be riven by factionalism and doctrinal disputes, just as parties are in America from time to time. But there is a strong incentive for political energy to flow toward getting party organizations ready for a short campaign rather than groom individual candidates for a long campaign.

The changes I have proposed would not necessarily produce sound policy. That would depend on the wisdom and skill of our leaders and the health of our culture. What they would do is remove the constitutional obstacles to coherent policy and improve the chances that the electorate could produce a government and then hold it accountable for its actions.

It is time to renew the American experiment in constitutional democracy. Its development has been fitful in recent years, as Congress and successive administrations have sought ways to adjust a 200-year-old framework to the insistent demands of modernity, and as the Supreme Court has groped for ways to decide which accommodations are sufficiently in accord with the framers' design and which are not. Despite these creative and dedicated efforts, the feeling has grown that we have lost our way, that our institutions no longer serve the principles that we share with the founding generation.

The proposals set forth here are imperfect, even on their own terms. They may be thought too timid, or too radical, as the nation comes to understand its situation and needs. But if they are seen as arising out of the American tradition, and if they seem to move in the direction of proposing a system of government that can be both effective and accountable to the popular will, perhaps other minds—or, even better, the collective mind of the American people—will deem them worthy of criticism and improvement.

Notes

PREFACE

1. E. S. Corwin, *The President: Office and Powers*, 3d ed. (New York: New York University Press, 1948), p. 2.
2. Clinton Rossiter, *The American Presidency*, rev. ed. (New York: Harcourt, Brace, 1960), ch. 1.

CHAPTER 1: THE PRESIDENCY AFTER
TWO HUNDRED YEARS

1. On eighteenth-century arrangements, see J. H. Plumb, *England in the Eighteenth Century* (Baltimore: Penguin, 1950); for the nineteenth century, Walter Bagehot, *The English Constitution* (first published in 1867; Ithaca: Cornell University Press, 1963); and for twentieth-century constitutional developments, R. H. S. Crossman, *The Myth of Cabinet Government* (Cambridge: Harvard University Press, 1972).
2. *Newsweek* (November 18, 1963), P. 29. See also the interview of Walter Lippmann by Charles Collingwood, in *The New Republic* (May 18, 1963), in which Lippmann traced the stalemate in national affairs to Kennedy's reluctance to give offense to his fellow politicians.
3. This period of hope and expectancy produced two of the durable classics about the presidency: Rossiter, op. cit., and Richard Neustadt, *Presidential Power* (New York: John Wiley, 1960), revised in 1980.
4. Norman Mailer, *Miami and the Siege of Chicago* (New York: World Publishing Co., 1968).

5. For an account of how and why the Democrats in Congress abandoned President Johnson, and with what consequences, see David S. Broder, *The Party's Over* (New York: Harper & Row, 1972).

6. Memo dated January 3, 1969; published later by the *New York Times*, March 11, 1970, p. 30.

7. Theodore White, *Breach of Faith: The Fall of Richard Nixon* (New York: Atheneum, 1975), especially pp. 136–38; see also Jonathan Schell, *Time of Illusion* (New York: Random House, 1975).

8. Richard P. Nathan, *The Plot That Failed: Nixon and the Administrative Presidency* (New York: John Wiley, 1975), p. 63 ff.

9. For a discussion of these and other problems with impeachment, see Hans A. Linde, "Replacing a President," *George Washington Law Review*, vol. 43, no. 2 (January 1975), pp. 384–402.

10. *New York Times*, December 17, 1985, p. B11.

11. See "A Presidency for the 1980s," a report by a panel of the National Academy of Public Administration, cochaired by Don K. Price and Rocco C. Siciliano, in *The Illusion of Presidential Government*, Hugh Heclo and Lester M. Salamon, eds. (Boulder, Colo.: Westview Press, 1981), pp. 303–07; also Arnold J. Meltsner, ed., *Politics and the Oval Office* (San Francisco: Institute for Contemporary Studies, 1981); and Kevin Phillips, "An American Parliament," *Harper's Magazine* (November 1980), pp. 14–21.

12. See the remarkable memorandums written during the 1980 campaign by pollsters Richard Wirthlin (for Reagan) and Patrick Caddell (for Carter). They are printed in an appendix to Elizabeth Drew, *Portrait of an Election* (New York: Simon & Schuster, 1981).

13. *New York Times*, loc. cit.

14. William H. Gray, "Expect Chaos," *New York Times*, December 19, 1985, p. A31.

15. Letter to Samuel Kercheval, July 12, 1816.

CHAPTER 2: THE IDEA OF THE EXECUTIVE

1. Max Farrand, ed., *The Records of the Federal Convention of 1787* (New Haven: Yale University Press, 1911, 1937), vol. II, P. 278 (August 13). Hereafter cited as II Farrand 278.

2. Circular Letter, dated June 8, 1783, in John C. Fitzpatrick, ed., *The Writings of George Washington* (Washington, D.C.: Government Printing Office, 1938), vol. 26, p. 485.

3. Quoted by Ralph Ketcham, *Presidents Above Party* (Chapel Hill: University of North Carolina Press, 1984) p. 6, from an essay by Madison published in 1792.

4. Quoted by Gerald Stourzh, *Alexander Hamilton and the Idea of Republican Government* (Stanford: Stanford University Press, 1970), p. 4.

5. Zera Fink, *The Classical Republicans*, 2d ed. (Evanston: Northwestern University Press, 1962), p. viii.

6. Ibid., p. 30.

7. Printed in Charles Blitzer, *An Immortal Commonwealth: The Political Thought of James Harrington* (New Haven: Yale University Press, 1960), p. 237.

8. S. B. Liljegren, *Harrington's Oceana* (Heidelberg: Carl Winters Universitäts Buchhandlung, 1924), pp. 112, 114; cf. Niccolò Machiavelli, *The Prince and the Discourses* (New York: Random House, 1950), Book I, ch. 34, pp. 201–04. Unfortunately there is no modern edition of the full text of Harrington's *Oceana*. For selected excerpts, see Charles Blitzer, ed., *The Political Writings of James Harrington: Representative Selections* (New York: Liberal Arts Press, 1955), which contains a brief sketch of Harrington's life (pp. xiv–xxv). Blitzer argues (p. xii) that, to discover "the original rationale of many of the characteristic features of the government of the Untied States—such as the written constitution, the secret ballot, and the rotation of the membership in the Senate—one must not look to *The Federalist* or to the other writings of our Founding Fathers, but rather to Harrington's *Commonwealth of Oceana*." For interpretations of Harrington's influence in America, see H. F. Russell Smith, *Harrington and His Oceana: A Study of a Seventeenth Century Utopia and Its Influence in America* (Cambridge, England: Cambridge University Press, 1914), and J. G. A. Pocock, *The Machiavellian Moment: Florentine Political Thought and the Atlantic Republican Tradition* (Princeton: Princeton University Press, 1975), ch. XIV and XV, in which Pocock argues that "the American Revolution and Constitution in some sense form the last act of the civic Renaissance" (p. 462).

9. Peter Laslett, ed., *John Locke: Two Treatises of Government*, rev. ed. (Cambridge, England: Cambridge University Press, 1970), Sections 134 and 150 of the *Second Treatise*. All citations in this chapter from Locke's work are from the *Second Treatise*; hereafter I will cite as *Second Treatise*, Section 134. Some scholars insist that Locke's *Second Treatise* was not widely known among the American founders. The boldest statement of this thesis is Garry Wills, *Inventing America* (Garden City: Doubleday, 1978). For a review of this debate and an assessment of Locke's influence, see Isaac Kramnick, "Republican Revisionism Revisited," *American Historical Review*, vol. 87 (June 1982), pp. 629–64. For a careful discussion of Locke as a source of the American doctrine of separation of powers, see W. B. Gwyn, *The Meaning of the Separation of Powers* (New Orleans: Tulane University Press, 1965), ch. V; also, M. J. C. Vile, *Constitutionalism and the Separation of Powers* (London: Oxford University Press, 1967), pp. 58–67.

10. Locke, *Second Treatise*, Section 213.

11. Ibid., Sections 143, 144.

12. Ibid., Section 222.

13. Ibid., Section 144. Some commentators, stressing that Locke relied on trust rather than institutional checks to ensure the proper functioning of his system, insist that he was not truly a source of the American doctrine of separation of powers. However, on the crucial point concerning the need to keep the legislative and executive "in distinct hands" for the sake of the rule of law (Section 153), Locke did anticipate the American tradition.

14. Ibid., Section 153.

15. Ibid., Section 156; cf. Section 167.

16. Ibid., Section 159.
17. Ibid., Section 160.
18. Clinton Rossiter, *Constitutional Dictatorship: Crisis Government in the Modern Democracies* (New York: Harcourt, Brace, 1963), pp. 138, 218–19 et passim.
19. Locke, *Second Treatise*, Sections 147, 148.
20. M. J. C. Vile, *Constitutionalism and the Separation of Powers* (London: Oxford University Press, 1967) emphasizes this point (p. 60).
21. Locke, *Second Treatise*, Section 152.
22. Ibid., Section 153; Locke's emphasis.
23. Ibid., Section 214–19.
24. Ibid., Section 168.
25. Ibid., Sections 223 and 225.
26. Ibid., Section 168.
27. David Wallace Carrithers, ed., *The Spirit of Laws, by Montesquieu* (Berkeley: University of California Press, 1977), Book XI, ch. 6, paragraph 5. Hereafter citations to *The Spirit of Laws* will be in the following form: XI:6,5, which means that the passage is taken from Book XI, ch. 6, the fifth paragraph. *The Spirit of Laws*, published in 1748, was available in an excellent English translation as early as 1750. Paul Spurlin, *Montesquieu in America, 1760–1801* (Baton Rouge: Louisiana State University Press, 1940), assesses its influence.
28. Ibid., XI:6,3.
29. Ibid., XI:6,30.
30. Ibid., XI:6,31.
31. Ibid., XI:6,45–46.
32. Ibid., XI:6,50.
33. Betty Kemp, "Sir William Blackstone," *Encyclopaedia Britannica*, 15th ed. (1974), "Macropedia," vol. 2, p. 1098.
34. William Blackstone, *Commentaries* (Philadelphia: J. B. Lippincott, 1863), vol. I, Book 1.
35. Ibid., pp. 105, 116–117.
36. Quoted in E. Neville Williams, *The Eighteenth-Century Constitution, 1688–1815* (London: Cambridge University Press, 1960), p. 75.
37. Blackstone, op. cit., pp. 105 and 111–12.
38. Ibid., p. 203.
39. Ibid., p. 252.
40. Ibid., p. 253.
41. Trevor Colbourn, ed., *Fame and the Founding Fathers: Essays by Douglass Adair* (New York: W. W. Norton, 1974), p. 95.
42. I borrow this term from Stanley Elkins and Eric McKittrick's classic essay, "The Founding Fathers: Young Men of the Revolution," *Political Science Quarterly*, vol. 76 (1961), pp. 181–216.
43. Charles Hendel, ed., "Perfect Commonwealth," in *David Hume's Political Essays* (New York: Liberal Arts Press, 1953), p. 157. Two works containing Hume's political ideas were read by political leaders in America: *Essays, Moral and Political*, originally published in 1742 and 1752 and available in America in a two-volume

edition published in 1758; and *History of England*, published in several volumes between 1754 and 1762. For a precis of the *History*, see Hendel's Introduction, ibid., pp. xxvii-xli. On the influence of Scottish thinkers in America, besides Adair's seminal essay (in Colbourn, op. cit., pp. 93–106), see Wills, *Inventing America*, especially Part Three; also Garry Wills, *Explaining America* (Garden City: Doubleday, 1981), which Wills dedicates to Douglass Adair, "who saw it first."

44. Hume, "Of the Independence of Parliament," loc. cit., pp. 73–76; see also pp. 69–70.
45. Hume, "That Politics May Be Reduced to a Science," loc. cit., p. 13; "Of the Parties of Great Britain," loc. cit., p. 89.
46. Hume, "Idea of a Perfect Commonwealth," loc. cit., pp. 145–46.
47. Hume "That Politics May Be Reduced to a Science," loc. cit., pp. 14–15.
48. Hume, "Of Parties in General" and "Of the Parties in Great Britain," loc. cit., pp. 77–92. As Douglass Adair noticed, Hume's typology of parties closely parallels Madison's account of the sources of faction in *The Federalist*, Number 10. Adair thought there was no doubt that Madison had studied Hume's *Essays* closely (Colbourn, op. cit., pp. 98–106).
49. Hume, "Idea of a Perfect Commonwealth," loc. cit., pp. 149, 152.
50. Max Farrand, ed., *The Records of the Federal Convention* (New Haven: Yale University Press, 1911, 1937), vol. I, p. 376. Hereafter cited as I Farrand 376.
51. Rossiter, *Constitutional Dictatorship*, pp. 12–13.

CHAPTER 3: FIRST EXPERIMENTS IN GOVERNMENT

1. Robert J. Taylor, ed., *The Papers of John Adams* (Cambridge, Mass.: Belknap Press, 1977), vol. 4, p. 88.
2. Evarts B. Greene, *The Provincial Governor in the English Colonies of North America* (New York: Longmans, Green and Co., 1898), ch. III.
3. Francis N. Thorpe, ed., *The Federal and State Constitutions* (Washington, D.C.: Government Printing Office, 1909), vol. IV, p. 2452. hereafter cited as IV Thorpe 2452.
4. Blackstone, op. cit., (1863), vol. I, pp. 227–32; and J. L. DeLolme, *The Constitution of England*, new ed. (London: Robinson and Murray, 1789), pp. 63, 71–74.
5. Allan Nevins, *The American States During and After the Revolution, 1775–1789* (New York: Macmillan, 1974), pp. 7–8.
6. Bernard Bailyn, *The Ordeal of Thomas Hutchinson* (Cambridge, Mass.: Belknap Press, 1974), especially ch. V.
7. Gordon S. Wood, *The Creation of the American Republic, 1776–1787* (originally published in 1969; New York: W. W. Norton, 1972), pp. 155–59.
8. William C. Morey, "The First State Constitutions," *Annals of the American Academy of Political and Social Science*, vol. IV, (1893–1894), p. 218.
9. IV Thorpe 2452–53.
10. James Wilson, "Considerations on the Nature and Extent of the Legislative Authority of the British Parliament," in Robert G. McCloskey, ed., *The Works of James Wilson*

(Cambridge, Mass.: Belknap Press, 1967), vol. II, pp. 721–46; Thomas Jefferson, "A Summary View of the Rights of British America," in Julian P. Boyd, ed., *The Papers of Thomas Jefferson* (Princeton: Princeton University Press, 1950), vol. I, pp. 121–35; and John Adams, "The Letters of Novanglus," in Taylor, ed., op. cit., vol. 2, pp. 216–387.

11. Thomas Paine, *Common Sense and Other Political Writings*, Nelson F. Adkins, ed. (Indianapolis: Bobbs-Merrill, 1953), pp. 4, 11–14.

12. Ibid., pp. 14–15, 16–18. The emphasis on "an ass" is Paine's.

13. Ibid., pp. 7, 31–32.

14. Letter dated March 19, 1776. Taylor, op. cit., vol. 4, p. 68. See also Adams's letters to William Tudor, April 12, 1776, and James Warren, May 12, 1776 (ibid., vol. 4, pp. 118 and 182.)

15. Ibid., vol. IV, pp. 70–72.

16. Ibid., vol. IV, p. 87.

17. VII Thorpe 3812–19.

18. Dumas Malone, *Jefferson the Virginian*, vol. I, *Jefferson and His Time* (Boston: Little, Brown, 1948), chs. XVIII–XX.

19. Malone's account is more sympathetic. See ibid., chs. XXII–XXV.

20. Ibid., pp. 361–66.

21. Thomas Jefferson, *Notes on the State of Virginia* (New York: Harper & Row, 1964), p. 113.

22. Ibid., pp. 120–24. Compare Locke's ideas about prerogative. In some ways Jefferson was a very naïve man.

23. Ibid., pp. 198–99.

24. Richard Barry, *Mr. Rutledge of South Carolina* (New York: Duel, Sloan and Pearce, 1942), pp. 226–33.

25. Ibid., pp. 264.

26. VI Thorpe 3248.

27. Quoted by Rossiter, *Constitutional Dictatorship: Crisis Government in the Modern Democracies*, loc. cit., p. 213.

28. V Thorpe 2623–83.

29. Ibid., 2628–29.

30. Morey, op. cit., p. 227.

31. V Thorpe 2628–29.

32. Wood, op. cit., p. 157.

33. V Thorpe 2633–34.

34. Oscar Handlin and Mary Handlin, eds., *The Popular Sources of Political Authority: Documents on the Massachusetts Constitution of 1780* (Cambridge, Mass.: Belknap Press, 1966), pp. 59–60.

35. Ibid., p. 337.

36. Ibid., p. 345.

37. Ibid., p. 364.

38. III Thorpe 1893–94, 1899–1905.

39. Nevins, op. cit., p. 182n.

40. IV Thorpe 2453–70, especially 2462–66.

41. Charles Page Smith, *James Wilson, Founding Father, 1742–1798* (Chapel Hill: University of North Carolina Press, 1956), pp. 112–13.
42. "Minutes of the Council of Censors, 1783–84," *Pennsylvania Archives*, 3d series (Harrisburg: Clarence M. Busch, 1896), vol. 10, p. 804 (hereafter cited as "Minutes"). Pages 787–809 of this volume contain the report, dated January 19, 1784, of the Council of Censors while it was dominated by the Republicans, including the Constitutionalists' dissent.
43. V Thorpe 3081–92.
44. V Thorpe 3091–92.
45. "Minutes," pp. 789–90; cf. Robert L. Brunhouse, *The Counter-Revolution in Pennsylvania, 1776–1790* (Harrisburg: Pennsylvania Historical Commission, 1942), ch. 6.
46. "Minutes," pp. 790–02.
47. Ibid., p. 808.
48. Brunhouse, op. cit., pp. 159–61.
49. Council of Censors, *A Report of the Committee of the Council of Censors* (Philadelphia: Francis Bailey, 1784), pp. 12–16. This document contains the Constitutionalists' analysis of the performance of the Pennsylvania government since 1776. It was used, somewhat ironically, by Madison in *The Federalist*, Number 50, as evidence for his argument that unicameral legislatures tend to encroach on the constitutional turf of other branches.
50. Ibid., pp. 3–4.
51. V Thorpe 3987.
52. Wood, op. cit., Part III; also, pp. 403–10, 432 et passim.

CHAPTER 4: THE CONVENTION OF 1787

1. Dispatch to French foreign secretary, Comte de Montmorin, April 10, 1787, in Max Farrand, ed., *The Records of the Federal Convention* (New Haven: Yale University Press, 1911, 1937), Vol. III, p. 15. Hereafter cited as III Farrand 15.
2. Alexander Hamilton was one. See Clinton Rossiter, *1787: The Grand Convention* (New York: Macmillan, 1966), p. 53.
3. Winton U. Solberg, ed., *The Federal Convention and the Formation of the Union of American States* (Indianapolis: Bobbs-Merrill, 1958), p. 54.
4. Ibid., p. 59.
5. III Farrand 559–86.
6. The analysis in this section is based on material presented in my essay, "The Inventors of the Presidency," *Presidential Studies Quarterly*, vol. XIII (Winter 1983), pp. 8–25.
7. John Conway, "Politics, Culture and the Writing of Constitutions," in Harvey L. Dyck and H. Peter Krosby, eds., *Empire and Nations* (Toronto: University of Toronto Press, 1969), p. 5.
8. Ibid., p. 8.

9. Rossiter, (*1787*, p. 147) estimates that more than half of the fifty-five delegates had practiced law.

10. Ibid., p. 145.

11. June 1; I Farrand 65.

12. See Franklin's speech, June 4; I Farrand 102–03.

13. June 4; I Farrand 100.

14. July 24; II Farrand 101.

15. June 4; I Farrand 110–14. J. G. A. Pocock, from his studies of republican ideas, stresses the centrality of the republican citizen as soldier; see *The Machiavellian Moment* (Princeton: Princeton University Press, 1975). ch. XIII. Mason was expressing this faith when he said, "Every husbandman will be quickly converted into a soldier when he knows and feels that he is to fight not in defense of the rights of a particular family, or a prince, but for his own" (June 4; I Farrand 112).

16. June 4; IV Farrand 19; compare I Farrand 113.

17. September 8; II Farrand 548.

18. June 1; I Farrand 65–66.

19. June 1, 4, 6, 9; I Farrand 65–66, 96, 132–33, 179–80.

20. See Bernard Bailyn, *The Ideological Origins of the American Revolution* (Cambridge, Mass.: Belknap Press, 1967), ch. III; and Wood, op. cit., pp. 18–27.

21. Wood, op. cit., ch. XIII.

22. June 22–23, August 14, September 3; I Farrand 375–77, 386–90; II Farrand 283–90, 489–92.

23. September 7; II Farrand 541.

24. For Mason, see September 7; II Farrand 537. For Wilson, September 6 and 7; II Farrand 522–23, 538–39.

25. August 20; II Farrand 341, 342–44.

26. September 7; II Farrand 542.

27. June 6; I Farrand 134.

28. It still does. See an anonymous note, "The United States and the Articles of Confederation: Drifting Toward Anarchy or Inching Toward Commonwealth," *Yale Law Journal*, vol. 88 (November 1978), pp. 142–66.

29. June 22; I Farrand 375–376. For Madison's emphasis on separation as "absolutely necessary," see July 17; II Farrand 35.

30. McClurg's motion came on July 17; II Farrand 33. Hamilton also proposed that presidents serve "during good behavior" (June 18; I Farrand 292), Hamilton was on the defensive for the rest of his life for making this proposal.

31. September 6; II Farrand 524.

32. September 4; II Farrand 500.

33. Quoted by Morton White, *The Philosophy of the American Revolution* (New York: Oxford University Press, 1978), p. 139 n.

34. June 1; I Farrand 68.

35. July 19; II Farrand 52–54.

36. July 17; II Farrand 31. For Mason's commitment to democracy, see his speech on May 31; I Farrand 48. For Wilson's, June 6; I Farrand 132.

37. July 17; II Farrand 19, 30–31.

38. July 17; II Farrand 29–32.
39. I discuss this problem in *Slavery in the Structure of American Politics, 1765–1820* (New York: W. W. Norton, 1979), pp. 243–45.
40. July 17; II Farrand 32.
41. July 19; II Farrand 57.
42. July 25; II Farrand 109–11.
43. For early discussions of the use of electors, see June 2; I Farrand 80–81, where Wilson first introduced the idea, and July 19; II Farrand 57–58. For a perceptive analysis, see Schlomo Slonim, "The Electoral College at Philadelphia: The Evolution of an Ad Hoc Congress for the Selection of a President," *Journal of American History*, vol. 73 (June 1986), pp. 35–58.
44. July 24; II Farrand 99, 103, 105–6.
45. II Farrand 497–98.
46. September 6; II Farrand 523.
47. September 4 and 5; II Farrand 501 and 512.
48. II Farrand 500–03, 510–15.
49. September 6; II Farrand 526.
50. September 6; II Farrand 527.
51. September 4; II Farrand 500.
52. August 6; II Farrand 185.
53. II Farrand 160, 171. Concerning Pickney's use of the term, see II Farrand 135 and 158 and III Farrand 606.
54. I Farrand 21.
55. June 13; I Farrand 232–33. Also, July 21; II Farrand 80–83.
56. II Farrand 614.
57. September 15; II Farrand 639.

CHAPTER 5: CHIEF EXECUTIVE

1. Corwin, op. cit., p. 2.
2. I owe this image to Theodore J. Lowi, *The Personal President* (Ithaca: Cornell University Press, 1985), p. 52.
3. Charles Thach, *The Creation of the Presidency, 1775–1789* (Baltimore: Johns Hopkins Press, 1923, 1969), pp. 141–42.
4. Joseph P. Harris, *The Advice and Consent of the Senate* (Berkeley: University of California Press, 1953), p. 32; from *Annals of Congress*, vol. I (Washington: Gales and Seaton, 1834), p. 518. See also Thach, op. cit., pp. 151–52.
5. Thach, op. cit., p. 148.
6. Harris, op. cit., pp. 30–33; see also Thach, op. cit., ch. VI.
7. For the evolution of these practices during the nineteenth century, see Joseph Story, *Commentaries on the Constitution of the United States*, Melville Bigelow, ed. (Boston: Little, Brown, 1891), vol. II, pp. 352–57. Also see Harris, op. cit., p. 430, n. 3.
8. James M. Burns, *Workshop of Democracy* (New York: Knopf, 1985), p. 56.

9. *Myers* v. *United States* (1926), 272 US 52.
10. *Rathbun, Humphrey's Executor* v. *United States* (1935), 295 US 602.
11. Martin P. Wattenberg, *The Decline of American Political Parties* (Cambridge, Mass.: Harvard University Press, 1984), pp. 17–23.
12. Printed in Richard B. Morris, ed., *Great Presidential Decisions: State Papers That Changed the Course of History* (Greenwich, Conn.: Fawcett, 1966).
13. Stephen Skowronek, *Building a New American State: The Expansion of National Administrative Capacities, 1877–1920* (Cambridge, England: Cambridge University Press, 1982).
14. See Madison, *The Federalist*, Number 51.
15. See Marver H. Berstein, *Regulating Business by Independent Commission* (Princeton: Princeton University Press, 1955), and Gabriel Kolko, *The Triumph of Conservatism* (New York: Free Press, 1963).
16. James Sundquist, *The Decline and Resurgence of Congress* (Washington, D.C.: Brookings Institution, 1981), pp. 130–40.
17. Quoted from *Congressional Record*, August 22, 1921, pp. 5415–21; ibid., p. 132.
18. Sundquist, *Decline and Resurgence*, p. 132.
19. Richard E. Neustadt, "Presidency and Legislation: The Growth of Central Clearance," *American Political Science Review*, vol. 48 (1954), pp. 641–71.
20. Edward S. Flash, Jr., *Economic Advice and Presidential Leadership: The Council of Economic Advisers* (New York: Columbia University Press, 1965), pp. 308–19.
21. See James L. Sundquist, "Party Decay and the Capacity to Govern," in Joel L. Fleishman, ed., *The Future of American Political Parties* (Englewood Cliffs, N.J.: Prentice-Hall, 1982), pp. 63–69.
22. Sundquist, *Decline and Resurgence*, p. 436.
23. David R. Mayhew, *Congress: The Electoral Connection* (New Haven: Yale University Press, 1974).
24. Rexford Guy Tugwell, *The Enlargement of the Presidency* (New York: Doubleday, 1960).

CHAPTER 6: COMMANDER IN CHIEF

1. Rossiter, *The American Presidency*, p. 25.
2. Walter Millis, *The Constitution and the Common Defense* (New York: Fund for the Republic, 1959), p. 32.
3. Richard Neustadt, *Presidential Power*, rev. ed. (New York: John Wiley, 1980), pp. 91–111.
4. Quoted by Louis Herren, *The New American Commonwealth* (London: Weidenfeld and Nicolson, 1968), p. 103.
5. R. Ernest Dupuy and William H. Baumer, *The Little Wars of the U.S.* (New York: Hawthorn Books, 1968), p. x.
6. Harold Stein, *American Civil-Military Decisions* (Tuscaloosa, Ala.: University of Alabama Press, 1963), pp. 27–42.

7. Ernest May, "McKinley," in Ernest R. May, ed., *The Ultimate Decision* (New York: George Braziller, 1960), p. 107. The emphasis in the quotation is May's.

8. Leonard D. White, *The Jacksonians* (New York: Macmillan, 1954), p. 66.

9. Cf. Samuel P. Huntington, *The Soldier and the State* (Cambridge, Mass.: Belknap Press, 1957), ch. 3.

10. Edward S. Corwin and Norman Small eds., *The Constitution of the United States of America: Analysis and Interpretation* (Washington: Government Printing Office, 1964), p. 336.

11. John McCloy, "Turning Points of the War: The Great Military Decisions," *Foreign Affairs*, vol. 26 (October 1947), pp. 52–72.

12. Almond, *The American People and Foreign Policy* (New York: Harcourt, Brace, 1950), pp. 92–106.

13. McCloy, op. cit., p. 55.

14. William R. Emerson, "F.D.R. (1941–1945)," in May, op. cit., pp. 141–142.

15. Harry Truman, *1945: Year of Decisions* (New York: New American Library, 1955), pp. 561–62.

16. Emerson, op. cit., p. 170; Herbert Feis, *Churchill—Roosevelt—Stalin*, (Princeton: Princeton University Press, 1957), p. 270.

17. Truman, op. cit., p. 563.

18. Ibid., p. 563.

19. Walter Millis, ed., *The Forrestal Diaries* (New York: Viking Press, 1951), pp. 487–88.

20. Harry Truman, *1946–1953: Years of Trial and Hope*, (New York: New American Library, 1956), pp. 450–67.

21. Foreign Relations Committee Report on the "North Atlantic Treaty," June 6, 1949, 81st Congress, 1st Session, p. 14.

22. Merlo Pusey, *The Way We Go to War* (Boston: Houghton Mifflin, 1969), pp. 101–08.

23. Ibid., pp. 34–35.

24. Ruth Leger Sivard, *World Military and Social Expenditures 1985* (Washington: World Priorities, 1985), p. 13.

25. Department of Defense, *Annual Report to the Congress*, Fiscal Year 1986 (Washington: Government Printing Office, 1986), p. 300.

26. Quoted in Pusey, op. cit., pp. 24–25.

CHAPTER 7: WINNING ELECTIONS

1. Jimmy Carter, *Keeping Faith: Memoirs of a President* (New York: Bantam, 1982), pp. 117–21.

2. James M. Burns, *Roosevelt: The Lion and the Fox* (New York: Harcourt, Brace and Company, 1956), pp. 376–77.

3. Lowi, op. cit., table, p. 128.

4. The quoted term is borrowed from Hugh Helco, *A Government of Strangers: Executive Politics in Washington* (Washington, D.C.: Brookings, 1977).

5. Lowi, op. cit., pp. 72–73.

6. *Mandate for Reform* (Washington: Democratic National Committee, 1970), pp. 40, 49.

7. Ibid., pp. 50–51.

8. Howard Reiter, *Selecting the President* (Philadelphia: University of Pennsylvania Press, 1985), p. 3.

9. Austin Ranney, *Participation in American Presidential Nominations, 1976* (Washington, D.C.: American Enterprise Institute, 1977), p. 6.

10. *Cousins* v. *Wigoda*, 419 US 477 (1975).

11. Nelson W. Polsby and Aaron Wildavsky, *Presidential Elections*, 6th ed. (New York: Charles Scribner's Sons, 1984), p. 149.

12. Walter Dean Burnham, "The 1980 Earthquake," in Thomas Ferguson and Joel Rogers, eds., *The Hidden Election* (New York: Pantheon Books, 1981), p. 101.

13. Calculations based on tables in Reiter, op. cit., pp. 64, 66.

14. Herbert Alexander, *Financing Politics* (Washington, D.C.: CQ Press, 1976), p. 20.

15. *Report of the Select Committee on Presidential Activities*, Report No. 93–981, 93d Congress, 2d Session, June 1974, pp. 415–59. See also Alexander, op. cit., p. 195.

16. Alexander, op. cit. pp. 88–89.

17. *Buckley* v. *Valeo*, 424 U.S. 1 (1976).

CHAPTER 8: BUILDING A GOVERNMENT

1. Hamilton's emphasis; *The Federalist*, Number 66, p. 405 (Mentor edition); see also Number 76.

2. Herbert Kaufman, "The Growth of the Federal Personnel System," in N. Wallace Sayre, ed., *The Federal Government Service*, 2d ed. (Englewood Cliffs, N.J.: Prentice-Hall, 1965), ch. 1; cited by Lowi, op. cit., p. 29.

3. John Macy, Bruce Adams, and J. Jackson Walter, *America's Unelected Government* (Cambridge, Mass.: Ballinger Company, 1983), pp. 5–6.

4. G. Calvin MacKenzie, *The Politics of Presidential Appointments* (New York: Free Press, 1981), p. 4.

5. Helco, op. cit., p. 84.

6. Bruce Adams, *The Senate Rubberstamp Machine* (Washington: Common Cause, 1977), p. i.

7. Personal communication, Sheldon Goldman, 1978.

8. David Margolik, "Stalled Federal Court Nomination Raises Concern," *New York Times*, June 24, 1984, p. 25.

9. "Lawyer Sworn in as Federal Judge," *New York Times*, March 29, 1986, p. 26.

10. Sheldon Goldman and Thomas P. Jahnige, *The Federal Courts as a Political System*, 3d ed. (New York: Harper & Row, 1985), pp. 39–51; for modifications introduced by the Reagan administration, see Sheldon Goldman, "Reaganizing the Judiciary: the First Term Appointments," *Judicature*, vol. 68 (April–May 1985), pp. 315–16.

11. Quoted in Harris, op. cit., pp. 116–17; see also p. 421, n. 4.
12. Ibid., pp. 317–20.
13. Goldman, "Reaganizing," loc. cit., pp. 319, 325; see also, by the same author, "Carter's Judicial Appointments," *Judicature* vol. 64 (March 1981), p. 351.
14. Larry Berkson, Susan Carbon, and Alan Neff, *A Study of the U.S. Circuit Judge Nominating Commission: Executive Summary* (Chicago: American Judicature Society, 1979), pp. 3 and 44.
15. Harris, op. cit., p. 416, n. 26.
16. *Congressional Quarterly Almanac 1977*, vol. 33 (Washington, D.C.: Congressional Quarterly, 1978), p. 575; see *Congress and the Nation 1969–1982* (Congressional Quarterly Service, 1973), vol. III, p. 303, for other examples of judicial breakdown during this period.
17. Goldman, "Carter's Judicial Appointments," loc. cit., p. 354; for Senator Humphrey's reaction, *CQ Almanac 1980* (Washington: CQ Press, 1981), p. 18-A.
18. These figures, and other data in this paragraph, are drawn from Goldman, "Reaganizing," loc. cit., pp. 313–39.

CHAPTER 9: ENFORCING THE LAWS

1. See Locke, op. cit., chapter XIV, for his definition of prerogative and an argument that it is inescapably part of constitutional governance.
2. See Louis Fisher, *President and Congress* (New York: Free Press, 1972), ch. 1 and Appendix.
3. Seth King, "Carter Signs a Bill to Protect 104 Million Acres in Alaska," *New York Times*, December 3, 1980, p. A-20.
4. *Encyclopaedia Britannica*, 15th ed. (1974), *Micropedia*, vol. VIII, p. 791b.
5. P.L. 91-504, *U.S. Code Annotated*, Title 16, Section 1133, p. 198.
6. U.S. Department of the Interior, *Assessment Report*, January 1982, p. 10.
7. Alaska National Interest Lands Conservation Act, 94 Stat 2475 (1980).
8. *National Audubon Society et al.* vs. *Department of the Interior*, civil action No. 83-425, U.S. District Court (Alaska), "Answer of Cook Inlet Region, Inc. to Complaint," September, 1983.
9. *National Audubon Society v. Hodel*, 606 Federal Supplement 825 (1984).
10. Paul Taylor, " 'Thin Cats' Sought: Presidential Hopefuls Scramble for the Early Money," *Washington Post*, May 12, 1983, p. A10.
11. *The Federalist*, Number 70. Compare Theodore Lowi, *The End of Liberalism* (New York: W. W. Norton, 1969), ch. 8.
12. Robert F. Cushman, *Cases on Constitutional Law*, 5th ed. (Englewood Cliffs, N.J.: Prentice-Hall, 1979), p. 568.
13. Laurence I. Barrett, *Gambling with History: Ronald Reagan in the White House* (New York: Penguin Books, 1983), pp. 415–21.
14. Ibid., p. 418.
15. Tom Wicker, "Fixing Mr. Reagan," *New York Times*, February 5, 1982, p. A 31.
16. Barrett, op. cit., p. 426.

17. Quoted by Michael Wines, "Administration Says It Merely Seeks a 'Better Way' to Enforce Civil Rights," *National Journal*, vol. 14 (March 27, 1982), p. 537.
18. *Swan* v. *Charlotte-Mecklenburg Board of Education*, 402 US I (1971); and *Davis* v. *Board of School Commissioners*, 402 US 33 (1971).
19. Barrett, op. cit., p. 422.
20. *CQ Almanac 1978* (Washington: Congressional Quarterly, 1979) p. 741.
21. *City of New Haven* v. *United States*, decided in U.S. District Court (D.C.), May 16, 1986; opinion by Judge Thomas Penfield Jackson.
22. Fisher, op. cit., especially ch. 3.
23. Handlin and Handlin, op. cit., p. 447.
24. Everett Ladd, "Clearing the Air: Public Opinion and Public Policy on the Environment," *Public Opinion*, vol. 5 (February / March 1982), pp. 16–20.

CHAPTER 10: MANAGING THE ECONOMY

1. Quoted by Rossiter, *The American Presidency*, p. 37.
2. Herbert Stein, *Presidential Economics*, rev. ed. (New York: Simon & Schuster, 1985), pp. 399, 401.
3. Lester Thurow, "The Moral Equivalent of Defeat," *Foreign Policy* (Spring 1981), pp. 114, 123–24.
4. *World Military and Social Expenditures 1985*, op. cit., pp. 38–42.
5. Janet L. Norwood, commissioner of labor statistics, quoted in the *New York Times*, August 3, 1956, section 4, p. 4.
6. Peter T. Kilborn, "The Sudden Wilting of Reagan's Rosy Economy," *New York Times*, July 27, 1986, section 3, pp. 1, 8–9.
7. *Economic Report of the President: 1984* (Washington, D.C.: Government Printing Office, 1984), p. 57.
8. These proportions are drawn from Everett Carll Ladd, *The Ladd Report #2* (New York: W. W. Norton, 1985), p. 6.
9. The story was told by William Greider, "The Education of David Stockman," *Atlantic Monthly*, vol. 248 (December 1981), pp. 27–54), and repeated by Stockman himself, *The Triumph of Politics* (New York: Harper & Row, 1986), ch. 5–7.
10. Stein, op. cit.
11. *National Journal*, vol. 13 (November 28, 1981), p. 2107.
12. Peter Kilborn, "The New Clash with Volcker," *New York Times*, December 26, 1984, p. D4.
13. Milton Friedman, "The Case for Overhauling the Federal Reserve," *Challenge*, vol. 28 (July–August 1985), pp. 4–12.
14. Flash, op. cit., pp. 308–19.
15. Sundquist, *Decline and Resurgence of Congress*, ch. VIII. For an argument that "the gap between promise and performance has been awesome," see Louis Fisher, *Constitutional Conflicts Between Congress and the President* (Princeton: Princeton University Press, 1985), pp. 239–42, and sources cited there.

16. Richard Fenno, Jr., *Home Style: House Members in Their Districts* (Boston: Little, Brown, 1978).

CHAPTER 11: MAKING WAR

1. Arthur Schlesinger, Jr. *The Imperial Presidency* (Boston: Houghton MIfflin, 1973), p. 43. Lincoln's letter is printed in Roy P. Basler, ed., *Collected Works of Lincoln* (New Brunswick: Rutgers University Press, 1953), vol. I, pp. 451–52. The emphasis in the quotation is Lincoln's.
2. For details of these and other "military actions to achieve diplomatic and economic objectives," see the useful compendium and annotations in Christopher H. Pyle and Richard M. Pious, *The President, Congress and the Constitution* (New York: Free Press, 1984), esp. ch. 5.
3. Theodore Sorensen, *Kennedy* (New York: Bantam, 1965), pp. 791–92.
4. Quoted in Pyle and Pious, op. cit., p. 318.
5. *Administration of National Security*, Hearings Before the Subcommittee on National Security Staffing and Operations, Committee on Government Operations, U.S. Senate, 88th Congress, 1st Session, 1963 (Washington: Government Printing Office, 1965), p. 77.
6. *The Pentagon Papers*, published for the *New York Times* by Bantam Books (New York: 1971), pp. 27–32.
7. Ibid., p. 32.
8. The Dillon and Dulles cables are printed in ibid., pp. 38–40.
9. Lansdale's report on his team's activities between August 1954 and August 1955 is printed in ibid., pp. 53–66.
10. Townsend Hoopes, *The Limits of Intervention* (New York: David McKay, 1969), pp. 13–14; see also *The Pentagon Papers*, p. 87.
11. This account of President Kennedy's decisions to escalate the American involvement in Vietnam is based mainly on *The Pentagon Papers*, ch. 3; Hoopes, op. cit., ch. 1; and Schlesinger, op. cit., ch. 6 and 7.
12. *Pentagon Papers*, p. 109.
13. Quoted by Rossiter, *American Presidency*, p. 32.
14. *Pentagon Papers*, p. 80.
15. Hoopes, op. cit., pp. 25–26.
16. Leonard C. Meeker, "The Legality of United States Participation in the Defense of Viet-Nam," *Department of State Bulletin* (Washington: Government Printing Office, 1966), vol. LIV (March 28, 1966), pp. 484–85.
17. Hoopes, op. cit., p. 76.
18. Ibid., p. 104.
19. Austin Ranney, *Channels of Power: The Impact of Television on American Politics* (New York: Basic Books, 1983), p. 5.
20. Hoopes, op. cit., pp. 172–80.
21. Ibid., pp. 182–84.

22. Ibid., p. 203.
23. Ibid., p. 224.
24. Lyndon B. Johnson, *The Vantage Point* (New York: Holt, Rinehart & Winston, 1971), p. 424.
25. Ibid., p. 380.
26. Ibid., p. 418.
27. Ibid., p. 424.
28. P.L. 91-652, 85 Stat. 1942, January 5, 1971.
29. P.L. 92-156, 85 Stat. 423-430, November 17, 1971.
30. Henry Kissinger, *The White House Years (1969–1972)* (Boston: Little, Brown, 1979), p. 1424.
31. *DaCosta* v. *Laird*, 471 F.2d 1146 (1973).
32. Wyzanski, senior district judge, quoted in Pyle and Pious, op. cit., pp. 350–51.
33. Ibid., p. 361.
34. P.L. 93-148, 87 Stat. 555, 50 USC Section 1541–48. See also Section 8 (d) (1): "Nothing in this joint resolution is intended to alter the constitutional authority of the Congress or of the president. . . ."
35. S. 440, 93d Congress, 1st Session, 1973, Sec. 3.
36. *War Powers: A Test of Compliance.* . . . Hearings before the Subcommittee on International Security and Scientific Affairs, Committee on International Relations, U.S. House of Representatives, 94th Congress, 1st Session, 1975, pp. 90–91.
37. P.L. 93-52, 87 Stat. 130, July 1, 1973.
38. A transcript of President Ford's comments appears in *War Powers and the Constitution* (Washington, D.C.: American Enterprise Institute, 1984), pp. 27–29.
39. Carter, op. cit., p. 437.
40. Ibid., p. 448.
41. Ibid., p. 457.
42. Ibid., p. 511.
43. Ibid., p. 514.
44. Ibid., p. 514.
45. Defense Department comments, quoted in Pyle and Pious, op. cit., p. 373.
46. *Crockett* v. *Reagan*, 558 F. Supp. 893 (D.D.C. 1982).
47. Statement by President Reagan on signing S.J. Res. 159 into law, October 12, 1983.
48. See Johnson, op. cit., pp. 402–03, and Carter, op. cit., pp. 449–450.

CHAPTER 12: ROUNDING OUT THE "CONSTITUTIONAL REVOLUTION"

1. Reprinted in Richard Loss, ed., *Presidential Power and the Constitution: Essays by Edward S. Corwin* (Ithaca: Cornell University Press, 1976), pp. 157–77.
2. The 1980 Republican platform is printed in the *CQ Almanac 1980*, pp. 58B–84B.
3. Reinhold Niebuhr, *The Children of Light and the Children of Darkness: A Vindication*

of Democracy and a Critique of Its Traditional Defense (New York: Charles Scribner's Sons, 1944), p. xiii.

4. For an analysis of Madison's use of this term, see Robert Dahl, *Preface to Democratic Theory* (Chicago: University of Chicago Press, 1956), pp. 12–27.

5. Fisher, op. cit., pp. 251–70; and Wood, op. cit., ch. XIII.

6. See Clinton Rossiter's discerning analysis, in *Constitutional Dictatorship*, Part IV; also, Donald L. Robinson, "The Routinization of Crisis Government," *Yale Review*, vol. 63 (Winter 1974), in which I first argued that the habit of resort to crisis government was becoming inveterate.

7. See "Political Economy and Constitutional Reform," Hearings before the Joint Economic Committee, 97th Congress, 2d Session, November and December 1982, Part I, p. xi.

8. Hugh Heclo and Lester M. Salamon, eds., *The Illusion of Presidential Government* (Boulder: Westview Press, 1981), p. 305.

9. Willmoore Kendall, "The Two Majorities," *Midwest Journal of Political Science*, vol. IV, no. 4 (1960), pp. 317–45.

10. For a thorough discussion of these difficulties, see James L. Sundquist, *Constitutional Reform and Effective Government* (Washington, D.C.: Brookings Institution, 1986), ch. 6.

11. Calculated from tables in Norman Ornstein, Thomas Mann, Michael Malbin, Allen Schick, and John Bibby, *Vital Statistics on Congress, 1984–1985 Edition* (Washington: American Enterprise Institute, 1984), pp. 49–51.

12. Lloyd Cutler, "Party Government under the Constitution," published in *Reforming American Government: The Bicentennial Papers of the Committee on the Constitutional System*, Donald L. Robinson, ed. (Boulder Westview Press, 1985), pp. 104–05 and passim; see also pp. 175–77, where the pros and cons of the proposal are analyzed.

13. Michel Debré, "The Constitution of 1958: Its Raisin d'être and How It Evolved," *The Fifth Republic at Twenty*, William Andrews and Stanley Hoffman, eds. (Albany: State University of New York Press, 1981), pp. 11–24; reprinted in Robinson, ed., *Reforming American Government* (op. cit.), pp. 313–27.

14. See Sundquist, *Constitutional Reform and Effective Government*, p. 149.

15. Ibid., pp. 65–66; cf. pp. 135–40, 143–51.

Index